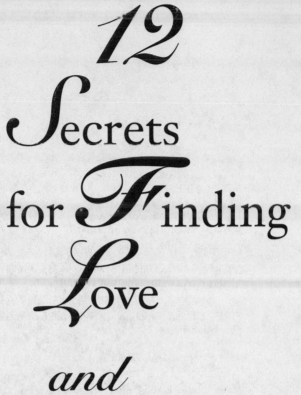

12 Secrets for Finding Love and Commitment

Jeffrey Ullman

Founder of Great Expectations

A FIRESIDE BOOK
Published by Simon & Schuster
New York London Toronto Sydney Tokyo Singapore

FIRESIDE
Rockefeller Center
1230 Avenue of the Americas
New York, New York 10020

Copyright © 1995 by Jeffrey Ullman

FIRESIDE and colophon are registered trademarks of
Simon & Schuster Inc.

DESIGNED BY BARBARA MARKS

Manufactured in the United States of America

10   9   8   7   6   5   4   3   2   1

Library of Congress Cataloging-in-Publication Data

Ullman, Jeffrey.
12 secrets for finding love and commitment / Jeffrey Ullman.
p.   cm.
"A Fireside book."
1. Mate selection. 2. Man-woman relationships. 3. Self-help
techniques.   I. Title.
HQ801.U39   1995
646.7'7—dc20   94-34864
                                                      CIP

ISBN 0-671-89207-X

Contents

Special Note: The author will donate all his royalties from the sale of this book to child abuse prevention groups.

Acknowledgments

This is truly the decade of love in a confounding climate. More than 90 percent of the world's population marries at some time in their lives. And, it seems that I have spoken to a great many of those people! Since I started Great Expectations in 1976, tens of thousands of singles have shared their heartfelt opinions with me. I could not have written this book without their honest and vocal expressions of what it's like to be single. Special thanks go to my favorite Member Services staff in Los Angeles and Encino who helped identify many of the most pressing issues facing singles in the 1990s.

I've been married most of my adult life, and during the time that I was unattached, fancy-free, and footloose, I always had my eye on marriage. Although I was very good at dating (and for the first time have revealed some of my most effective techniques in this book), I really didn't much like it and I learned to accept and deal with it effectively. Whether they realized it or not, many of the women whom I had the pleasure to meet helped inspire me to unscramble the more puzzling and annoying parts of dating.

Fortunately, I was successful in finding the right woman

through my best efforts. What made the difference for me was that I applied the same attitudes, approaches, and actions in my own personal search that are contained in this book. And I would like to add that this incredible woman helped me more than I can say in finally finishing this book.

Thank God I found Cindy. She has exceeded my greatest expectations. John Lennon was right: love *is* the answer.

*"Loneliness and being unwanted
is the most terrible poverty."*

—MOTHER TERESA

Introduction

"Why can't I meet anyone really wonderful?"
—CURRENT WORLDWIDE LAMENT OF MILLIONS OF
  SINGLES

*O*ne *is* the loneliest number. And if you're like one out of every three adult Americans, you're single and not too happy about it either. In all, there are 75 million singles out there, and experts predict that by the year 2000, half of the U.S. population will be living alone. It's a shocking statistic. And the numbers are just as disturbing abroad, from Mexico to Japan, England to Argentina, Germany to Australia, France to Canada.

That's the reason for this book. It's my chance to tell you about a step-by-step system that I have developed for finding a life mate. I have already taught the system to more than a quarter of a million people. Since 1993, at least two couples get married every day because they have utilized the basic elements of my system, and thousands more were married since I first started offering my system in 1976.

I work with people who tell me that it's their deepest heart's desire to find a true love and life companion. Everyone longs for and has an enormous need for love—a love that fills us, exhilarates our being, inflames our bodies, stimulates our spirit, and satiates our soul to give us a profound sense of peace within.

This book is for people like my friend Larry, a forty-two-year-old cardiologist living in Miami. Larry was married for nine years, but he's been divorced for the past seven. While he's not a knock-'em-dead Romeo, he's a charming and pleasant-looking guy. He's very successful, has a fabulous condominium in South Miami Beach, dresses impeccably, and is a genuinely good person. He is currently seeing a woman but the relationship is, as he puts it, "heading nowhere." Still, Larry does not want to give it up. He doesn't want to be alone . . . again. So he spends a lot of free time at weekend seminars, learning to "make love work."

It's also for Gina, a thirty-five-year-old advertising executive based in Chicago. Gina is everything a man could want. She's competent and outgoing, attractive and charming. She recently redecorated her apartment and turned it into a really creative living space. A few years ago Gina rarely spent a Saturday night alone. But despite all her good qualities, that's begun to change. She's now approaching her late thirties, and she's very much alone. One by one, her friends have all fallen in love, married, and started to have kids—while she's watched them from the sidelines.

This book is for Doug, an up-and-coming journalist in New York City. Barely twenty-seven, he's got a great job with a major magazine. He's exceptionally bright. He's committed to excellence in everything he does. Anytime he's sent out of town on an assignment, he's encouraged by his boss and coworkers to take an extra day for himself. "Have some fun," they tease him. "Meet somebody!" Knowing that he's a little shy, several friends have even tried to set him up with young women who might be right. But it never works out.

And it's for Arlene, a fifty-four-year-old drama teacher in Los Angeles. Although she's never been married, Arlene partied with the best of them through the seventies and eighties. She ran with a fairly bohemian theater arts set, and went through a lot of casual (and a few serious) relationships. But as middle age sets in, her efforts to find new partners have slowed. Ten years ago, she talked openly about her hopes of meeting someone wonderful. Today, she never brings up the subject. It's as though the word "romance" had been dropped entirely from her vocabulary. In appearance and attitude, she seems to have settled into permanent singlehood.

None of these people want to be alone. None of them need to be. They are as appealing and well-balanced as all kinds of married and otherwise mated folks. So what's the problem?

The problem is that they all share a set of false expectations about love and partnership. They all believe in the myths of romance that this society perpetuates among the young and the old alike. Unfortunately, the myths did not work for them.

To be fair, they do seem to work for some people. More to the point, some people don't get caught in the huge gap between the myths and the reality. They are the lucky ones: men and women who manage to find one another through a college classroom, a mutual friend, the office, or their athletic club. But "lucky" is the all-important word that describes them. They merely had the good fortune to be in the right place at the right time.

Everybody else has become the innocent casualty of escalating modern-day isolation. The much-praised, high-tech, streamlined, fine-tuned communication systems of the nineties have certainly failed them. They're not getting in touch with anyone. Often for no identifiable reason, fate just didn't work in their favor. Instead, it's been their misfortune to wander through their twenties, into their thirties, and often beyond—looking, hoping, waiting.

Forget the myths and forget that *passive* approach to falling in love! If you do not recognize and accept the obsolescence of that romantic expectation, then you are doomed to years of uninterrupted loneliness. If you learn nothing else from this book, learn these six words:

Romance is different in the nineties.

Those words offer you the key to a happier and busier love

life. Romance is a new game. It's played by new and different rules. This book is going to teach you those rules and tell you how to put them to good use. I will make arguments that will prove to you that the courtship, dating, and relationship practices that might have worked before aren't likely to work as well now. But it's not enough just to do something; it's essential to see the world differently so that you know what your options are and how to apply your resources. W. Somerset Maugham said it well: "It is a funny thing about life; if you refuse to accept anything but the best, you very often get it."

My goal is to help you get it. I can't guarantee that my system will work for you unless *you* work at it. If you want real love in your life, you've got to pursue your goal with passion and dedication. Highly successful people push toward their goals relentlessly until they achieve them. Patience and diligence, like faith, move mountains. Perseverance is the key to their success.

I'm not an academic. I'm not a therapist. I'll leave the theories and psychologizing to the people best trained to offer that kind of information. I do recognize that every moment of life is an opportunity to make your life better. I also realize that when you bought this book we made a commitment to each other: you by putting your faith in me to share my secrets to romantic success, and me by presenting those to you as clearly and generously as possible.

What I will offer you is more than twenty years of experience in helping mutually interested singles meet one another. I created, built, and continue to lead the largest relationship service in the world. Many people know it as "Video Dating," but it's not really about dating because its focus is on creating loving, committed relationships. My company, Great Expectations, is clearly the largest service in the world with almost 200,000 Members in North America alone, and future Membership Centres to be opened on other continents. Over the years my fabulously sensitive and bright "G/E" employees and franchisees have helped me understand and perfect a system that continues to help relationship-minded single people meet and fall in love. The entire G/E system is based on a unique combination of practical advice and sensitive reassurance. Best of all, it works. Great Expectations has brought together hundreds of thousands of people and helped spark thousands of marriages (approximately 10,000). There are also a lot of men and women out there who will testify to the wonderful way in which they've changed their own lives after trying our system of introduction.

But what if you don't live in any of the cities where Great Expectations has a Membership Centre? Or what if you don't want to make a financial investment in yourself and buy a membership? What if you don't believe that video dating is the right thing for you now? The question then follows: "Do you have to become a Member of Great Expectations in order to benefit from my system?" No, you don't. Yes, it helps (or could make the difference), but the fundamental elements of the system can work for you wherever you are, so long as you are willing to commit yourself to following them.

The elements to this system are simple. First, there's the reassurance that nothing is wrong with you. It really is harder than ever to meet someone wonderful. But then there's the tough-love message that you can do it. In fact, only *you* can take responsibility for doing it. This book will give you the right system. It will present the facts. It will show you why so many smart, sexy, compassionate people spend so much of their leisure time alone, wishing they had someone to share it with. It will identify the obvious and subtle ways in which many of us set ourselves up for one emotional loss after another. No matter who you are you can enhance your future relationships by applying my strategies and action steps.

It's my life's passion to help as many people as possible to find their true love: a love that lasts, a love that grows with your journey toward personal growth, and a love that brings you endless joy.

If you are committed to falling in love with someone of your own choice, and if you want control over your love life, then you have to stop looking to your family, religious institution, friends, and fate for help. It's no one else's job to make your love life work. That job is all yours.

So open your eyes and see the singles world as it really is. Get real. **All the good ones aren't taken.** They may be tough to find, but by applying the positive principles and action steps from this book you will be on your way. This book is meant to be your personal magnifying glass. It will clear out the meaningless, fuzzy details that surround modern dating. It will zero in on what is most important. It will tell you where the good ones are. And it will show you how to find the special person who is right for you.

Will the system work within thirty days? A year? I won't promise that it will. I do promise that if you can reach past all the outdated definitions of romance and relationships, if you can get beyond your own cynicism and insecurity—then you will discover inside yourself the confidence that's always been there. Your own wisdom will help you keep trying until it does work.

Put It into Practice

At the end of each chapter in this book, you'll come to a "Put It into Practice" section. These are easy exercises, meant to help you translate the principles of the chapter into real-life action. For many of them, you'll need a convenient and private place to write your revelations, such as a separate notebook.

So many tens of thousands of relationship-minded singles have applauded my system and encouraged me to share my principles and procedures even with nonmembers of Great Expectations. I am utterly convinced that if you follow my suggestions and spend just a few minutes doing these exercises, you will stand a better chance of succeeding, sooner rather than later. Expect to reread your entries many times, as the next several weeks will take you on a whirlwind adventure of self-analysis and romance. As the little old lady quoted by E. M. Forster once said, "How can I know what I think till I see what I say?" In other words, you will absolutely, positively, and most assuredly gain clarity about your life because writing and thinking go hand in hand.

By the time you get to Chapter 12, "Twelve Secrets About Finding Love and Commitment," you will recognize how you can apply the basic ingredients of my plan (and what will soon become *your* plan). They should serve as reminders of your new love motto: *It's my love life. I control it.*

1 Want Love? Get Real

"Limited expectations usually mean limited opportunities."
—JEFFREY CRAIG ULLMAN

*I*t's not your imagination. It really *is* harder than ever before to find the right someone to love who will return that love. Meeting a mate has become a matter of chance for tens of millions of perfectly normal and desirable single people. With technological know-how that boggles most minds, we have invented countless timesaving devices to make life easier. In virtually every other facet of life—from career advancement to physical fitness—experts can offer reliable guidance for success. Yet when it comes to meeting and mating, most people just bumble along, waiting for good fortune to smile their way.

Fortunately, it doesn't have to be that way for you. Disappointing, maddening, and even pointless as the search may sometimes seem, you can find a loving and lively relationship. But you have to know how to go about getting it. The good looks, smarts, and muscle that once guaranteed romance and marriage are no longer any insurance against a lifetime of lonely nights.

I have spent almost twenty years working with single people who want a committed partnership with someone. I regularly hold seminars and conduct discussions on the subject of modern relationships. I have been interviewed by hundreds of newspaper, magazine, radio, and television reporters from around the world about everything from making the most of single life to meeting a mate, living together before marriage, reentering the love market after divorce or widowhood, and the keys to balancing romance with single parenthood. And wherever I go, I hear the same question: "I'm a good person. Why can't I meet someone wonderful to fall in love with and share my life?"

Like most serious questions, this one calls for a complex answer. Just for starters, consider the profound social, sexual, and emotional changes that have taken place over the past twenty-five years. Most traditional ways of "getting together" aren't very realistic options for today's singles. School, religious institutions, family, and friends—when was the last time you met somebody fabulous that way?

The last quarter century has changed us, too. In general, single men and women of the nineties know more about themselves and their needs than their parents ever did, and they expect more from their mates. Much as they want someone, most still prefer the loneliness of being alone to the frustration of living with a spouse they don't really like.

How about you? Are you like most American singles? Do you know the facts about single life in the nineties? Let's find out. The following quiz will give you the chance to test yourself. I should warn you that the point is not to get all the "right" answers. It's the process of asking and answering these questions that can help get you started on the right road to romance. This quiz is meant to help you examine your own ideas about attracting and keeping a mate. These ideas play a crucial role in how well you currently run your love life. Are they right for today's single scene? If they aren't, then they're holding you back from finding someone.

You can begin whenever you're ready. Take as much time as

you want, and feel free to change your answers as often as you like. When you're done, fight the temptation to turn to the end of this chapter for the correct responses. Read through the following pages first. Then see what you've learned. See if you know why the actual answers are what they are.

1. You're at a Fourth of July barbecue. As it happens, the 100 guests are a perfect mirror of national averages. What percentage are single?
   (a) 25
   (b) 30
   (c) 44
   (d) 55

2. If the same party were held in the year 2000, what percentage would be single?
   (a) 50
   (b) 40
   (c) 30
   (d) Fewer than 10

3. In the year 2000, what percent of Americans will never be in a committed relationship?
   (a) 5
   (b) 10
   (c) 20
   (d) 35

4. If a TV journalist were to interview shoppers at any mall in this country, what percentage would tell her that it's perfectly fine to be single?
   (a) 80 percent
   (b) 60 percent
   (c) 40 percent
   (d) 25 percent

5. How many of those same people would feel perfectly fine about being single themselves?
   (a) Around 40 percent
   (b) Around 20 percent
   (c) Around 10 percent
   (d) Only 2 percent

6. The most common complaint among single women is:
   (a) Men are so selfish. I don't even want to try forming a faithful relationship.
   (b) All the good ones are married.
   (c) Why is there is so much pressure to commit? I want a relationship, but not right now.
   (d) What's wrong with me? I'd give almost anything to be committed to someone who's committed to me.
7. The most common complaint among single men is:
   (a) What's wrong with me? I'd give almost anything to be committed to someone who's committed to me.
   (b) Women are so selfish. I don't even want to try having a faithful relationship.
   (c) Why is there so much pressure to commit? I may want a relationship down the line, but not right now.
   (d) Even before I'm ready for dinner, she's ready for marriage.
8. Almost 90 percent of all Americans are married by the time they're:
   (a) 25 years old.
   (b) 30 years old.
   (c) 35 years old.
   (d) 40 years old.
9. Research indicates that each of us could be truly compatible with what percentage of the people we meet?
   (a) 15 percent
   (b) 10 percent
   (c) 5 percent
   (d) Only 1 percent
10. The best way to meet somebody really right for you is:
   (a) through friends.
   (b) by joining a local health club.
   (c) by trying absolutely any means possible.
   (d) at work.

EVERY NUMBER TELLS A STORY

Of course, everybody thinks it's fine to be single. A survey recently conducted by one of New York's leading market research companies found that 80 percent of Americans said there's nothing at all wrong with it. But there seems to be a big gap between what people think about everybody else and what they want for themselves. For instance, a Virginia Slims Poll in 1990 found that just one woman in fifty (and only one man out of every 100) would choose to live alone. Everybody else wanted to be solidly and eternally attached to one person.

For many of us, this is a realistic vision of the future. After all, 90 percent of all men and women who marry do so by the time they're thirty-five. Nevertheless, researchers warn that between now and the year 2000, more and more people will remain forever single—whether they like it or not. Some sources even predict that the number of never-marrieds will double, to 10 percent of all adults, before the end of the decade.

The best-publicized hoopla has focused on the plight of single women. There just aren't enough men to go around, we always hear. Remember the two professors at Yale and Harvard whose study on white, college-educated women found that if such a woman is not married by age thirty, she has only a 20 percent chance of still finding a husband? That story hit the newsstands with great gusto. They further reported that by age thirty-five, her chances drop to only 5 percent. And if she is still unmarried by age forty, she has a better chance of being killed by a terrorist than of ever finding a spouse.

Pretty frightening, wouldn't you say?

The trouble is, *none* of their research was true!

One of the most accurate critics of this "man shortage" research is noted writer Susan Faludi. In *Backlash*, her landmark book, Faludi reports that the only real "shortage" is of women! She draws upon recent U.S. Census statistics to show that there are nearly 2 million more bachelors than single women between the ages of twenty-five and thirty-four living in this country today, and about a half million more men than women between the ages of thirty-five and fifty-four! So if anyone faces a shortage of possible mates, it's men in their prime marrying years: Between the ages of twenty-four and thirty-four, there are 119 single men for every 100 single women.

In the face of these facts, we have to wonder why the Harvard study so captured the public's attention—and why so many people were willing to believe it. In my view, it's because women are so much more willing than men to talk about their dating problems. Women like to share their heartaches (as well as their happiness) with one another. It's one way that they cement friendship. In the process, they begin to feel there is somehow strength—or at least comfort—in numbers. "Penny feels the same way, and so does Mara. It's good to know I'm not alone."

Men, on the other hand, are known for keeping it all inside. They would rather create a bond with their friends by discussing politics, business, or sports. Topics as personal as appeal to women, failed relationships, and romantic ineptitude or performance are totally off-limits for most men.

Still, there's a big difference between choosing not to share feelings and denying them. Contrary to prevailing myth, most men don't deny their feelings. They just don't see the point of sharing information that's unlikely to bring a quick, satisfactory solution. Being largely analytical, men look at the world in a problem/solution manner that doesn't encourage much sharing. On the rare occasion that a man does share a personal problem with another man, the friend usually reaches for some kind of concrete solution. Nodding in passive agreement just doesn't match the male temperament.

The point is, when social psychologists prepare their research, they generally get more and clearer information from women than from men. The result is a body of misinformation upon which a universe of self-help manuals have been based. Is it any wonder that they have failed?

Getting Past Your Old Mind-Set

Why are so many singles unhappy and alone? With all those single people out there, and the countless bars, gyms, dating services, and personal columns intended to introduce them, why haven't they all found somebody?

Part of the answer has to do with the realities of human personality. Psychologists tell us that even the most outgoing among us aren't able to genuinely hit it off with all that many people. In fact, the experts say most of us are truly compatible with only 1 percent of those we meet! And that only addresses temperament compatibility. It doesn't even begin to look at sexual attraction. I can think of several men and women with whom I am basically in tune. But that doesn't mean I find them attractive. So, in truth, the universe of really appropriate mate possibilities is very small.

All too often, single people don't try hard enough to overcome that enigma. Most people simply give up too fast. If you're like the average American single, you spend too much time at home. Sure you tried the personals ads. (Once.) And you joined a gym. (Five years and fifteen pounds ago.) You even looked into a video dating service. (But it just seemed like something you didn't want to do yet.) So, ultimately, you chose the easy way out. You decided to sit alone in your easy chair, watching countless Saturday nights go by, dreaming of looks across a crowded room and romantic violins in the moonlight. Be honest: *you expected love to find you.*

Another reason so many singles remain unhappily alone is this: They get a lot of really bad advice on how to find a mate. There are an incredible number of so-called personal matchmaking services out there, but most of them send out a very mixed message. They promise to help you save time and discreetly find your match, but usually end up making things worse. They tell you to take a giant step toward finding someone, but by following their directions, you find yourself a little closer to believing that you'll never meet anyone.

Let me explain. In most "foolproof plans for finding love," there's a direct or implied suggestion that you undergo a complete makeover. Consultants ask you to take an inventory of your own assets and liabilities. You wind up convinced you're either too fat or too thin. You've got too little hair or the wrong haircut. Your sense of style is either too trendy or too drab. In short, your looks doom you to a lifetime of complete social and sexual isolation.

If you are getting advice from a pop psychologist, you'll probably find that your personality is all wrong, too. Either you're too aggressive or too passive. You expect too much from love or you're willing to settle for too little. You take things too seriously or not seriously enough. You are, in other words, so utterly mixed up that you will end up alone forever.

Don't get me wrong. I believe in critical self-analysis. It's among the very first things that any searching single must do. You must take a close look at yourself and decide who you really are, warts and all. Look at yourself through the eyes of the opposite sex. What do they see when they look at you? I don't even take exception to suggestions about changing your outer self. Sometimes an outward change can positively affect someone inside. Then, take a good look at who you're looking for. What kind of person do you believe is right for you? What kind of person do you usually settle for?

I do find it extremely offensive that, in pursuit of love, so many people are made to feel that they aren't good enough for somebody wonderful, just the way they are. Frantically, they go on a diet, buy a new wardrobe, get a hair transplant, join a gym, or begin seeing a therapist to unearth the real problem. Many stay on the regimen for some time, and when it fails to produce the mythical mate they've been hoping for, they're left with only one possible conclusion: they must not have made the right changes. That sends them back to square one, where they make themselves over again, and hope to get it right this time.

None of these solutions are able to address the enormity of a problem that belongs to an entire generation. Think about it. The single population, as a segment of society, is getting bigger all the time. Personal imperfection—whether physical or emotional—is not the main reason people are alone. Imperfection has been around since the Stone Age and cavemen and women still managed to get together. Don't put on an act; don't try to be anyone except yourself, flaws and all. It's important that others get to know the real you.

Too many singles turn to costly cosmetics and quick-fix therapies for the answer to a problem that affects people of every race, economic class, geographic region, and political bent in this country. My experience is that these cure-alls will not get you what you want—not unless you include them as just one part of a practical plan for finding a mate.

Not until you "get real" will you get love.

GETTING REAL ABOUT WHY SINGLES ARE ALONE

The great majority of people who are alone will stay alone if they don't find ways to meet more possible partners. Unless you interact with enough other single people, you could easily become one of the 10 percent of Americans whom the Census Bureau reports will *never* marry.

That may not sound like a very earth-shattering piece of information, but it sums up the basic problem that faces most single Americans. Why can't more singles do what their parents and grandparents and great-grandparents did? Chances are, they don't know where to go to find that special someone.

At one time, there were people who really *did* marry the boy next door—because he was one of only twenty-five or thirty possible candidates for the job. People in the 1920s and even 1930s lived in much smaller communities. Even in cities, young men and women were most at ease with the people in their own neighborhood. The raciest thing that ever happened was to meet and fall in love with someone from out of town.

By the 1940s, the pool of eligibles was getting a little bigger. Towns were becoming small cities. Cars and bus lines extended the limits of single people's stomping grounds. High school was the most common way to meet life mates. By the 1950s, college was operating the same way for an increasing number of people. Classroom sweethearts actually made the decision to marry and begin families right after graduation. In fact, by the time men and women were in their junior and senior year of college, they were teased, urged, and nagged by parents and friends to finally get serious and settle down with someone nice. Life was much less complex back then. Expectations were different, too; people didn't require as much knowledge about others as they do in the nineties.

Then came the social and sexual revolutions of the 1960s, and "nice" became just another four-letter word. Out went many of the tried-and-true methods of mating. College graduation became the beginning of adulthood, not the signal to get married. People didn't want to marry at nineteen or twenty, or even twenty-four. Feminism was happening and the birth control pill helped women stay free from unwanted pregnancies. They were in control and they wanted to enjoy the sexual freedom that went with it.

Religion was out and fun sex was in. People dropped out of their church choir and joined a consciousness-raising group. A lot of people left their small-town upbringings behind. In the process, they moved away from the social cocoons where they were a known (if sometimes imperfect) commodity. In droves, singles volunteered to participate in some of the most daring social experiments of this century: open marriage, communal living, group sex, and the like.

The problem was that most singles failed to shift their fundamental expectations about life and love. They waltzed into the freedom of the 1970s and early 1980s with ideas about mating that belonged to the 1940s and 1950s. Singles dabbled in new lifestyles but somehow planned all along to end up with one of the most conventional of all social choices, a permanent faithful relationship.

For many, it simply didn't work. So here we are, in the 1990s, a little older and a lot more experienced, wondering why our lives aren't following the unspoken plan we had for them. It's not that you are undesirable or incapable of making a commitment. Often, it's just that you have not seen how or when your plan went wrong. You haven't fully accepted the fact that the traditional ways of meeting are out of date and useless. Relationship-minded singles in the 1990s must be more efficient in their search for a life mate.

Our country's changing economic environment (and the ever-shrinking amount of leisure time that results) have wreaked havoc with your dating life. Think about it. Don't you find that you have to work harder and harder, just to keep earning the same amount of money? You are likely to pay as much for your next new car as your parents paid for their first house! In that sort of economic environment, there's very little free time left. Forget about the old notion of work hard/play hard. Today it's all about work hard/work *harder*.

This mentality has even entered our homes, in the form of the new home office. In the 1990s, more and more people find that they are better off working from home, although that means harder work and even less free time. The value we place on professional independence doesn't come without a high price, though. It takes an enormous toll on modern singles. It's created a stressful environment that has led to a general feeling of social burnout. Who has the energy to date after a long day of dealing with people who are depending on you to perform for them?

Also, working from home cuts out much of the average single person's means of meeting new people by limiting social contact to phone calls or fax memos.

Of course, there are also social factors that have brought us to the trying nineties. Women are now a normal part of the working world, but they have not given up family values. Today's woman wants (and often has) it all: career, child, and happy family life. This puts a greater strain on the already uncertain male, because now he must take into account a woman's career and how it might affect the relationship.

Some women want to have it all so badly that they are willing to accept less to gain more: they will compromise some of their romantic ideals for a man who would make a good companion and an excellent father. While compromise is part of any successful relationship, you won't have to compromise nearly as much if your search for the right partner lets you meet more potentially compatible singles. So once again, lifelong relationship happiness is directly affected by the effectiveness of your attitude and actions in your search.

Also, with women's increased economic independence, there has been a shift in what they expect from their relationships with men. Women want men who can communicate and articulate their feelings on an emotional level. Therefore, in the nineties men need to meet more sophisticated emotional needs, not just simply provide shelter, food, and clothing.

The nineties have also been plagued with HIV and AIDS. This deadly virus is one of the major factors in changing the face of modern dating. Unsafe sex can lead to death. It is a serious matter that has made many singles too frightened to date anybody they don't know a lot about—even before the first handshake.

THINK LIKE A WINNER

Singles are often their own worst enemy. Asked why their love life is a mess, many will point to real-life problems that limit their opportunities to find a partner. Single parents, for example, almost always complain about the limited time and resources they have available for romance. Yet the power to break the loop of missed chances or unfulfilling relationships rests with each individual. You make your choices. You have the power to do something different.

One of the most often misused words in singles' vocabularies is "loser." The typical definition is someone who is a combination of ugly, socially inept, unsophisticated, and uneducated—in short, someone who is not worthy of you.

I strongly disagree. I think a loser is someone who wants more out of life than he or she is getting. Losers reenact the same behaviors that got them into their current troubles. They stay in ruts whether or not they create them. They hold onto go-nowhere relationships because they're afraid of being alone. They don't venture out to places to look for new people to meet because they're fearful of being uncomfortable, and they worry about what others might think of them. Losers make excuses. Losers blame others for their failures and problems. They hold themselves back. They're easy to identify because they're the ones who complain the loudest that all the good ones are taken or gay. They're the ones who moan and groan about the opposite sex being "no good." Losers hide out; they don't go out. Basically, losers give up control of their lives.

A "winner" is not always someone who's physically attractive, rich, sophisticated, or well-educated. A winner can be anyone, anywhere. Winners know that they don't have the kind of romantic relationship that they deeply desire. But they also know—and this is the key—that romance and risk go together like salt and pepper. They know that the only way to find Mr. or Ms. Right is to take calculated romantic risks. Winners take control of their life. If necessary, they break off bad relationships in search of the right one. They identify new chances to meet new people, even though they might have to go it alone. The new way of thinking is that winners don't complain; they take meaningful action to increase their exposure to new people. Winners give themselves *decent* exposure.

Of course, not-so-obvious psychological dynamics can also make it hard to find someone. For instance, lots of single people stumble across one another without ever taking note of it. Why? Because they're too preoccupied with disguising themselves. They haven't got enough energy left to see (much less see through) the next person. Maybe Pogo, the comic strip character, was right: "We have met the enemy and he is us."

Recently, I witnessed this exact ritual of oversight taking place. It was at a local Chamber of Commerce mixer at the end of a workday. One of the people attending was a woman, perhaps in her early or mid-thirties. She was very attractive—short blond hair, well-dressed and sensual. She seemed to be coming from work and was engaged in a conversation with another woman. "It's true," I heard her say. "All the good ones *are* taken. The only guys I ever meet are married, gay, or afraid to make a commitment."

I noticed that as others heard what she said, she began directing her attention to the people—mostly men—around her. She was obviously outgoing, and made conversation with just about everyone. She commented to one man on the weather, and joked with another about the misery of Monday mornings. Clearly, every guy who caught her eye enjoyed talking with her. She was pretty and outgoing.

Still, as the conversation turned toward business subjects, I couldn't help wondering if one of those men might have been really right for her. Obviously, she wanted to meet someone. She had said so to her friend. But all her actions managed to (good-humoredly) keep men at a comfortable distance. She behaved like someone who wanted to talk in fun, but not in sincerity. What did she do wrong, you may ask? If she had been less outgoing or less talkative, she still wouldn't have met anyone. At least this way, she didn't hit some poor guy over the head with her desperation.

That's a word I hear a lot from single people: "desperation." Nobody wants to appear to be desperate. So we all make a real effort to be cool and casual. That's what is expected. Imagine what would have happened if that woman had decided to look at each of those people and blurted out her wish to be involved with some wonderful man? People would have hidden in their briefcases. For real reasons, nobody wants to expose their loneliness; nobody wants to be caught asking for love or companionship.

Nevertheless, it's strange that in a world where tens of millions of single people want a mate, we're all so afraid to appear too interested. At some level, it's silly and self-defeating. We say we're looking for intimacy, but we pack ourselves into a hard shell of friendly disinterest. I guess it's simple self-protection. We must ask ourselves: how is it that we've come to see the basic human need to love and be loved as the mark of a rash fool? Why don't we realize that love really is just the need to love and be loved back?

What about all our different disguises? We're one person at work, where we try not to need anyone at all because that could easily be mistaken for professional weakness. We're someone else with our close friends, who generally expect mutual caring but not out-and-out openness. (That could appear wimpy, whiny or, worse yet, truly neurotic.) Of course, we must be still another person with our tennis partners, because they're looking for a friendly competitor. We try to be someone else again with our love interest because we all know that within such relationships there shouldn't be competition. We wear our "mommy/ daddy/ son/daughter" hats and need to appear in total control, when inside we may not feel quite so secure.

And the truly amazing thing is that modern living makes it possible; it allows us to remain quick-change artists, switching our disguises over and over again. We aren't part of a tightly knit community in which everyone knows about us or what we do. We're part of many social and professional circles, most of which never overlap. So we can divide ourselves up, explore different sides of ourselves with different people, and experiment with a number of personas. We live by a fast-food mentality that allows us to change our personalities as often as we change our clothes.

On the downside, this sort of split leaves us all without an anchor in the waters of personal identity. Who are you? Where— and with whom—do you really belong? Is your professional self the real thing? Or is it just a mask you wear in order to make money and support yourself? Are you most yourself with your family? Your friends? Or the people you date?

What kinds of people do you date? Are they complementary to your personality and values? Are they so much like you that you're with them more for comfort than love?

Until you can answer those questions, it's going to be pretty hard to even know where to begin looking for the right relationship. At work? While shopping? At the gym? Or over chicken soup one Friday night with your mother (who wants to introduce you to the nice girl who lives on her block)?

PUT IT INTO PRACTICE

To make my love search system work for you, you must first get real about who you are. Remember, I don't want you to remake yourself in the image of some fantasy Mr. or Ms. Right. I want you to know yourself as you truly are, well enough to begin looking for a compatible partner. So get out your notebook. It's time for your first practical exercise.

Remember the crayon-colored self-portraits you created when you were a little kid, in kindergarten and first grade? Well, this is going to be a similar sort of project, but it will be done with words instead of crayons. At the top of the page write: "This is me." Now skip a few lines and begin to describe yourself, for nobody but you.

I've done this exercise in many seminar groups and I find that some people like to just let their description flow, like a stream of consciousness. For others that's a little unfocused. If you have trouble getting started, think about dividing the page into sections. One section can be for a description of your physical self. Another will let you write about your professional side. One for your sexual self. Your spiritual orientation. Your free-time persona.

The trick to benefiting from this exercise is found in forcing yourself to describe who you really are in any or all these facets of life, not who you have come to assume yourself to be. You see, that's what we all do. We get into a rut in terms of our self-image. We forget to check in with ourselves every now and then. We continue to act like the person we were five years ago. Or ten. Sometimes even twenty or thirty years ago. The image doesn't actually fit anymore, but we don't realize that. It's little wonder that we have trouble communicating who we are to other people. If we have trouble clearly identifying ourselves, it's no wonder that we have difficulty finding our soulmate.

When you're done, take a look at yourself. What do you think of you? And what sort of person would best suit the person you've become? You've got to arm yourself with this information. It's the only way to win in the virtual battlefield of modern dating.

ANSWERS TO THE QUIZ

1. c
2. a
3. b
4. a
5. d
6. d
7. a
8. c
9. d
10. c

2 The Rules of the Dating Game

"Control your own destiny, or someone else will."

—JACK WELCH

My work lets me travel a lot. Sometimes a trip takes me to a city where I appear on radio or TV to talk about love in the nineties. I also speak at seminars where I meet singles from all around the country. You know the question I hear on virtually every one of those trips? "Why does dating have to be so difficult?"

Dating is complicated because nobody really knows how to do it very well. And we don't know how to do it well because dating hasn't been around long enough to have had the rough spots rubbed smooth. That might sound strange, but dating, as we know it today, is a relatively new pastime. Until the early twentieth century, courtship amounted to gentlemen from the middle and upper classes "calling" on respectable young ladies. Where did they "call"? In parlors and sitting rooms of the girl's parents.

In other words, just two generations ago, courting couples stayed at home, supervised by a watchful family. In fact, it's no exaggeration to say that many of our great-grandparents got married before they'd ever been alone together.

Then, sometime between 1910 and the early 1920s, automobiles entered the picture and courtship changed forever. Singles started getting to know one another by leaving home to spend time away from home, by themselves. Dating was born.

No wonder we're all so confused. Here we are trying very hard to be casual and confident about a complex behavior that is still so new to human history. To make matters worse, we aren't even honest about not knowing what to expect from ourselves, or the people we date.

We act as if the rules of courtship were widely known and accepted. For no real reason, we expect people to act in very definite ways. What's more, we place the same tough expectations on ourselves. Meanwhile, the people we date are acting and reacting in ways that have nothing to do with our expectations. That's because they have their own notions about love and romance. All in all, it's amazing that any of us ever get past a first date.

A "Date" with History

Before we look at all that changed once "backseat" came to mean more than a lousy theater ticket, let's start with a brief quiz on how dating came about.

1. What changed dating most in this century?
    a)   parents
    b)   rock and roll
    c)   the automobile
    d)   none of the above
2. Dating is a tradition that's always been around.
    a)   true
    b)   false
3. Until recently, men who paid for dates expected something physical in return from women.

a) true
b) false
c) neither—many men still think buying dinner entitles them to sex

4. The word or phrase that best describes modern dating is:
   a) shopping
   b) "war between the sexes"
   c) driving
   d) running in circles

5. The most graphic description of how singles themselves often perceive one another is as:
   a) peachy keen
   b) a piece of meat
   c) candy
   d) none of the above

6. Advertising and the media play on singles' strongest inner need to feel:
   a) superior
   b) intelligent
   c) sexy and attractive
   d) capable of solving any problem

7. What tends to affect our perception the most of what couples should be like?
   a) our parents
   b) books
   c) television and print ads
   d) pop psychologists

8. The second-best modern metaphor for dating in the nineties is:
   a) a job search
   b) a walk in the park
   c) "Love Connection" reruns
   d) none of the above

9. In a more primitive time, males courted females for what reason?
   a) division of labor
   b) food
   c) sex

    d)   companionship
10. Until quite recently, females "played the game" of courtship
    with males in order to:
    a)   acquire goods and services
    b)   acquire status
    c)   procreate
    d)   all of the above

THE BACKSEAT AND BEYOND

In 1920, men controlled the overwhelming financial resources of the country. So it wasn't at all surprising that they were the first to use the power of the automobile. In most cases, it didn't take much for a man to persuade a woman to take a ride with him in his exciting machine. After all, the invitation was a double thrill. First, it meant that she was sexually desirable. Second, it meant that she could evaluate her new beau by herself, without her family members along to enforce their authority.

Once the pair left the watchful eye of the girl's family, things really began to change. While they were around her home, the man's behavior was directly influenced by her family's presence and importance. Once away in his automobile, any woman was much more under his influence. The only real price he had to pay for such newfound power was an economic one. He had to cover all dating expenses.

Some experts say that when courtship took this turn, out of the young woman's home and into the commercial world, it became subject to all the economic rules that governed other social institutions of the period. The most basic of those rules involved economic exchange. When money was spent on courtship, something was expected in return. That rule continues to function today.

To this day many men think that if they spend money on a date, the woman should "repay" with physical affection. The more money he spends, the more payback he expects. Of course, a great many women have come to reject this notion and, again, we face a collision of different expectations.

This economic view of courtship is not new. In researching mating behavior, anthropologist Margaret Mead found that by the end of World War II, the average person's idea of dating had changed. Where once it had been viewed as a "give-and-take" between the sexes, it was now considered a game of gift and "repayment." In other words, by the 1950s dating had become a kind of economic bartering system, a status-oriented rating game.

This dating as rating was based on the idea of a woman "selling" her appeal to the highest bidder. For instance, a young woman who had many dates with wealthy men increased her social status and was therefore made even more desirable to even wealthier men. Eventually, when she determined that she had attracted as impressive a suitor as possible, she cashed in her chips. In most cases, that meant she married and settled into a life of trying to keep her mate and the economic stability he provided.

Being competitive by nature, men adapted well to this ritual.

THE NATURE OF THE GAME

There's actually an academic explanation for the economic exchange of dating. It's got a fancy name, too: "biological imperative vs. acquisition of goods." Anthropologist Helen E. Fisher covers it in her book *Anatomy of Love: The Natural History of Monogamy, Adultery, and Divorce.* She says that many cultures (especially primitive ones) rely on two parallel systems of mating. In the first, men seek women primarily for sex. In the second, women seek the companionship of men in order to acquire certain goods (e.g., a roof over her head, food, and clothing).

Perhaps this is at the heart of why everything has become so difficult for men and women who are dating in the nineties: the system we used to rely on has become outdated. Women can acquire their own goods and services. What, then, happens to the man? Whether he admits it or not, he has always been expected to provide dinner and gifts in exchange for a little physical affection. What can he offer now to get the things he so desires?

Interestingly enough, we're finding that women of the

nineties don't want tangible things as much as they do the intangible. Simply put, women want men to perform on *their* terms. They want men who can give them emotional support, love, and equality. This is a kind of paradox for most modern men, mainly because they weren't brought up to be emotionally open. It's not easy for them. Yet that's exactly what is necessary in order to please today's woman.

Once men learn the unfamiliar language of emotion and the art of open communication, they will be surprised at how many of their needs can be met in a loving relationship. Men and women can give equally to a relationship—both in tangible and intangible ways—and that is the essence of understanding dating in the 1990s.

BETTER SHOP AROUND

Some of you are probably thinking, "Yeah, but those values are totally out of date. Men don't expect physical favors just because they pick up the tab at dinner. Not nowadays."

You're right. And wrong. Especially among younger singles, there has been a trend away from that sort of thinking. I still believe, however, that a lot of guys say one thing while they really think another. They say that they don't expect a kiss after paying for the theater, but they really do. What's more, if they don't get one, they're sure they've been used, or they don't feel good.

For the moment, though, let's put aside these old dating problems. Instead, let's look at newer ones. In 1960, Smokey Robinson and the Miracles recorded "Shop Around." One reason for the song's success was the clever way that it described smart singles. The smart ones looked before they bought. Of course, the song was only a small part of a much larger social tendency: people—especially single people—were becoming objects. Sometimes desirable and other times not. Expensive, cheap, hard-to-get, or easy. They were changing from distinct individuals to a general "consumer class" that could be the target of promotion and selling.

In their fascinating 1991 study called "Market Metaphors for

Meeting Mates," researchers Aaron C. Ahuvia and Mara B. Adelman examined the tremendous growth of singles-oriented businesses like matchmakers, video dating services, singles ads, and singles bars. All these moneymaking ideas are, they say, evidence that love has come to have incredible marketability. I agree. Most of us in the nineties do see love as something we can buy. After all, we have the opportunity to buy a personals ad, attend a singles mixer, fly off to a Club Med singles week, or spend money to make a video that will attract suitable partners. But this buy-and-sell mentality also has a downside.

The commercialization of dating has led some people to see women and men as commodities—nothing but products that can be purchased, used, discarded, and quickly replaced (usually with a new improved model). It's important to realize that when you seek out one or more singles-oriented services, you are in the role of dating consumer. Remember that this is an entirely different kind of "investment"; you invest in yourself, in something emotional, versus something material.

But what about marketing strategies as they apply to the products we actually do buy?

To market and sell a product, you've got to make it attractive to potential buyers. That fact applies to everything from shampoo to international flight fares. How do you make a product attractive? You need your customers to connect your product with something they want very badly. That's why shampoo companies don't just sell hair cleansers. They sell a gorgeous, sexy self-image. Airlines don't just ask you to buy a seat on a crowded plane. They encourage you to purchase a fantasy of Paris in the springtime.

It's the same with the modern marketing of relationships. Singles-oriented gyms don't just sell you a membership. They promote the idea that your wildest romantic dream can come true, effortlessly. All you need is a one-year sign-up fee and the right workout clothes. Unfortunately, nothing is that easy. And after a few aerobics classes, a lot of singles get the idea that many of these meeting places are not worth the money or energy they cost. As our society grows increasingly market-driven, it's not at all surprising that writers, business people, and advertisers are beginning to think of courtship in more and more entrepreneurial terms. The book *You Are What You Wear* proudly proclaims: "People are also products. Are you packaged to gain attention, confidence and respect?" (How's that for a completely offensive approach to building self-image?)

Today's marketing minds also play on our personal need to feel attractive. We're constantly told that, if we wear this particular cologne or drink that special light beer, the opposite sex will find us irresistible. The unspoken message is that it's the product that makes us sexy and inviting. It's not us, just as we are. That's absurd! Do you really think anyone believes your eyelashes are that long *naturally?* Or that your body is flawless perfection when those expensive clothes come off ? Of course they don't. Yet despite the fact that we know such ideals are unrealistic, a lot of us strive for them anyway. That's why we are so often disappointed. It's hard for us to grasp that ordinary people don't live like our favorite TV characters. They don't all have exciting jobs, or perfectly adjusted kids, or wonderful love affairs.

Don't kid yourself. Our unrealistic view of the world definitely affects modern courtship. It seems that many singles see themselves on a shopping spree, in search of the most desirable partner. It's a competitive world, they figure, and to get the best deal on a lover they've got to sell themselves intelligently. At the very least, they've got to put themselves out there so that other singles can do comparative shopping—evaluate their assets against everybody else's.

It's true, of course, that romance doesn't just find you. You've got to make it happen. And in the great shopping mall of dating, it does pay to comparison-shop. Nevertheless, don't go nuts. Stop and think about when and how to market yourself. If you approach your dating life in this manner, you will not feel forced to go out with absolutely anybody who asks. Wouldn't it be great if you could know all of the pertinent information about a potential date ahead of time, so you could both avoid wasting time with someone who's completely incompatible?

THE "DREAM JOB" APPROACH

The dating process is not all that different from a job search. For instance, in the job market, applicants try to promote themselves to employers because they hope to find their "dream job." At the same time, they try to judge each prospective employer. Is this company really right? Are its benefits appealing? Does it offer enough security and opportunity for advancement? In relationships, the same two-way evaluation happens. We sometimes refer to a good romantic partnership as a "match." That's a good word for it because it has to work from both sides.

Let's take the metaphor a bit further. Most high-paying professional jobs involve a long-term commitment. So does a long-term relationship or marriage. In both, two people decide to work together over the long haul for a common and mutually beneficial end, even during periods of conflict. And who wouldn't agree that both a good job and a good marriage require a lot of work and compromise if they're going to be successful?

In fact, the work can be quite overwhelming. And that's where some of the new businesses of the nineties can help. In today's marketplace, those businesses come in the form of personals ads, singles clubs, matchmaking agencies, and video dating services that offer you a library of possible dates to choose from. They're helpful because they let you intelligently narrow your pool of partner applicants. Instead of wandering from club to club, from party to party, they put you directly in touch with single people who are expressly interested in a relationship.

I won't hide my bias. I think dating companies (like my relationship service) are the most helpful of these singles introduction services because they are efficient and practical. With video dating you get to screen people *before* you meet them. You see what they look like and you learn about them as unique individuals. You make the choice. Then you decide if meeting them seems like a good idea. Personals ads don't offer those benefits. Neither do matchmaking services. Best of all, a good dating service offers you the chance to meet people who have screened you, too, and have liked what they've seen. *You are assured of mutual interest before you initiate the first date.*

With all the talk about the "Information Highway," it only makes sense for you to be in control of your own information flow. Video dating—unlike matchmaking services of any kind—is perfectly fit for this new age. An ideal way to date in the 1990s is to have information about those people you'd like to meet, and *then* be able to decide if you want to meet them. Video screening also removes the fear that so many people have: the fear of rejection.

LET THE BUYER BEWARE

Your being single has created big business for the singles industry. That means you need to know how to protect yourself. How do you know which service will work best for you? How can you be sure you're not being financially or emotionally ripped off as a result of your personal vulnerability?

Used carefully, the following pointers can help you select a singles introduction service that is right for you:

1. How does the service actually work? How does it introduce people? You may want someone to select dates for you (i.e., a matchmaker). In this manner, you give up your control to someone who doesn't know you. Or you may prefer to screen and select people yourself (i.e., video), and in this manner, you maintain 100 percent control, because you know yourself best. Both methods can work. Be sure the service you choose offers the approach that most appeals to you. Remember that when you use any matchmaker, you essentially give up all authority because you let someone else choose for you a person *they* think is appropriate.

2. How long has the service been in business, both in the office you might join and in other locations? What is their business reputation?

3. Does the service seem to be in business for the long run? Or do you sense that they've rented all their furniture and might leave town at any time with your money, hopes, and expectations?

4. Does the service offer a three-day right to cancel your membership contract? It should, just in case you decide at the last minute that the whole idea isn't right for you. And three days is plenty of time to decide whether your decision was right for you now.
5. Do you get a good feeling from the employees you meet?
6. What has the media said or written about the service? This isn't always easy to find out, unless you take a trip to the library; but even then, libraries usually only archive print media.
7. What has the local Better Business Bureau and/or consumer affairs agency said about it? Dial Information and ask for the local numbers in your area.
8. What is the service's success rate? Don't just listen to what they tell you. Look for testimonial evidence that what they say is really the truth and they back up their claims. You can sometimes obtain this information directly from the service when you visit. If they don't have any information of this kind, look out!

Perhaps most important, understand that a bargain isn't really a bargain if the service won't work. By that, I mean that a service (or a classified ad) that costs only a few dollars may actually be a bad investment that also wastes your precious time and energy. Some services count on quantity of volume, not the quality of service. By the same token, services that cost several thousand dollars aren't always a "rip-off." Sometimes you do get more service and a better class of clientele when you pay more. You should always consider fees in your decision-making process.

PUT IT INTO PRACTICE

If you decide to use a service, you will still need to take charge of your love quest. A lot of people think that once they've signed up, they've done their job, and their dates will now start flowing very swiftly and smoothly. They believe it should now be up to the service to do the rest. All an introduction service can do is provide you with only the very basic ingredients for a good partnership. *You* need to mix those ingredients together. *You* must take the time to review information you receive on others looking for possible dates. *You* must make choices and respond (with a yes or a no) to people who express an interest in meeting you. Joining a service is only the beginning—not the end—of your search.

Salespeople know that it's ridiculous to "burn leads"—i.e., to attempt to make a sale before you are really familiar with your prospective customer and his needs. Likewise, with dating you must similarly prepare yourself so that you don't miss tremendous opportunities. Before you start randomly meeting and dating, I would also suggest that you take the time to sit quietly and think through what you're looking for in a mate. What do you want most from a partner? What are you simply not willing to tolerate in one? Divide a blank page into two columns. On the left, make a list of the qualities you hope to find in someone. Include all the attributes you want, making sure that you cover at least these four concerns: looks, personality, favorite pastimes, and values. This exercise will help you focus on what you really need, and what you definitely don't want or need.

On the right side of the page, make a list of the qualities that bug you or turn you off. Include what you will not tolerate. (And I don't just mean physically.) Jot down mannerisms, fashion taste, political perspectives, and any other quirks that signal "dead-end" for you.

Maybe you're thinking, "But wait, the reason I bought this book is to discover what I want. I don't want to start out by limiting my choices this way!" That's a very open-minded attitude, and I respect it. However, everybody has minimum standards. Ignoring them doesn't make them go away. It just sets you up for disaster. If you have not yet identified these qualities, you will not likely recognize them if and when they appear.

So whether you start with a fully-fleshed-out fantasy mate or just a bare-bones list of minimum standards, start with something. And start now. You will probably revise your list more than once as your needs come more clearly into focus. By the way, I'm not asking you to do this exercise because I think you should be certain about what you want or not be open to someone who may not fit what you thought you wanted. I'm asking you to do it because I think it will serve as a path to discovering what you want, and who you are.

When you've finished both lists, please don't refer to your lists for a day or two. When you come back and review the material, how does it strike you? With a little reflection you may find that not all your "wants" are equally important; not all your "red lights" are equally offensive. Take the time to distinguish between what you'd like to find and what you absolutely must have. See the difference between what you could not tolerate and what you might be willing to overlook under the right circumstances. Remember to respect yourself and your needs. Don't compromise your true values, as this will only come back to haunt and ultimately hurt you. Be true to yourself.

Even if you're sophisticated or highly experienced at love, I bet you can benefit from this exercise. Even if you feel that love is magical and undefinable—and even if you want to keep it that way—making these notes will identify patterns that might prevent the repetition of past mistakes.

Remember: learning to be wiser about love doesn't make it any less romantic. In fact, it sets you up for *more* romance because you are better equipped when the opportunity presents itself. Healthy love *is* magical and undefinable. When you compromise your basic needs, comfort levels, or values, it' s both unhealthy and unproductive, and probably not even love at all! It could be equally undefinable, but certainly not miraculous. Beware of this kind of "love relationship"; you deserve better. But it's up to you to get the kind of healthy love that is built upon a solid, positive foundation.

ANSWERS TO THE QUIZ

1. c
2. b
3. c (Trick question—unfortunately, we haven't come that far yet.)
4. a
5. b
6. c
7. c
8. a
9. c
10. a (Gotcha—bet you thought it was all of the above!)

3 Are You a Victim of Love?

"Any fact facing us is not as important as our attitude toward it, for that determines our success or failure."
—NORMAN VINCENT PEALE

*O*ddly enough, the first step to a happier love life is a careful look at your past romances. Why? Because if you understand what went wrong the first time you fell in love and built a relationship with that person (and all the times after that), you can avoid making the same mistakes next time. As George Santayana said: "Those who cannot remember the past are condemned to repeat it."

By the time we're sixteen, we've all loved and lost at least once. By the time we're twenty-five, we've attached and split up many times. The question is, how have you reacted to the ups and downs of love? Do you, like most of us, wear the scars of a few intimate wars? Are they surface wounds that mark your bravery in love's unavoidable combat? Or do they go much deeper, down to a gut pain that makes it difficult for you to establish and maintain satisfying relationships? Do you learn from these? Do you do soul-searching? Before you can move forward, reflect upon your role in your past.

The most important question you can ask yourself when looking at your past relationships is this: Am I a victim of love? If you discover that you repeat the same mistakes, you are, more than likely, a victim, doomed to repeat unsuccessful (and sometimes quite unhealthy) patterns—unless you recognize the pattern and work on changing it.

How to Avoid the "Walking Wounded"

Okay, so maybe you're not a "victim of love"—but how can you protect yourself against getting involved with one? What are the signs to watch out for?

The number-one sign of the "walking wounded" is their constant urge to talk about past relationships. They especially want to tell you everything that went wrong. These people carry a big chip on their shoulders. They tend to blame others and avoid taking responsibility for their role in these relationships. Beware. Don't think that your love can change anything.

Of course, these repeat offenders aren't the only ones to watch out for in your quest for love. Far worse are what I call the singles saboteurs. They are people hell-bent on ruining their chances for a relationship even before they get a first date. You can usually spot them by their whiny complaints or aloof mannerisms or attitude. They say they want a "relationship." However, they don't put forth the effort, and only complain about what you haven't done, or what you've done incorrectly. These folks could depress or annoy even Mother Teresa. For example, they'll agree to go to a dance with a date, but then spend the whole time talking about how they really don't like crowds or dancing. Or they go out to dinner when they're tired and didn't really want to go out, then spend the rest of the evening complaining about the service, the food, anything and everything. Naturally, things don't work out—which was the plan all along; a self-fulfilled prophecy that is self-sabotaging.

The other day I had lunch with Jake, a friend of mine who's always flying between the heights of romantic bliss and the depths of rejection. Offhand, I can think of four different wildly passionate relationships he's had in the past year. Each of those women left him. Among other things, Jake and I talked about this book, and he asked me to write a chapter for people like him, who can walk into any room, anywhere, anytime, and within ten minutes fall madly in love with the meanest or most inappropriate person in the place.

Well, here it is, Jake. For you and millions of other men and women who want nothing more than one love that will last forever, but who end up on an endless treadmill of emotional commitment and collapse.

TESTING FOR DAMAGE

Actually, Jake is not so unusual. A lot of us, whether we like to admit it or not, go from one painful affair to another. So many of us tend to choose to stay in an unhealthy relationship, instead of being alone. But ask yourself: isn't it worse to be *alone within* a relationship? In fact, according to the National Institutes of Health, at least half of all romantic relationships involve abuse. Sometimes it's physical. Usually it's emotional. And more often than you might imagine, the abuse is a two-way street, and a continuous vicious circle. So when the breakup finally comes, at least one person (and most likely both) walk away licking their wounds.

Will time heal the hurt? The experts say it won't. They tell us that every loss takes its toll and burdens us with even more emotional baggage. That makes it just a little tougher to walk into the next relationship open and willing to take a risk.

The following quiz will help you test your knowledge of how people react to breakups and how they recover from them. It will also help you to identify what works or hasn't worked for you. Do you think a bad affair should always end—no matter the consequences? Or do you feel that the benefits of having a mate, even an imperfect one, outweigh the drawbacks of being alone?

1. For the past two years, Ron's been involved with a self-centered woman who rejects many of his sexual advances, knocks his lack of social skill, and calls him "Baldy" to comment on his receding hairline. Ron is living like:
   (a) 10 percent of all men.
   (b) 25 percent of all men.
   (c) 50 percent of all men.
   (d) more than half of all men.

2. If Ron ends the relationship, his closest friends are likely to show their support by:
   (a) sympathizing at first but then pushing him to date again.
   (b) leaving him alone to work things through.
   (c) thinking of ways to get him back in touch with his ex.
   (d) belittling his ex and reminding him of her faults.

3. But if he really loves her, Ron will mourn the relationship:
   (a) less time than he expects; it's easy to recover from neurotic attachments.
   (b) a few weeks, or until he meets someone equally abusive.
   (c) forever because that's how long true love lasts.
   (d) maybe weeks; maybe years; it depends on his basic nature.

4. Barbara is successful in her field. She has never been married, but for the past three years she's been in love with Mark, a controlling man who refuses to cohabitate with her. He insists he'll marry her one day and argues that his occasional "outside affairs" should not threaten her because he only loves her, and not the others. Then he criticizes her for voicing her concerns and feelings. Barbara is living like:
   (a) 30 percent of all women.
   (b) 50 percent of all women.
   (c) 75 percent of all women.
   (d) nearly all women.

5. Despite his abuse, when Barbara thinks about giving up the relationship, she feels afraid and like a failure as a woman. She blames herself for the problems in their relationship. This suggests that she's:
   (a) too insecure to handle a man like Mark.

(b)   perfectly normal. After all, a breakup feels a lot like failure.

(c)   unable to face life without the man she really loves.

(d)   trapped more by her poor self-image than by Mark.

6. If she ever gets up the nerve to break away from this negative relationship and leave Mark, Barbara should:

(a)   give in to all the grief she feels.

(b)   begin dating other guys right away.

(c)   stay out of the dating circuit for at least six months.

(d)   sublimate her pain into some constructive activity.

7. If Mark decides to leave her, Barbara's first reaction is likely to be:

(a)   relief; at least it's all come to the surface.

(b)   anger; only a brute walks out like that.

(c)   disbelief; he'll be back once he cools down.

(d)   hurt; who will ever love him like she did?

8. Patty's mother has always been extremely loving, attentive, and giving. Even now she enjoys being at the center of Patty's universe. Patty is very dependent upon her mother. Patty finds herself often drawn to:

(a)   men who promise to take care of her.

(b)   men who complain about her dependency.

(c)   men who belittle her efforts at self-sufficiency.

(d)   men who openly disrespect her mother.

9. Intense and prolonged physical responses to separation—chest pain, headaches, nightmares, and insomnia—are signs of:

(a)   a compulsive attachment.

(b)   a rupture in true love.

(c)   normal breakup anxiety.

(d)   unacknowledged rage.

10. The fundamental difference between true love and compulsive attachment is:

(a)   love lasts forever; compulsions always end.

(b)   love coexists with independence; compulsion cannot.

(c)   love is easy to describe; compulsion is a vague sensation.

(d)   love makes you happy; compulsion never can.

Nobody Wants to Be a Failure

There's every reason in the world for us to try to maintain our relationships, even when we feel they're bad for us. We're told from grade school on to try and try again not to be a quitter. School ignores, however, the lesson that we must learn not to put ourselves in bad relationships in the first place. And if we unfortunately find ourselves in one, school does not teach us how to recognize it and get out fast!

To compound this dilemma, most people believe that real love lasts forever. So if your relationship doesn't, there are only three possible explanations: Either you did a really lousy job of picking a partner—in which case, you're not very bright. Or you didn't work hard enough. Or you had unrealistic expectations from your partner or your relationship.

In either case, you feel that *you* failed. And who likes failure? Nobody. Perhaps even more important, who prepares for failure? Only people who expect it. And sometimes if you expect the worst, it *will* happen! If you grew up imagining that you'd eventually find a successful love match, then you probably didn't spend much time thinking about how to end love relationships. Mating skills are highly valued in this society. Parting skills are not. So when the big bust-up appears on the horizon, most of us react with denial and/or fear. In our panic, we make all kinds of mistakes.

If we're the one who's being dumped, one of those mistakes is to build a wall around ourselves and start blaming our ex. He drank too much. She was too argumentative. He ran around with other women. She was obsessed with her career. He was too aloof. She was too immature. He was a control freak. She was too clinging. He was too sexually aggressive. She was frigid. Often with the support and encouragement of our friends and family, we begin to see the other person as a villain. We play the role of being the victim of circumstances beyond our control. We believe it was the other person's fault and don't come to grips with our accountability in the process.

When you put all this together, you get a general picture of what breakups mean to people: failure and victimization. As a result, we tend to avoid ending them at almost any cost. From virtually every angle, we're urged to "try a little longer," or "give it a little more time." For the sake of the kids. For economic reasons. For professional convenience. Because we don't want to give up our lifestyle, friends, and social opportunities. Sometimes just because it seems the honorable thing to do. But whose honor? And at what cost? Other times it's because we're afraid of what the other person might do: Move out of state with your kids. Follow through on threats to make your life a miserable wreck. So we wait and try to hang on—until somebody can't stand it anymore, until one partner finds someone else, or until both partners see their emotional investment as a total waste of time. But if you take the time at the beginning of your relationship to identify or set objectives for what would really work for your long-term needs, and not compromise on your true needs, you save yourself from endless pain later on. There's a saying that goes something like this: The woman believes that she alone can change the man after they are married ("*He'll* change!"). The man prays, "I hope she *doesn't* change after we're married!"

It's wonderful to have great expectations about the person you're in a committed relationship with; they just might be fulfilled. If you accept less, you'll get less. But there' s another old and appropriate saying: "You can't make a silk purse out of a sow's ear." So if you don't recognize and accept someone's significant shortcomings *before* you proceed to that relationship, you are dooming yourself to unrealistic expectations, frustration, and conflict.

Just recently, I was reminded of how we all tend to react when someone we know is going through a breakup. Donna is an executive secretary who works in a friend's office. I don't know her well, but she's always struck me as attractive, competent, and warm. One morning she came in with swollen eyes and running mascara. Naturally, everyone asked what was wrong.

The night before, she explained, her live-in boyfriend, Allan, had announced that he needed her to move out of the house they'd shared for nearly three years. He had been pretty vague, she said. He just kept repeating that they both weren't getting what they needed out of the relationship; he wasn't happy anymore, and he could sense that neither was she. He wanted a change in his life and he needed to be single again.

As Donna talked, she ran down the long list of sacrifices she'd made for Allan: She'd given up a great apartment near the trendy part of town to be closer to where he worked. She'd overcome her distaste for exercise and gotten into tennis just so they could share a common physical activity. She'd cleaned and cooked for him, and still kept a full-time job. She'd even played weekend mom to his two children. She built her life around his demands and needs. She felt she met all his conditions. What else could she have done?

Everyone just stood in amazement. "What a jerk!" one of her friends finally said. "Wimping out like that for no reason." But later, I heard one of Donna's coworkers say to another, "Poor Donna, she's so sweet, but she's so blind."

I repeat this story because I think it shows one of many double standards we maintain about our love affairs and marriages. We don't allow the person on either side of the breakup to come out of the experience smelling like a rose. Only cowardly creeps leave; only somebody who is basically unlovable is dumped.

Be aware that these judgments are not made exclusively by other people. We make them about ourselves! We take on the role of abuser or abused, villain or victim. Most of us play the same part over and over again. We memorize all the best lines for leaving or being left. We master the behavior of the one who dumps or the one who gets dumped. And whether we realize it or not, we go from one affair to another, acting like the emotionally lopsided lover we've become.

Donna knowingly chose to adapt her life to accommodate Allan's needs. Yet now she complains about "all the sacrifices" that she made for Allan. She now assumes the role of "the self-sacrificing victim," when she consciously made her own choices. She probably would have continued to stay in that compromised relationship had Allan not left. And there's no doubt that she would have continued to be dissatisfied and unhappy, as would he. She should really be thanking Allan for allowing her to get out of this relationship that obviously wasn't right for her!

EVERY ENDING INVOLVES A LOSS

Whenever a relationships ends, it leaves emptiness behind. If the attachment was a fairly insignificant one, the void is fleeting. When it's a major relationship or a marriage, it feels like an enormous hole in our lives; even the bad ones do that! But whatever the nature of the relationship, when two people part they both lose something; everyone loses. Even if they lose what they don't want, there's an opening in their lives that wasn't there before. Whether you learn from this and follow an entirely new direction, or continue to make the same mistakes by following the same patterns, it's how you've responded to these openings in your life that determines whether you've been brutalized or just bruised by love.

Most of us react to endings by moving through a normal and predictable series of grief stages. The first of them is denial. Your lover walks out and, although you accept that things are in crisis, you refuse to admit that they're over. Instead, you may begin plotting ways to win your partner back. Or comfort yourself with the thought that today's just been a really bad day, that things are bound to get better. Or you think a vacation together is the solution. Maybe your kitchen remodeling is the problem. We can all be extremely inventive at finding excuses for the tension, and very imaginative at concocting the best remedy for it. Instead of this, we should take a reality check and objectively see it as it is.

At some point the truth sinks in. It's really over; you won't be getting back together. Now you're ready to enter the second stage of grief: depression. Suddenly, your world comes to an end, and in all likelihood, you blame yourself for that. "If only I'd spent more time with her." Or "If only I'd lost weight after the baby was born." Or "If only I'd had more money to shower on her." Or "If only I'd gotten along better with his friends." You look at the incredible loss in your life and you assume total responsibility for it. Even if your ex did the abandoning, you spend time reproaching yourself. You convince yourself that you weren't worth the effort to stay. Your new negative mantra becomes: "I'm not worthy!"

Often we put up with thoughtless treatment and stay in unfulfilling relationships because we convince ourselves that we don't deserve better. But self-love should always be our model for the love we may reasonably expect from others.

Eventually, though, you'll replace your depression with blind anger. When you do, you've gotten in touch with resentment, the third stage of loss. Instead of blaming yourself, you turn your rage on your ex—the one who left or who made your life so miserable that you had to leave. In either case, your anger is likely to at least dim any pleasant memories you have of the relationship. The bottom line is that you loved a louse or a witch, and got trampled in the process of finding that out.

Ultimately, and usually without knowing when or why, you adjust to life without the person who once meant so much to you. Part of the adjustment comes simply from living, from getting caught up in the details and concerns of your new everyday life. Before long, the desire to try again arises, and you become open toward looking for another mate.

One word of warning. We don't all enact this "grief" process in the perfect sequence that I've described here. Not everyone passes neatly from denial to resolution. A lot of us in fact, move back and forth from one stage to another several times before resolving the relationship. You can be angry one day and deny the loss the next. You may think you're over it and ready to move on with life until, suddenly, you run into your ex at a restaurant, come across an old photograph, flash back on an old memory, and plunge right back into depression or rage almost as bad as the one shortly after your breakup.

BEWARE REPEAT OFFENDERS

For a lot of very complicated reasons, some of us aren't able to mourn and learn from that relationship and then spring back, healthy and ready to enter another. In fact, some people are obsessed with dead-end relationships. They hold onto unrealistic perceptions about their dream mate, and it's no wonder that no one in real life can ever live up to these lofty standards! Since they don't ever let go of their fantasy, they're unable to allow anyone new into their life who might be really right for them.

They're what you might call repeat offenders, continuously hooked on somebody who's all wrong for them. They feel comfortable with their new relationship not because there is true compatibility, but because they haven't yet recognized that they are perpetuating the same scenario. Like my friend Jake, who always falls passionately for women who don't love him back.

What amazes me most about repeat offenders is the way they seem to land in exactly the same kind of abusive affair, over and over again. Granted, one lover's eyes may be green and the next one's brown. Not every object of their desire will be physically alike or have the same job. It's not as simplistic as that. But the same basic qualities keep coming back in each of their future partners. Maybe they're needy or demanding, insecure or controlling, narcissistic or generous. That's because while most of us like to think we have put the past to rest, we have actually held on to our confusion about compatibility. And, oddly enough, the more we consciously try to repress and resist the reality, the more we unconsciously seek out partners who arouse a negative pattern all over again. We tend to accept these repeat patterns because it's comfortable, and we can identify with it; unconsciously it's not a stranger to us.

If our earliest experiences with deeply intimate bonds are not healthy, then our lifelong response to loss is likely to be less than ideal. There's a popular explanation for certain relationship patterns. It says that when you don't get what you need during childhood you are likely to spend your entire adulthood working through the problem. If, for instance, your mother was too harsh or insensitive in responding to your earliest needs, then you may find yourself drawn to one obsessive relationship after another, always looking to find and keep what you didn't get when you wanted it the most. You may tend to replay this pattern over and over by being with someone still too harsh, or insensitive, but whom you expect to give you what your mother couldn't.

By the same token, if your early efforts to establish independence were unnoticed and unacknowledged, or if they were met with cruel criticism, then you are likely to get involved with an endless series of would-be Supermen (or Wonder Women), mates you imagine will teach you perfect competence.

Everybody needs more love. We're all looking for the love that we either got (or never got enough of) when we were children. The truth is that most of us perceive that we didn't have a "perfect" childhood. Some of us feel that we didn't get enough recognition, praise, affection, or unconditional loving. Everybody needs lots of love. More love. Surrounded by love. The Beatles said it well: "The love you take is equal to the love you make."

In either case, you've got a problem because what you want and what you know how to handle are two very different things. In the first case, you want to find the ultimate caring partner, but you only know how to deal with relatively uncaring "mothers." So that's who you look for. In the second case, you want to be personally independent, but your established pattern is to be ignored or put down for any attempt at independence. So, again, that's what you find.

Like homing pigeons who always return to the roost, we spend our lives going back to what we know and feel comfortable with. If our earliest lessons in attachment and separation were healthy, then we probably have a pretty wholesome response to mating. Things may not always work out perfectly. After all, even normal and well-adjusted people get involved in relationships that need to end. The point is, they end them; they go through a period of loss; and then they feel ready (and usually anxious) to try again.

Frankly, I don't believe that any single theory can contain the full range of human behavior, but I do think that unless we consciously work to identify and break the pattern, we re-create the familiar. Even if we hate it, we know what's expected if we've done it before. So we get into habits that eventually harden into patterns. And then we wonder in astonishment why we keep making the same mistakes.

ARE YOU A VICTIM OF LOVE?

Does your love life suggest normal ups and downs? Or are you one of those repeat offenders, a virtual love addict who craves what isn't good for you?

There are a number of "red flags" that suggest you may be crossing the fine line between passion and compulsion. Every case is different, of course, but I think the following four rules can serve as a guide for deciding just how badly you've been hurt on love's fierce battleground. And remember, just because all's fair in love and war doesn't mean we can't change the way we fight.

Rule One: Most People Give Themselves Time to Grieve; Love Addicts Never Do.

Almost as soon as a relationship ends, there are various pressures to reenter the dating circuit. On one level that's because, in a world of fast food, instant "on/off" switches, and disposable everything, it's hard to accept that loss cannot be tossed aside and replaced immediately with something more enjoyable. There's also the wonderful comfort in feeling part of a couple. Well-meaning friends might encourage you to get out there again.

On a more important level, remember that people tend to assume true love lasts forever. So, obviously, this relationship wasn't the real thing. Friends and relatives are likely to tell you to dust yourself off and resume the search for your true soulmate.

The healthy response to that pressure is to dismiss it. Only you can know the amount of grieving you need to do. Only you know how important the affair was to you. Only you know the depth to which you feel each loss. And only you know when it's time to at least start meeting new people to date.

A less healthy response is wholehearted acceptance. People who jump from one relationship to another are usually not taking the time to recover from any of them. They're too busy trying to get those primal needs met by somebody, anybody.

They're hooked on that relationship "fix." Until that pattern stops and is replaced by self-reflection, love addicts will keep hopping from one dissatisfying attachment to another. When the next relationship ends, they scratch their heads in bewilderment as to what went wrong. I know all too well about this because I've allowed it to happen to me.

But there can be an exception to this (and this, too, has happened to me). When you've been in a committed relationship that's been painfully dissatisfying for so long—when you've exhausted every solution that could possibly address and possibly heal your relationship problems—it's possible that you slowly disengage, analyze what needs of yours are not being met, and actually go through your own grieving process while still appearing to be a couple.

Rule Two: Most People Don't Experience Love "Withdrawal"; Love Addicts Do.

Clearly, love addicts rush from one relationship to another because they don't want to deal with the tremendous loss they really feel. As bad as the panic is when they think about losing someone they care about, it's nothing compared to the withdrawal that goes along with living without their love addiction. It's actually as bad as what smokers, drug addicts, and alcoholics feel when they try breaking their habits cold turkey. Some addicts get light-headed and dizzy. Others suffer from severe stomach or chest pain, even insomnia. It's okay for this to temporarily be the case, but not if it becomes a chronic problem. You think you'll only feel "normal" again by getting back together with your ex.

Some people mistake this craving for a sign that the relationship—as wrong as it was—really fulfilled their needs. Not so. Don't let the strong physical reactions throw you off. It's just that, when you're caught up in the addiction, you want to believe in some legitimate reason for continuing the attachment. You want to enable yourself to justify keeping the pattern going even if this is a negative pattern.

Curiously, when addicts finally give up and let go of each

compulsive relationship, they can feel a powerful but unrealistic sense of liberation. They are overcome by the sudden illusion of self-awareness and a false sense of confidence that this horrible mistake could never happen again. Oddly enough, because of their obsessive/addictive behavior they usually jump right into another similarly destructive relationship. Soon, failure sets in, they lose it, suffer withdrawal, and then experience another false sense of liberation.

Rule Three: Most People Don't Make the Same Mistake Again and Again; Love Addicts Do.

We can all get sidetracked sometimes. A great body can lead us off in search of love when lust is all that was ever there to find. Money and its material comforts can be alluring. So can professional status, artistic talent, or even a great sense of humor. But if you can look back at all your disastrous affairs and see a common thread tying them together, then you're probably compulsive.

Usually, the trait that first ignites the flame is tied up with some fantasy about what would make a perfect mate. Like Jake. The four women I told you about, the ones he loved so madly (if not wisely), were superficially very different. One was an accountant, another a would-be actress. A third was involved in interior design, and the fourth was an elementary school teacher. Not too similar on the surface, but they shared one common trait: they were all fanatics about the outdoors. And Jake loves that. In fact, he somehow takes it as a sign of perfect desirability. To Jake, any woman who can start a fire with two twigs and loves the outdoors is destined to be his perfect match.

Unfortunately, perfection doesn't exist. And until Jake gets that straight in his own head, his idea of a fulfilling love life probably won't either.

Rule Four: Most People Want to Move Beyond Grief; Love Addicts Don't.

After a breakup, some love addicts retreat into themselves and seem completely unable to move beyond the separation. It's almost as if they're comatose about what's happened. Ironically, they become obsessed with it. They worry about the other person: how they're doing; whether they've found a new job; whether they're getting back with an old flame that wasn't good for them. They stay stuck because of their own actions. If this is you, you need to look honestly at the relationship that's ended and your genuine investment in it. If your need to mope around and feel sad seems out of proportion to what you think is appropriate, you may have too much wrapped up in the image of yourself as victim. That can be an addiction, too.

Remember, the keen sense of loss that follows a breakup may get you sympathy—at least for a while. It may even reinforce your image as the love-sick victim, completely blameless for whatever negative dynamics led to the end of the affair. But an unhealthy yearning for loss also forces you to see yourself as weak, ineffective, unaccountable, and fundamentally unworthy. Those are unhealthy and counterproductive labels you can do without.

CHANGING FOR THE BETTER

It's easiest to change your life when there's nobody else wrapped up in it with you. Being single actually offers you a unique opportunity to review your past relationships, gain perspective, and stop any of the patterns that you consider to be destructive.

All of us can become better individuals to ourselves and to our future lovers and mates through this process of self-examination. For most people, the desired adjustments will be a matter of emotional fine-tuning so that we reach an emotional homecoming. For some others, however, the internal shifts will be more fundamentally eye-opening and far more stressful. In either situation, if you want to realistically choose someone compatible to love and form a loving relationship with, and if you want to be freely chosen by them, then—like all of us—you've got to consciously decide to be open and willing to change.

True love demands that we alter our perspectives about ourselves and the people we choose to love. When we self-reflect we learn things that we are perhaps reluctant to admit, or didn't imagine that we even needed to know. It requires us to stretch ourselves, as well as to reach toward others. All this means that we must commit to change our behaviors both publicly and privately, emotionally and spiritually.

PUT IT INTO PRACTICE

It's time for more self-assessment. At the top of a blank page, jot down the names of those with whom you've had an unfulfilling relationship. Next to each name, I want you to write the most honest explanation you can for what went wrong.

Next, I want you to write the names of two people you admire for making their relationship work. And next to their names, put down your thoughts about how and why they've been successful.

After you finish don't look at it until tomorrow. When you do take it out again, review what you've written and do the whole exercise again. This time, write the name of someone else you've loved and lost. Why didn't that relationship fulfill your needs? Underneath that, identify another good relationship and explain why you believe it works.

This project should take a full week. Every day, add just one entry to each list. Feel free to review anything you've written to date. Even note down extra insights. But for the most part, let each day be an opportunity to think about one "failed" relationship and one apparent "success" story.

By the way, not all of the relationships on your list should be romances. In fact, I hope they won't be. By looking into old school friendships and family ties that ultimately fell apart, you can begin to put together an amazing profile of yourself. By the same token, you can learn a great deal about emotional give and take when you concentrate your attention on fabulous partnerships of business associates, relatives, neighbors, teachers, and students.

When the week is through, review your work. Do you see any patterns to what makes your relationships fall apart? Are there recurring elements in what you think makes other partnerships so good? Are these things that you can work on for yourself? Of course, you can't just abandon your own bad habits overnight or wake up one morning able to imitate somebody else's strengths. Still, the simple act of identifying those behaviors, strengths, weaknesses, and ruts will help you metamorphose.

Look at the difficult times in your life as invitations for personal transformation. You have the power.

Answers to the Quiz

1. c
2. a
3. d
4. b
5. b
6. a
7. d
8. c (Because as much as she hates it, that's what she knows.)
9. a
10. b

4 *Putting Chemistry to Work for You*

"Too many people tend to confuse emotional high theater with being in love."
—JEFFREY ULLMAN

They say that sexual attraction makes you find her as sexy as Sharon Stone, as smart as Hillary Clinton, as funny as Jerry Seinfeld, and as athletic as Michael Jordan. True love is when you realize that she's as sexy as Hillary Clinton, as funny as Michael Jordan, as athletic as Jerry Seinfeld, and nothing like Sharon Stone in any category. But you care about her just the same.

Put simply, the thrill of a crush is just the tiniest—but still a significant—step toward a solid relationship. Courtship without infatuation is nothing to write home about. People will rationalize that they can't have it all. Granted, your grandmother may have eventually grown to care for her bad-tempered husband, but that may have been just because his habitual presence was comforting. But who wants to follow that example? Most of us want to start out with a big dose of passion with the hopes of maintaining this electric connection forever. We want that indescribable something, a shared sexual synergy, a special yearning based purely on animal attraction. In a word, we all want chemistry. While sex won't solve your problems when things get dicey, it can help sustain some kind of special connection between the two of you.

Whether we're driven more by some notion of love or passion toward sex, we all crave the euphoria known as "chemistry." The butterflies-in-our-stomach feeling—the passion that enraptures you with the throbbing desire of a new romance. This romantic thrill rides on the tidal wave of impulsive, instant, physical attraction. But it is this magnetic pull together with the true love that we're searching for, that we must learn to recognize, enhance, and deepen between two lovers.

The question is, how do you increase your chances of feeling it? Are there ways to identify the physical and personality traits that will guarantee the magic spark? Astrology buffs look upward for the answer. It's all a matter of cosmic harmony, they say. He may appear to be a perfect 10, but if he turns out to be a down-to-earth Taurus while you're a hot-tempered Leo, the romance is over before it begins.

Most people are a lot less certain that there is a formula for love. They just move from one week to the next, hoping that luck will turn their way. They muddle through their workday, occasionally visit a singles bar, go to almost every party they can, and register for at least one night class a year. All the while, of course, they harbor the secret fantasy that from across a crowded room true love will appear!

Guess what? It might. Maybe not with movielike drama, but definitely with enough gusto to send you spinning into—what we call falling in love. Even in the 1990s, in this decade of step-by-step guidelines to forming "workable" relationships, it's important to remember that attraction really is the best way to begin a potential love affair. It's also important to learn how attraction operates in you, and in every person who feels it for you.

CAN YOU READ THE SIGNALS?

Do you know what a man instinctively does when he finds a woman attractive? Are you aware of the subtle ways in which he moves and how he holds his head when he wants to make an approach? And what about women? Have you learned to read the verbal and nonverbal signals they send to the males who attract them? Can you distinguish between the silence that happens when they're sexually excited and the withdrawal that means they're completely uninterested?

These important questions are at the very heart of how well you attract, meet, flirt with, and impress the opposite sex. The following quiz will help you test your skill at the language of attraction.

1. If you already find someone attractive, your body will chemically respond with heightened feelings of desire when:
   (a) you get a clear message that the feeling is mutual.
   (b) you get a mixed message and have to guess what's going on.
   (c) you get a clear message that you're in for a game of hard-to-get.
   (d) you get no message at all, just a cold shoulder.
2. What sense plays the most underrated role in sexual attraction?
   (a) sight
   (b) sound
   (c) smell
   (d) touch
3. If you're not sexually attracted to the person that everyone knows is right for you, expect that:
   (a) attraction will never happen; it's either there from the start, or forget it.
   (b) attraction will develop as you become increasingly aware of your partner's best qualities.
   (c) attraction may happen or may not. It's impossible to predict sexual response.
   (d) attraction won't matter after a while.

4. When a man stands near a woman he finds attractive, he's most likely to:
    (a) approach her, look straight into her eyes, and speak.
    (b) turn away and back again, looking to see if she's noticed him.
    (c) keep his eyes down, too uncertain to risk immediate rejection.
    (d) turn toward her, look for a few seconds, and then speak.

5. When a woman has just met a man she likes, and suddenly he touches her shoulder, she's apt to:
    (a) like him even more. Touch is a basic hurdle in the chemistry of courtship.
    (b) like him less. Touch is too familiar a gesture this early on.
    (c) like him the same so long as the touch is not too intimate.
    (d) become suddenly uncertain of his feelings and hers, too.

6. The best indication of mutual attraction is:
    (a) when people repeatedly move toward each other and then retreat.
    (b) when people's body movements begin to imitate each other's.
    (c) when people keep looking at each other, but can't think of anything to say.
    (d) when people irritate each other for no apparent reason.

7. The compliment most likely to impress an attractive woman is:
    (a) "You are the best-looking woman here tonight." People like to hear what they know is true.
    (b) "You have a real insight into human behavior." We all enjoy hearing something good and often unnoticed about ourselves.
    (c) "You're a lot smarter than you look." Most pretty women worry that people think they're dumb.
    (d) "You must resent being appreciated just for your looks." It's great to be understood instead of just admired.

8. Humor is sexy. In fact, when two people are attracted to each other, they instinctively laugh together. But:

    (a)   men usually laugh too much while women don't laugh enough.

    (b)   women usually giggle too much while men don't laugh enough.

    (c)   men and women both tend to overrely on laughter to disguise their nervousness.

    (d)   nervous laughter turns off both men and women.

9. If a man moves to stand across from a woman, aligns his upper body with hers, and gives her a perfect "mirror image," he is unconsciously:

    (a)   saying that he's uninterested and wants to take control before she does.

    (b)   saying that she confuses him.

    (c)   saying that she should be more assertive with him.

    (d)   saying that he wants to speak with her.

10. Chemistry is:

    (a)   the most important element in any satisfying relationship.

    (b)   a small but essential element in a long-lasting relationship.

    (c)   a delightful extra but not essential to a happy relationship.

    (d)   something that eventually grows when you're in a satisfying relationship.

IT'S ALL IN YOUR MIND

According to a growing number of research scientists, "chemistry" is an almost perfect word for the sudden rush of feeling that gets you when you meet someone special. An even more perfect word is "neurochemistry," shorthand for the complex hormonal activity that goes on inside your brain every time you get caught in a romantic whirlwind.

The brain chemicals most often linked to love are phenylethylamine, norepinephrene, and dopamine. Together with the sympathetic nervous system, they heighten activity within the body. They trigger rapid pulse, increased respiration, shakiness, feelings of happiness and excitement, a sudden urge to talk, and the ability to overcome shyness and make an advance.

Oddly enough, fear also causes the brain to produce these chemicals. Experts think that may be why sexual attraction is strongest in the beginning, when you're just a bit afraid of your new crush. Is the attraction mutual? Can this really be as wonderful as it seems? The anxiety that comes with not being sure may actually stimulate the production of brain chemicals that we experience as passion.

So maybe Italy's legendary lover, Casanova, was not off the mark when he wrote that he would walk through rooms looking for women with trembling hands. Quivering hands meant that she felt excited and even a bit frightened at the prospect of his approach. That shakiness, he said, was a signal of sexual readiness. She was in the palm of his hand before he ever uttered a word.

Chemistry and "animal magnetism" are increasingly being studied by scientists so that we can understand how they work. Once we identify this, we will be better able to apply these secrets of nature. Biologists believe many animals secrete behavior-stimulating chemicals called pheromones to attract mates. This has led them to theorize that pheromone odors might be able to alter the behavior of other humans. This falls into that undefinable and intangible attraction that two people might have for each other.

Experiments also suggest that smell plays a big role in attraction. Undoubtedly perfumes and colognes, lotions and creams, scented oils and even exotic shampoos are all supposed to capitalize on this form of appeal. But in truth, the smells that draw you to someone are not at all so intense. In fact, they're nothing more than traces, too tiny to even register consciously but still powerful enough to change your blood pressure, speed up your respiration, and increase your heart rate within a matter of seconds.

All this information points toward a scientifically based appreciation for the unspeakable something that attracts you to one person and turns you off to another. It's all just a matter of the right chemicals coming together in your brain. It doesn't matter how perfectly suited you are to one another. You can come from similar backgrounds, work in the same field, love all the same music, and agree on every political issue. But if those brain hormones aren't activated, your dreams of a steamy affair are likely to end up as little more than hot air.

That's because thought and sexuality come from different parts of your brain. They're controlled by totally unrelated segments of your brain. So, like it or not, you can't make a logical decision to fall for someone—even if you know that all the elements for a successful relationship are in place. By the same token, you can be drawn to someone with whom you have nothing in common (and may not even like very well). It's a primal, physical force that makes you want one person and not another. This is something that must be recognized for what it is: lust, not necessarily love or compatibility.

Unfortunately, nobody knows much about what exactly makes somebody turn you on. However, there are anthropologists who focus exclusively on the mating behavior of human beings. Their research indicates that despite our so-called civilized lifestyles, the courting movements of men and women are basic animal instincts. In fact, they generally agree that for gut-level sexual attraction to end in a mature agreement to deliberately see each other again, five distinct events must take place. Whether the encounter lasts sixty seconds or six years, men and women who move beyond meeting and toward relationship soulmating all travel the same road marked by the same five progress points:

1. The first of those points is an initial approach. All of us, even the shyest, tend to move physically closer to someone we find attractive. There is disagreement over precisely how close your instinct tells you to get during this first phase of attraction, but most experts agree that it's in the neighborhood of six feet. In Western culture we intuitively know that if we get any closer we may be seen as invasive. Yet if we stay more than six feet away, we will not be acknowledged as a potential partner.

2. Now it's up to the other person. If the chemistry is working two ways, he'll turn ever so slightly and look at you. By the way, a look is very different from a stare. In fact, staring does

not often play a role in sexual attraction. That makes sense when we think about it. If you can stare, you're very much in control. You're not nervous. Remember that attraction and anxiety go hand in hand. Your confident stare means that true sexual desire is not part of the picture.

3. The third progress point is talk. As the turn occurs, one of the two people must begin a conversation, and as they talk they must continue to turn until they are face-to-face. At this point, the attraction ritual becomes more frightening because it requires that you move even closer together physically, and it introduces the element of eye contact. Again, the experts are very clear. You will always move closer than three feet apart, and most often about eighteen inches from each other. This third phase is where most encounters end. That's because it destroys the mutual poise of silence and gives clear information about educational level and social status. These rational data often interfere with the instinct that's taken you this far.

4. If you haven't stopped the mating ritual after talking is introduced, then you're ready for the fourth progress point: touch. Even while talking and turning are happening, touch will begin. It's usually light, fleeting gestures. Maybe a touch on the hand to emphasize a point in the conversation, or a shoulder squeeze to convey appreciation. Touch is where most encounters break down. Even when the first three steps have been successfully taken, touch is moving. So it's quite possible that one person (or both people) back off. Yet touch can be extremely effective in pushing the mating advance forward. Research has repeatedly shown that when people have a tendency to like you, they will like you far more if you touch them. Conversely, if they already tend to dislike you, they will like you even less if you touch them. Physical gesture is a powerful progress point in human attraction.

5. The final progress point is "synchrony." That's just a fancy word for imitation, or mutually mimicked behavior, also called "mirroring." For example, a man and woman meet at a restaurant counter. They pass successfully through the approach, the turn, talking, and gentle touch. Now, if they are

really attracted to each other they will unconsciously begin to move in unison. They may pick up their glasses at the exact same moment, take the same number of sips, and lean forward at the same angle to put it down. Then with perfect timing, they will each lean back in their chairs and one will cross a leg toward the other. Broken down into tiny pieces like this, synchronized movement seems awkward and contrived. But when two people are enjoying genuine chemistry, they will fall into the pattern without any effort at all. In fact, research anthropologists maintain that mirrored behavior is the single best indicator of a mutual sexual interest.

WARNING SIGNS

Looking for signs that signal sexual or other chemistry between you and someone else is very helpful. But we had best not ignore certain signals or behaviors that tell us to stay away. Most of these signs are not so reliant on nonverbal communication. Most are communicated by words; the very omission of certain words can also serve as a clear warning sign.

Here are some helpful warning signs for both single men and women:

- Do they frequently criticize or find fault in others?
- Do they seem unable to take and utilize criticism?
- Do they appear happy in their job?
- Are they more positive or more negative persons?
- Do they seem to take on the role of "victim" on too many subjects?
- What about communication? Is there usually some important element missing from the story a person tells that makes a big difference in what it means?
- How affectionate are they?
- How confident are they?
- What about long-range goals? Are they absent? Unrealistic?
- How flexible or rigid are they?

- How do they treat others? Friends, family, fellow employees, the waitress or busboy at a restaurant?
- Do they follow up on their commitments?
- How dependable are they? Can you count on them?

MAKE IT ALL WORK FOR YOU

If it's all so easy, why are so many of us single? Shouldn't we all be perfectly paired off by now?

Well, for one thing, attraction is not always mutual. Unfortunately for millions of would-be lovers around the world, there's no guarantee that your overwhelming desire for that sexy stranger will be returned. It's sad but true: you actually can be crazy in love with a woman who doesn't even know that you're alive. You really can feel down-to-your-toes attracted to a man who would enjoy having you as a friend, but nothing more.

Another problem is what you might call mismatched levels of intensity at any one of an encounter's essential progress points. For instance, you see a pretty woman at a party and (to open up the possibility of a conversation) you ask, "Can I get you a drink?" In your mind, you've made a polite and friendly gesture of interest. Nothing more. For you, it's a low-intensity signal of attraction. Well, you may have made the offer to someone who interprets it as a pushy, brash come-on. Quite obviously, she views your invitation as a high-intensity signal. When that sort of misunderstanding occurs, things go nowhere fast.

Such difficulty will drive you crazy unless you remember the number-one rule of courtship: don't take it too personally. To make the rule easier to follow, remember this: the vast majority of approaches are going to end in failure. That means that occasionally you may approach someone who thinks you're totally disgusting. Far more often, though, it just means there wasn't enough chemistry between you to get the encounter past all five progress points. Rejection is an equal-opportunity annoyance. You may have to get a lot of "nos" before the right "YES!"

That news should make it easier for you to overcome the fear we all have about making an initial approach. Unfortunately, we figure that if we can't do it perfectly, we'd better not do it at all. And the more attracted we are to someone, the less willing we feel to take the risk. But if you make it too important, you're wasting a lot of energy. Even the best approach style will work only a small percentage of the time.

Trust me. You really don't have to be all that clever or bright. You don't have to make a dazzling first impression. You don't have to worry about whether your first comment was too aggressive or too passive. You don't need to do it perfectly. In fact, you don't even need to do it well. *You just need to do it.* Repetition gives you confidence and security and also softens the rejection factor.

With that on the record, though, let's look at what the experts say will increase your chances of moving confidently from the first glance to the request for a date. The following is really a distillation of what I know works. It's based on my review of just about every book ever written on the subject of pickup lines, conversation starters and "men talk/women talk," and on the feedback I get from real single men and women.

Fact Number One: During the First Conversation With Someone You Like, It's Good to Repeat the Person's First Name Three Times.

Nobody knows exactly why, but successful flirts all agree that you can improve your chances with a gorgeous stranger if you sincerely utter his (or her) name a few times during your first encounter. I say three times, not because three is a magic number but because three times will definitely convey your desire to connect. Just realize that the average length of time that you spend talking with any new acquaintance is just four minutes. So this three-time rule has to be done quickly.

If you don't think you'll remember, formalize the process. Use the name when you first meet. (And unless you mean it, don't comment on its beauty or strength. Just say it.) Then at some point during the encounter, say the name again. You might use it to emphasize a point. ("It's true, Judy, I've done my own taxes for the past five years, and I hate it.") Or you can use it to focus attention on a request ("Jerry, would you be willing to move over there? The music is a little too loud for me here."). Then, as you say good-bye, use their name a third time. All this shows that you care enough to remember this person's name, and that you have paid attention. It makes the person feel good, too.

Fact Number Two: Only Unexpected and Sincere Flattery Is Sexy.

Everybody knows that when you flirt, you should flatter. The problem is that most of us go for the obvious. We meet an attractive man and, wham, the first compliment out of our mouth is, "You look like you really take care of yourself!" It's nice, but let's face it, he already knows that. And many other women have probably used it. So take a moment to think of a compliment that he's not already heard that night. Maybe you can comment on his unusual watch, or on his insight when it comes to human behavior. Maybe after talking with a woman for a very few minutes, you can flatter her because she has such feminine hands or because of her sense of humor.

Remember, though, a compliment must be genuine because insincerity will always show through. If you're sincere, praise is effective. If you're insincere, it's manipulative. Don't forget to look the person in the eye when you talk! This adds substance to what you say, and indicates that you're really seeing the person. If you can't think of something you really like about the person, skip it. Besides, if you've talked with the stranger for four minutes and haven't discovered anything you like, your chemistry experiment is rushing toward washout anyway.

Fact Number Three: It's Good to Be Nice, But It's Bad to Be Too Nice.

It sounds too basic to mention, but you'd be surprised how often people forget to be nice when they flirt. In the desire to be up-front, I hear a lot of singles volunteer very unappealing information when it's inappropriate to do so. Like the guy who tells every woman he meets at a party that the women's movement has gone too far. Maybe it has. Maybe it hasn't. But why bring it up in the very first conversation? It's as though he wears a neon sign over his head: No Enlightened Woman Wanted. Well, guess what? He'll never have a relationship with one. There's plenty of time to opine—the first meeting, though, is not the time to offer political, religious, or potentially controversial opinions that might alienate the person whom you'd like to get to know.

By the same token, don't be too agreeable at the expense of compromising who you are and what you believe. For one thing, it can be misleading. Your attempt to convey interest may be seen as embarrassingly too much or phony. What's more, if you're too extending, you remove all the mystery. (And don't forget that sexual confusion—and I don't mean teasing or game playing—is a necessary ingredient in sexual attraction.)

Fact Number Four: Most Women Should Use Humor More. Most Men Should Use It Less.

People who study male/female behavior generally agree that attraction and laughter go together. When people like each other, they usually laugh during their earliest interactions. It may be nervous laughter, but it's still laughter. So expect it to happen. In fact, initiate it, as long as the giggle or chuckle is sincere. I suggest that you stay away from sarcasm as that might be too threatening, and you don't yet know whether your audience would find that appealing.

Psychologists also tell us that laughter comes easiest to men, largely because they use it so much with one another. Laughing with your buddies is a male fact of life. Women, on the other hand, like to talk more and laugh less. From my experience men appreciate women who not only have a good sense of humor, but are also positive and upbeat. This difference between the sexes can easily ruin the attraction ritual. Up against the high-pitched emotions that accompany sexual chemistry, men tend to laugh and joke too much. It's their attempt to lighten the moment, to keep it playful. Women usually laugh and tease too little, a sign that they're already after deeper-level conversation. So think about your natural tendencies and, if necessary, consciously adapt them to the one you're with.

Fact Number Five: The Best Time to Say Good-bye Is When You're Sure the Chemistry Is Working.

In attraction, it's best to follow the lead set by popular politicians, athletes, and entertainers: always leave 'em wanting more. When you flirt you give someone your undivided attention. That's very flattering. But it's an undeniable law of nature that we want what we can't have.

So, a good flirt will also say good-bye when things are going well. Don't wait around for things to hit a downward slide. Instead, politely leave as soon as you're sure you're interested in seeing or hearing from the other person again. And, of course, you both can exchange business cards. (Special note: If you don't have a business card, get a card with your name and phone number made up. It's not difficult at all. And it can easily and frequently help you reconnect with people whom you'd like to see again.)

READING THE SIGNALS THAT COME YOUR WAY

Even if you follow the rules and do everything right, how will you know if it's working? You can't very well come right out and ask if the other person's feeling the same lust that you are. So, short of a passionate kiss in the fresh produce section, is there any way to know if that person you meet at the grocery store actually likes you, too?

Absolutely! Although most of us are oblivious to them, men and women send each other sex signals all the time. Behavioral anthropologists have formally studied them, written them down, tested them, and found that they operate—not just some of the time, but all of the time.

Listen for the meaning between the actual words. Often what we say is *not* what we mean. We may hide our true feelings from what we're verbally communicating. Sometimes we are unable to actually communicate what we feel. So if you listen attentively and something strikes you as odd, look your companion in the eye and help the person out. Close watching will reveal what eyes and body language are trying to tell you. Often these are the true indicator of the real meaning behind the message.

For example, both males and females instinctively lift their shoulders when they find someone attractive. The movement inward and up is very slight but it's enough to covey the message that an approach is welcome. This same gesture will actually be made continuously throughout the courtship phase, always signaling that the next advance would be welcomed. In contrast, when we are near someone we don't like, we tend to cross our arms in front of our chest. You might think this forceful stance would at least attract women to men, but it doesn't. Instead, it's a coded way of saying, "Don't intrude. I'm threatening. I'm tough." As a result, it's a turnoff to all but the most self-destructive.

There are many other sex signals that you send out and receive every day. Like the tilting of your head, an ever so slight movement down and to the side. This timeless gesture of attraction has been caricatured by everything from high fashion to porno magazines. In its most natural form, however, the tilt is a subtle maneuver that communicates coy interest. There's even something called the "Tit Stance" for women: their shoulders are tilted slightly back, their breasts protrude, stomach is sucked in and head tilted.

Women, in particular, also pigeon-toe a bit when they're attracted to someone. Again, it's an unconscious body stance and experts say it's meant to convey openness and even mild intimidation. They even suggest that if a woman will deliberately toe in ever so slightly, it will indicate eagerness for a possible advance. That's one of the most fascinating things about sex signals: we understand and respond to them without conscious thought because they're part of our instinct.

When we're subjected to stress, our eyes blink faster and uncontrollably. They do the same thing when we're sexually attracted. You can bet that's what mascara and eyeliners were all about when first developed. They are a way to accent and draw attention to this signal of sexual arousal.

Eye contact is an equally powerful cue that attraction is happening. On average, a stranger's eyes will rest on your face for one or two seconds before moving on. When you like someone, however, it's hard to look away that fast. As I've already said, a cold stare is not alluring. In fact it's threatening and makes most people (both men and women) feel uncomfortable. But a slightly lingering look that just exceeds the acceptable two-second limit definitely signals attraction. When you get more than one of those three-second gazes, you can be sure there's more coming at you than simple curiosity.

Forward leaning is another attraction signal that most people notice unconsciously. When you sit across the table from someone you like, you will unintentionally lean your upper body forward. This signals that you would like to move closer; you're being drawn toward the other. Without realizing it, the other person will "know" your meaning. And if mutual interest exists, that person will lean up and toward you, too. Otherwise, you'll see an involuntary movement back, away from you—disengagement.

This two-way body leaning will ultimately lead to what's been called "body alignment," a kind of mating dance done by mutually attracted men and women. Slowly, they will aim themselves at each other and square off chest-to-chest for several minutes—as if to show that conversation is about to start. By squaring his chest with a woman's, a man indicates that he wants to speak. When this approach is rewarded by an eye gaze, blink, or touch, the attraction is mutual.

All these sexual codes happen without our trying to accomplish them. So watch yourself and see when you tend to utter the silent language of attraction. You may be shocked by who really draws you in, and who doesn't. Sometimes our minds are a million miles from understanding what excites us about that stranger living down the block or that woman who fills our prescriptions at the drugstore. So "listen" with both your ears and eyes to the unspoken and attend to what is not being said in words.

By the same token, there's no way to talk yourself into finding someone sexually enticing, because initial attraction is not about thinking. It's about feeling; it's about your body reacting on a subconscious level. It's about surrendering our thoughts and letting our most basic drives take control. It doesn't allow the mind even the least input. For that very reason, it should never be the sole (or even the most important) ingredient in any relationship. Men and women, for all their animal impulses, are ultimately controlled by drives far more powerful and more refined than sexuality. Unlike other beasts, we can subsume our urges in work, religion, creative expression, and even avocation.

But don't kid yourself. Chemistry should not be shrugged off as some adolescent fixation. It is very real. Without it, the most appropriate love affair in the world can't possibly live up to your own greatest expectations.

PUT IT INTO PRACTICE

Now you're armed with some practical information about what you do when you're physically aroused and what other people do when they're aroused by you. What's your next move?

Well, you could hit every singles bar and Caribbean cruise, and look for signs of lusty interest. Frankly, I don't think that would get you what you're really after. Those situations wouldn't provide you with the environment necessary to meet as many qualified relationship-minded singles. You've got to send the right signals to the right people, and give yourself the opportunity for this to occur. Even the best message is ineffective if it's not given to the right audience.

So before you let the Cave Man or Amazon Warrior in you go wild, think things through a bit. It's time to add to your "Notes to Myself." Once again, divide a blank page in half. On the top, list the qualities you like most in the opposite sex. Don't try to impress anybody with your desire for brilliance, political insight, or exceptional sensitivity. This list is for your eyes only. So get real. What really turns you on? Think about it and make a list. Some traits are bound to be physical. But jot down other turn-ons, too. What kind of clothes do it for you? What careers seem sexy? Political and religious inclinations. Race. Age. What about temperament? Do you like a talkative date, or a quiet one? Do you want someone who puts you on a pedestal? Or are you after the type who wants to be adored?

As you make your list, remember that I'm not asking you to create the image of the person you'd like to want—somebody perfect and well-balanced in every way. This exercise is about sexual chemistry, and we don't always like what our mind tells us we should want. Personal kinks are a part of each and every one of us, and your kinks have a lot to do with what turns you on. Let this exercise give you permission to explore exactly those physical traits, emotions, and behaviors that make you hot!

On the bottom half of the page, list all the qualities that you think might draw someone to you and what you have to offer. Be fair to yourself. For example, if you're bald, put that down. After all, there are women who don't just find baldness acceptable, they love it! The same thing goes for being a bit too thin or too fleshy; very tall or short; facial hair or not. Exceptionally bright or a bit wacky. And what about your personality? What features of your temperament and background could attract a person?

In the end, this exercise should teach you a great deal about yourself. It may unlock the door to a better understanding of what makes you tick as a sexual being. It should also serve to prove that almost everything about you has the potential for attracting someone. It just needs to be the right someone. And don't worry: by following my system, you will multiply exponentially your chances of meeting someone special.

ANSWERS TO THE QUIZ

1. b
2. c
3. a
4. d
5. a
6. b
7. b
8. a
9. d
10. b

5 Initiating the Ritual: The First Official Date

"To do anything in this world worth doing, we must not stand back shivering and thinking of the cold and danger, but jump in, and scramble through as well as we can."
—SYDNEY SMITH

A date. Almost every single person wants one, but more often that not won't muster up the confidence it takes to land one. We get sidetracked, trying to decide a whole list of questions. Who should ask whom for a date? And who should pay for it? Who decides location and when? Should the outing be planned down to the smallest detail? Or is it better to let things unfold naturally? Should sex be a part of early dating? Or is emotional exchange the goal?

Along with the craziness that comes with these routine questions, there are even more subtle ways in which we undermine ourselves. For example, we wonder if the woman we want to ask out is really a "Wonder-Cutie," or one of hell's "Fatal Attractions" in disguise. We ponder the possibilities and typically take the easy way out.

Even the word "dating" dredges up powerful uneasiness and embarrassment. I mean, who dates? "Teenagers date," goes one school of thought. And that reminds us of the insecurity and awkwardness of those teenage years. As adults, dating inflames our insecurities because we feel unsure and imbalanced. "Adults go out." Mature men and women let real relationships grow spontaneously from friendship and mutual understanding. Dating sounds so artificial. How could you possibly get to know someone *that* way?

Recently on one of the national talk shows I was asked a personal question about my own experiences as a newly single man. "I don't like it," I said with mixed feelings. "I enjoy meeting new people and learning about them. But at the same time I don't like feeling like I constantly have to sell myself. I feel that I have to prove who I am; how nice I am; my lifestyle and my real feelings to gain her interest and acceptance, all to someone whom I don't even really know!"

We all tend to want to resist exposing ourselves and the vulnerability that goes along with it by holding back some of the most important elements of who we are until we know that person better. At the same time I recognize that before any relationship can unfold, it takes considerable getting-to-know-you time: the basics of who you are, what you like, what makes you tick, and a long laundry list of your likes and dislikes.

In every culture, from the dawn of time, the same law of nature has applied: it's disconcerting to pursue someone you like. Unfortunately, today there are no defined cultural mores for us to follow. So single men and women in the 1990s face real challenges when it comes to dating and relating. First, they've got to move beyond the initial worry that they might be rejected. What's more, they must find ways to contact prospective and available partners. Falling in love and having someone to ourselves—that's what we're all after. But sexual interest is only a springboard to real romantic interaction. In other words, between attraction and commitment, there is a vast and terrifying place that we call dating. Most of us wait for it impatiently in our early teens, and dread it by our mid-thirties. But if you want a life mate, you've got to get out and date.

HOW WELL DO YOU DATE?

Whether you've been single all your life or have recently terminated a long-term relationship, you probably have some experience with dating. Take a minute to quiz yourself on the ins and outs of it all. Remember, like all the quizzes in the book, this one isn't looking for the absolutely right or wrong answer. It's just asking you to think about the ways to get a date.

1. Karen is a thirty-four-year-old single professional who recently settled in Houston. She is attractive, ambitious, bright, and always willing to go on a blind date arranged through a friend. Nevertheless, she has spent three years in therapy trying to figure out why she isn't in a permanent relationship. Karen's biggest problem is probably that:
   (a) she needs her friends to introduce her to more men.
   (b) she intimidates most men.
   (c) she needs to take more responsibility for meeting people.
   (d) she needs to decide what kind of man would make her happy.
2. When she thinks about taking out a personals ad, joining a dating service, or going to a singles bar, Karen feels uneasy and embarrassed. That's probably because:
   (a) she doesn't have enough genuine self-confidence.
   (b) she knows those actions would leave her open to rejection.
   (c) she doesn't want a relationship; she only thinks she does.
   (d) she worries about the kind of men she'd meet that way.
3. Risk and romance are:
   (a) always linked. You can't have one without the other.
   (b) mutually exclusive. You can't be open if you feel you're at risk.

(c)   sometimes connected, but usually not.

(d)   inseparable in unwholesome relationships but not in healthy ones.

4. The majority of singles prefer to meet people through:
    (a)   sheer luck. That's why they're still single.
    (b)   friends. That way, they'll start out with having something in common.
    (c)   singles bars. They offer lots of people who demand no commitment.
    (d)   their work. It suggests common goals.

5. The majority of singles report that their least favorite way of meeting is through:
    (a)   haphazard destiny. Who believes in love at first sight?
    (b)   friends. It's a sure-fire way to stay single and lose friends.
    (c)   relatives. There's nothing so boring as your aunt's new accountant.
    (d)   singles bars. They're the ultimate land of plastic people.

6. Research indicates that love at first sight happens for:
    (a)   one person out of 1,000.
    (b)   one person out of 100.
    (c)   one person out of 10.
    (d)   anyone whose heart is open to it.

7. The best way to meet a compatible dating partner is:
    (a)   through chance encounter. Fate may be fickle but it's always on your side.
    (b)   through off-hour pastimes. That's where you get to meet people as they truly are.
    (c)   through personals ads. It's great to let your fingers do the shopping.
    (d)   through a dating service. Here you meet only people who are available and looking as seriously as you are.

8. If a woman asks a man for a date, he's most likely to think:
    (a)   she's aggressive and unfeminine.
    (b)   she's "easy."
    (c)   she's desperate for any relationship.
    (d)   she's wonderfully willing to help start the courtship.

9. If the chemistry is right, a first date will be:

(a) awkward anyway.

(b) relaxed but without sexual contact.

(c) explosive!

(d) relaxed one minute and awkward the next.

10. Which of the following would make the best first date?

(a) A quiet dinner for two. That way you can really concentrate on each other.

(b) A hike in the woods. It combines exercise with lots of time to get acquainted.

(c) A trip to the zoo. When conversation falters you can laugh at the animals.

(d) A movie. You can just sit close, watch, and decide if the chemistry is right.

NO PAIN, NO GAIN

Not all the good ones have been taken. After all, *you're* still available, aren't you? Yet, what's the most common complaint that single people have against dating?

You're right: "I never meet anybody interesting."

Can you believe it? There are millions of unattached men and women out there looking. Yet most individual singles say they can't find even one person who's engaging enough to get to know. With this in mind, it's no wonder these same singles have a difficult time finding the one person who's right for them. Some people attract the wrong people because they're looking in the wrong places. Meeting people in a positive environment increases that person's attractiveness. Scores of advice books have been written on this subject. Most of them offer the same bottom line: *"If you're not meeting the right people, you need to change your expectations."* These authors warn against holding out for the best-looking, most intelligent, funniest, and warmest partner in the world. Unless you're a 12 on the scale of 1 to 10. The trouble is, what's the alternative? To settle for less than you want and deserve? Be open-minded—even if you're asked out by people who seem not to be your type—they may be your true love in disguise.

I don't think the solution to your love quest lies in pairing off with someone who can't fulfill your expectations of a life mate. (Remember the list you made at the end of Chapter 2?) In fact, that strikes me as a prescription for disaster. It's also an outrageously insensitive approach to mating. When you begin a courtship with poor intentions, you're only delaying the inevitable. One or both of you will feel dissatisfied and unfulfilled within your relationship. Save yourselves the heartache and time *now*! You both deserve the chance to date somebody you truly like.

The truth is, you probably don't meet anybody really worth meeting because you don't have easy access to enough singles. Dating is a numbers game. It's as simple as that. In all probability, prior to reading this book, nobody taught you how to compensate for that very real obstacle. So the problem isn't you; the problem is society. Despite the growing number of single men and women, we haven't developed good-enough ways to bring available people together. Why is the singles bar the place that we all think other singles go? What does *that* say about us? There's one thing you can be sure of: the old ways of meeting don't satisfy the needs of modern people. High school and college romance are great, but very few of us nowadays want to settle down so early in life. Religious affiliation can function well as a source of introduction, but only for the religious. And community—that supportive cluster of men and women with whom you share values and personal history—is all but extinct in this country.

Many traditional methods may work for some, although they frequently take a lot of time and energy. Many of today's new ways of meeting people don't provide such a friendly psychological mask. It's pretty hard to appear indifferent as you walk into a singles bar or dial the phone number you found through a personals ad. Even singles business networking mixers provide only a thin disguise for why everyone is there. Today, looking is a much riskier business than it used to be. Talk about vulnerability. You don't even need to say that first hello to feel rejected. You just have to walk into the room!

Frankly, that's not altogether bad. The bitter truth is that the riskier it is—the more it makes you feel exposed as a "seeker"— the likelier it is to produce results. That's a hard pill to swallow. It would be a sweeter world if love really did come to those who deserve it. But it doesn't. Now, more than ever before, love comes to those who seek it, and who do so intelligently. So if you're in search of a relationship, you must get out there and let your interest be known.

GETTING THE RIGHT PERSON'S ATTENTION

In the groundbreaking book *You Just Don't Understand Me*, author Deborah Tannen states, "Men and women might just as well be speaking different languages." We are raised and affected differently by our parents and socialized upbringing so that our styles of communication and expectations of how we interpret what others say to us are not the same.

Men and women seem to speak so differently because we have a different understanding of what the other sex is really saying. When it comes to communicating and socialization skills, women are more evolved. Numerous studies have shown that women communicate more to create relationships, while men communicate to gather information. Men seem to feel threatened by women's open communication style. They are less able than women to expose their internal conflicts and emotions.

Both sexes need to learn to accept that we may see things differently, learn to compromise, and negotiate new behaviors and create their own unique language.

There's a handy acronym that will help you remember communication techniques useful for both your personal and business life. It's called "AIDA" (and it's even more powerful than the Italian opera by the same name).

"A" = Attention. Use opening verbal remarks and nonverbal cues to gain someone's attention and interest. Why bother complaining that "all the good ones are taken" when you see or hear people who pique your interest? Take the first step and get that person's attention. Sure, you might get rejected, but isn't that an expected part of dating? Don't concern yourself over objections or rejections. Take joy in the knowledge that you are one of the "good ones." Think positive. Feel good about yourself. You don't

have to be obnoxious, overtly intrusive, or phony. All you have to do is make a move. Get eye contact. Hold eye contact. Smile. Say something nice. Say whatever comes to mind and forget about memorizing "1,001 Best Opening Lines."

"*I*" = *Interest.* Create mutual interest and intrigue. Learn as much as you can about the other person in as brief a period as possible. We're all flattered by someone who is sincerely interested in us. Create a safe environment so that others will want to give you some information about themselves. Naturally, it's a two-way street, so share some mutually interesting things about yourself.

"*D*" = *Desire.* Build desire in you by giving reasons why you are worth getting to know. While conceit and "I-did-that-I-do-this-I-am-great" are certain turnoffs, good self-esteem will shine through. Remember who your audience is: it's the opposite sex. So identify those qualities, activities, and areas in which you might share common interests, and talk about them.

"*A*" = *Action.* Motivate the other person to take action, to want to get to know you better by spending some time alone with you. Feel good about yourself and people are likely to want to be with you. Then, make a date!

Remember, you never get a second chance to make a first impression with a prospective date.

MEETING FOR MATING

To save you time and trouble, I've put together the following list of common how-to's for meeting other singles. I call it the Six Levels of Risk and Romance Potential. It proves my basic premise: if you want to discover love you've got to get real. You must declare yourself an explorer, a romantic adventurer who follows a realistic route.

Level One: The Faith-in-Destiny Approach

Do you believe in love at first sight? You should, because it happens. But only to one person out of every hundred. Or is it one out of a thousand? Anyhow, it's pretty rare. And it happens more in the movies than in real life. So if you're holding out for life to drop the ideal mate in your lap, you'd better find a soft cushion to sit on because you've got a long wait ahead.

When it appears in front of you on the printed page, this destiny approach can seem too naïve to be taken seriously. But don't kid yourself. Research tells us that it's still the form of introduction that people want most. Believe it or not, a tremendous number of single men and women even expect it. They think that, in time, their soulmate will magically appear. And, best of all, they don't have to do anything to hurry love along. That's part of the modern myth of romance: you don't need to *do* anything because fate, karma, or cosmic intelligence will bring love into your life at precisely the right moment.

It's important to repeat this . . . get *real!*

I'm convinced that it's actually the fairy-tale simplicity of this approach that makes it so popular. It gives you such an incredibly easy role to play in the mating game. Nothing is demanded of you. You aren't asked to take any risks. You don't need to expose yourself in any way. You just have to wait. And wait. And . . . wait. That's the downside to putting all your faith in destiny. Fate has all the power. You have none.

This method of meeting rates a lowly 2 (out of ten points) on both risk and romance potential. You may take no risk, but you probably get no romance when you want it most.

Level Two: The Relying-on-Friends-and-Relatives Approach

About ten years ago, a study revealed that nearly 35 percent of all single men and women met most of their dating partners through friends and relatives. Today, the percentage has fallen to less than 18 percent.

The biggest problem with this approach to dating is that you usually have to rely on coupled friends for help. Why? Because all your single acquaintances keep the best people for themselves. Or, if they "recycle their dates," they've already rejected them. Unfortunately, couples tend to know couples. They just don't have a lot of single friends. So if you depend on them to find you a catch, realize that you're fishing in a small pool.

If it's so ineffective, why do people continue to accept dinner party invitations from friends who promise an introduction to someone "really great"? Because there's a giant safety net beneath the relatively small risk you take in showing up. You can walk in, size up the prospect, and, if you like what you see, settle in for a great evening. If, on the other hand, you feel you've been set up with an extra from Hollywood's most recent horror film, you can still relax because you are among friends.

Despite the anxiety that blind dates create, they have worked for many. Sure, they're a gamble, but if you've got enough time and personal stamina, they can help you meet lots of new people. My friend Cynthia swears by them. She's about as picky as they come, but she trusts her friends enough to take their suggestions.

This method of meeting rates a shaky 3 for both risk and romance potential. It might work. Just like you might win the lottery tomorrow. But who wants to lose time and risk a lifetime of happiness on those odds?

Level Three: The Run-a-Personals-Ad Approach

No one is sure how many people place or answer these open mating calls, but we assume a great many do. A few years ago, *New York* magazine estimated just its share of responses at over 6,000 per week. The biggest alternative weekly in Los Angeles recently added a techno twist to its classified personals section. By instituting a personals 900 telephone number, it brought in nearly 25,000 minutes of individual responses per issue. And that was only in its first month of operation! There's no doubt about it: personals ads have appeal to the masses.

Research indicates that most single people who use the personals would rather place an ad than answer one. Why? Because it gives *them* the power and reduces their chances of being rejected. When you place an ad, you get to ask for what you want, reveal only what you choose to reveal about yourself, and sit back to await results. Then, as the letters or calls of interest come in, you can pick and choose the ones that you like best. (Be sure to keep in mind that these ads easily lend themselves to hype and misrepresentation on the part of the ad placers.) Because personals ads rely on the written word, it's quite possible to meet up with a modern-day Cyrano de Bergerac, where the person who you think wrote the wonderful ad isn't the person who actually shows up at your front door for your first date!

Actually, there is even more risk when you try to find love through the personals columns. At some point, you have to pick up the phone and dial a number that's been submitted to you. Unfortunately, even this venture is unavoidable. That's the problem with personals ads. You can look over the response letters for as long as you like. Forever, if you choose. And who will ever know the difference? Even the respondents won't know that you couldn't bring yourself to call. They'll just figure you weren't interested in them.

This method of meeting rates a solid 5 for both risk and romance potential. All things considered, you've got about a fifty-fifty chance of finding someone—but not necessarily one with whom you might form a committed and satisfying relationship—through the personals, if you force yourself to answer *every* letter of interest.

Level Four: The Business-Mixer Approach

Since the mid-1980s, a new twist on the age-old party mixer has been tried in cities all around the country. It's called "networking for singles," and here's how it works: You go to an upscale restaurant, bar, or hotel lounge after work one day. You pay your money (usually about ten or twenty dollars) and are instantly surrounded by an ocean of singles, all of them looking to "network." It's important to bring plenty of your business cards, because, after all, that's why you've supposedly come in the first place.

Of course, the real reason you're there is to meet people for entirely social reasons. The flimsy excuse of being there to enhance your professional connection is just a psychological crutch that helps everyone feel a little more at ease while they do the same things that they would do at any other ordinary social mixer.

On my ten-point scale of risk and romance, I'd rate these mixers a near 7. So long as you feel comfortable talking about business, they do give you a fairly comfortable environment in which to meet new people.

Level Five: The Singles-Bar Approach

Try this sometime: walk into a singles bar and act nonchalant. I predict that within thirty minutes, you'll either mimic the usual behavior that characterizes these night spots, or you'll leave. That's because when you spend time among people who have gathered for no reason but to meet possible dates, you've got to acknowledge that you're looking, too.

Frankly, that's the best thing to be said of the bars. They force you to take some degree of risk. Just being there says you're looking.

Virtually every study on the subject indicates that people hate bars for two specific reasons. First, they don't like the people they meet in bars. Over and over again, single people say that they expect little more than "rank dishonesty" and "game-playing" from anybody they initially get to know at a singles bar.

The second criticism has to do with how people view their own behavior while they're in these lookout towers. Sociologists Margaret O'Connor and Jane Silverman interviewed hundreds of men and women on the subject, and found that both sexes admitted to acting less like themselves in bars than in any other place. Men act their most macho and try to appear uninterested—until they're ready to make an approach. Then they're gruff and fairly aggressive. Women try to look lively and amusing. They laugh too much and toss their heads back at virtually anything, trying to show how much fun they are to be with. Game playing is the operative word at bars.

Perhaps one of the most dangerous aspects of singles bars is that they give everyone equally unknown marital status (I think we should rename singles bars "unknown-marital-status taverns"). There is no way to tell whether a person is married or not, and that can pose real problems. Sometimes a person who is temporarily separated goes to a bar believing that he or she should be free to pursue a liaison, at least for the night. More often, though, a married person purposely pretends to be single. In these situations, it's too easy for an innocent person to be hurt emotionally.

Still, experts tell us that one out of every five single men and women uses the bars to meet prospective dates. They go partly because the clubs are specifically called "singles" bars. They buy into the name, and are likely to participate in anything else branded "especially for singles."

I also suspect that the bars provide an acceptable "out" for people. Since research tells us that most people visit them in groups of two or three, they can always tell themselves (and anyone else) that they went for a friend. They weren't personally interested, they claim; it was just an act of friendship.

This method of meeting slides in with a slippery 3 for both risk and romance potential. If you're willing to behave in bar fashion, you're quite likely to meet prospective dating partners. But, given the two-way personality deception that goes on, how will either of you know if you really like each other?

Level Six: The Dating Service Approach

Think about it. The so-called riskiest of all introductions come through dating services. That's because both the man and woman are totally exposed (in a good way). There's absolutely no way that either of them can deny the fact that they're looking for love or friendship. In fact, they've put their money and their ego on the line to buy a membership. Ask the members of virtually any service whether they're there for a date, and they'll quickly respond with an emphatic "NO!"; they're there for a *relationship*. (So why did they join a "dating service"? They would have liked to have joined something with a more fitting name—"relationship service"—but that's not what they're called.)

Whatever they're called, dating services are generally divided into two principal types: matchmaking services and self-selection services. The former are much more common and range from the "momma-poppa" variety where the owner might run the service out of her home, to the large-scale franchise and/or chain type. Regardless of their business size, they all work pretty much the same: they match you with someone of their choice. Sometimes they use psychological tests; sometimes they rely on proprietary "what-do-you-like?-what-don't-you-like?" questionnaires; and sometimes they rely on gut instinct. Who you go out with is strictly *their* choice.

If you like to make your own selections, then video dating is the path for you. You are responsible for doing your own research. First, you read autobiographical information on other members. You learn about their values, interests, attitudes, height, weight, age, whether they smoke, drink, have kids, want to have kids, and of course, what they're looking for in a relationship. There are also plenty of *current* photographs with the bio. A video brings it all together. The combination of the autobiographical profile, photos, and video gives an unequaled amount of information that other dating services do not give you.

Now that you understand a little more about both systems' selection processes, there is both good and bad news about their results. The trouble is, it might initially seem confusing! With matchmaking services, you are guaranteed dates (the more you pay, the more you get, and/or the harder the owner might work on your behalf). With self-selection services you are responsible for your own success because they don't "fix you up"; you do. You meet someone only when there is "mutual consent"—when either of you who initiates the selection receives a "yes" response from the other person. Therefore, there is less blindness from your first meeting.

So while it is entirely possible to meet people from a matchmaking service, there is no guarantee or reasonable assurance that they will either want to meet you, or that you will have anything meaningful in common. And with self-selection services it is possible that while you may choose people to meet, others may not respond with a "yes." However, when you do meet someone that person definitely wants to meet you! When you actually meet the person face-to-face, you both have seen each other's videos, read each other's autobiographical profile, and talked on the phone. No wonder your first date is more relaxed ... you both already know so much about each other!

Both services' approaches have a higher nonphysical risk level than any other approach to meeting. True, it's set up to protect you from actually hearing "No, thank you" to your face. But a self-selection service does put your ego on the line. That's exactly why it offers the highest potential for finding romance.

The very thing that makes a self-selection service so scary is what makes it work: you express your interest only to people who have likewise expressed a desire to find someone. And that brings us to yet another of the associated risks. They actually make it possible for you to get what you've asked for!

My enthusiasm over this particular meeting style is obvious, I know. My career has been built around that enthusiasm. For almost twenty years, I've watched the number of dissatisfied singles grow while the means to available and appropriate introductions have continued to shrink. Dating services are the one and only exception to that rule. There are more of them opening all the time, and more singles join them each and every day.

I conclude that matchmaking services—because they take away all your individual power, but still help you find potential mates—rate a middle 5 on my scale.

In my view, self-selection services (actually video dating) rate higher than all other meeting styles for both risk and romance potential. They challenge you to take the biggest risk. But in exchange, they offer you the best chance at finding romance. They rate a logical 9.

MAKING A DATE

Outside of dating services, meeting is only your first concern. Once you've exchanged the superficial niceties, you need to move toward the first date.

Who should ask? It doesn't matter, really. Yes, a large number of women still view themselves as traditional and insist that they "would never make the first move." Research has shown that many single women worry that they will appear aggressive if they bring up the idea. Not true. Several studies indicate that, in fact, men either don't mind if women extend the invitation or actually like to be asked out. Everyone has a need to be desired; we all want to be pursued and courted. True, you're more vulnerable if you decide to ask. But we've already talked about the inescapable risk that goes along with courtship. So don't wait to feel invincible. It's never going to happen. In most other aspects of our lives we don't hesitate to make important decisions, so why should dating be any different? Why should we let the good ones get away just because we waited and pondered and deliberated about whether we should or shouldn't ask him or her out? Don't wait. Ask! Success in dating and relationships comes to those who take individual responsibility for their thoughts and feelings, and then act upon them.

Also, it can help to remember that saying "yes" involves its own kind of risk. It reveals interest, too. By the same token, refusing is not easy. People don't realize that. Caught up in the nervousness of wanting to ask and hoping to be accepted, it's hard to understand that when that other person declines your invitation, he or she risks being considered an arrogant snob. Who wants that? So the asker is more exposed—but only for the thirty seconds it takes to make the invitation. After that, the other person becomes vulnerable, too.

It is also true that dating requires someone who will pursue and someone who will be pursued. Whoever asks first falls into the role of pursuer. If you simply cannot handle being more aggressive over an extended period of time, it might be better to wait for an approach to come your way. Of course, it might never happen. That's the risk you take with passivity. Opportunities may pass you by unless you take action.

The basic rule of dating should not be ignored: don't begin playing a role you aren't willing to assume for at least the initial phase of courtship. In most healthy relationships each of you will share the aggressive/passive roles.

Once the invitation is extended and accepted, you've passed the first hurdle. The ritual is under way. Remember, it's the initial wooing that's hardest to survive. That's because it goes against human nature: you must trust and expose yourself to a near-total stranger. So don't expect to be particularly relaxed or self-confident on those first hours together.

Whenever you plan a first date or romantic outing, it's best to keep things fairly simple. This is not the time to plan an all-day picnic in the park or a hike alone through the mountains. You need to offer yourself and your date something upon which to focus attention when the conversation falls off into silence (a.k.a. "the Pregnant Pause"). So think about an event: a street fair, a particular exhibit at a new museum, a ballgame, miniature golfing, an outdoor art show, a trip to the zoo, a day at the races—anything that lets you talk and watch at the same time. In fact, the more off-beat (without being threatening, of course), the more exciting and fascinating your experience will be. You both will have no shortage of things to talk about!

Personally, I never liked meeting a first date for a meal because it was always so uncomfortable and stifling for me, It felt too formal; there was too much "interviewing" going on. And for those who know me well, such a setting was not very workable for my outrageous sense of humor and attempts at instant emotional and intellectual connection on a deeper level. I always sought something—almost anything—that would allow both of us to relax more and show our real personalities, versus our "Date Face." If I absolutely had to, I'd have lunch or dinner. It wasn't the money that I spent, it was the venue. If given the choice for a meal, I'd prefer breakfast. Why? Because it let me know how positive and energetic (qualities that I absolutely had to have in my soulmate) that person was in the morning; it showed me how well she was either naturally, or through motivation to be positive.

If it's any comfort, your date is also feeling awkward. Both people on a first date are caught in the sticky business of getting to know each other. So don't think it's up to you to make it perfectly comfortable for both of you. That isn't possible. It's both your responsibilities to put forth your best efforts. If you don't get a cold brush-off at the end of the date, assume you've passed the first of many tests with flying colors. Sometimes the date will feel comfortable and when it ends, you may feel it went well. However, the other person is still a virtual stranger and therefore might be difficult to gauge. Your date may have enjoyed your company, laughed at your jokes, appeared interested and stimulated—yet still not want to see you again. That's okay, too, because if it's not right, it's not likely to get right. Don't take it personally; you're not being condemned. The person just doesn't think it's a love match. Dating is a numbers game. You wouldn't want to waste time or energy with someone if the feeling wasn't mutual. So it's time to move on to your next step, and allow the ritual to unfold.

PUT IT INTO PRACTICE

Question 1: What's the first obstacle that prevents you from finding the love of your life?

Answer: You aren't meeting enough available candidates.

Question 2: What's the other barrier to your getting more first dates?

Answer: Your own fear of rejection.

Again and again in this book I've said: "Want love? Then get real!" Before you get results you need to take action. And before you take action you need to have the right attitude. It's not enough just to say to yourself, "I'm going to do things differently." What's important is that you actually *do* what you promise yourself!

What to do about rejection? I want you to set yourself up for it. Really. I want you to make it happen soon. You pick the day. And on that day, I want you to walk up to the very first stranger (of the opposite sex, and who isn't wearing a wedding ring) that you see and ask: "If I asked you for a date, would you accept my invitation?" If it's someone walking a dog around the block, ask. If it's someone you pass on your way to work, stop and ask. I don't care how ridiculous it seems: I want you to ask a total stranger for a date.

In all probability, you'll get turned down. And that's okay. In fact, that's exactly what I want. I want you to get turned down. Why? Because I'll bet you've lived the past I-don't-know-how-many years protecting yourself from being turned down. I think you're long overdue for some rejection.

This exercise is meant to teach you that rejection is part of any romantic's life. Rejection is also part of every successful professional, sporting, educational, or business success story. And it's not nearly as bad to experience it as to fear it. Everyone gets rejected! (I will confess that I am the recipient of more than my fair share of rejections both professionally and personally. Yet would you call me a "failure"? I have learned to strengthen my inner resolve so that when I receive a rejection, I learn from it, rather than fear it and all subsequent attempts at success.)

If you need further convincing about why you need to engage in a little exercise in order to conquer your fear of rejection, let me ask you a simple question: if you had a presentation to make to someone in business or school, wouldn't you practice before you performed? Of course you would!

Now, what if you walk up to that first stranger, ask for a date, and—shock of shocks—you hear, "Yes, I'd love to." Well, as Jiminy Cricket said, "Let your conscience be your guide." Then I want you to repeat the exercise with the next stranger who enters your field of vision because this is not an exercise about getting a date. It's not just an exercise about getting rejected, either. It's about learning that you can survive it and try, try, try again!

ANSWERS TO THE QUIZ

1. c
2. b
3. a
4. a
5. d
6. b
7. d
8. d
9. a
10. c

6 Intimate Connections

"When men and women are able to respect and accept their differences, then love has a chance to bloom."
—JOHN GRAY

*A*fter working with so many singles for twenty years, what became apparent to me was how little we know about how to date. In school we're taught the 3R's: "Reading, 'Riting and 'Rithmetic." Unfortunately, what we're not taught is the fourth "R": Relationships. And we've never been taught the fundamental basics of dating, and how to create an atmosphere of relationship making, maturing, or maintaining.

For example, it's funny the way we say good-bye after a pleasant first date and, without even knowing why, find ourselves fantasizing about an entire lifetime with that person beside us. From a simple pasta dinner and Saturday-night movie, we slip into rose-colored dreams of marriage, family, and old-age retirement—all with someone we still don't know very well.

That's because the ultimate goal of every date is the intimacy of connecting with that one special person. Granted, most romantic pursuits do not result in a serious commitment. But that's not for lack of trying. The truth is, most of us date in the effort to find a close, caring relationship. Once we catch scent of one, we get carried away. We work at a fiery speed toward wherever it is that we think attachments should lead. To bed, to marriage, to Hawaii, anywhere. Especially among people who are eager for true love, there is the tendency to push for too much too fast.

Unfortunately, if you see romance and seduction as a race, you deny yourself (and your partner) the chance to delight in those initial love signals. You try so hard to get down to the nitty-gritty of a real relationship that you miss the fun of courtship.

Remember, the beauty of romance is found in re-creating something timeless. So as you move beyond your first date, try to maintain your sense of perspective. If you don't, you're likely to initiate the ritual again and again without ever really enjoying it. When you're too worried about where you're headed, you may completely miss the beauty and adventure of the journey. Slow down. Don't view dating as a bullet train speeding toward your final destination but as a leisurely walk down a thrilling, winding road. Slow down and enjoy the scenery.

DO YOU PLAY YOUR CARDS RIGHT?

How well do you handle the transition from first date to romantic intimacy? Some people have a real knack for saying and doing just the right thing at just the right moment. They make it seem so easy. They're the lucky few. The rest of us approach courtship and seduction with a mix of excitement, uncertainty, and fear. No matter what hand of love cards we're dealt, we always seem to discard the ones we later wish we'd kept, and hold on to those we think we can't really use.

Do you belong among the lucky few, or somewhere among us mere mortals? Try taking the following quiz. It may help you find out.

1. A good first date is the result of mutual attraction. The next few dates are most likely to result from:
   (a) heightened sexual attraction.
   (b) genuine interest.
   (c) a sense of obligation.
   (d) pure social habit.

2. Most couples take four steps toward romantic intimacy. The typical order of those steps is:
   (a) retreat, return, conversation, and sex.
   (b) conversation, retreat, return, and sex.
   (c) conversation, sex, retreat, and return.
   (d) retreat, conversation, return, and sex.

3. If there's real chemistry between two people, their first attempt at conversation will probably be:
   (a) remarkably relaxed and easy.
   (b) silly but a lot of fun.
   (c) filled with sexual innuendo.
   (d) embarrassing and awkward.

4. Sexuality and the need to express it by making love are:
   (a) universal drives in all men and women.
   (b) biological facts of life for men, but not for women.
   (c) culturally determined drives.
   (d) the lowest form of romantic expression.

5. A recent national survey found that most men and women think of a sex-filled weekend with an attractive stranger as:
   (a) not very romantic.
   (b) a little romantic.
   (c) extremely romantic.
   (d) too romantic to ever really happen.

6. In a good relationship, sex usually leads (at least temporarily) to:
   (a) genuine closeness between the lovers.
   (b) an unexplained retreat by one of the lovers.
   (c) an unexplained retreat by both lovers.
   (d) a false sense of security between the lovers.

7. After two people make love, the one who actively sought the affair is likely to:
   (a) work hard to maintain the balance of power within the

relationship because that's what attracts him or her.

(b) lose power within the relationship because he or she will try hard to maintain the affair.

(c) willingly relinquish power as a way of expressing real emotional commitment.

(d) gain power within the relationship because he or she suddenly backs off and waits to be pursued.

8. Telling a lover what his or her behavior says about internal feelings is a good way to attract:

(a) very analytical people.

(b) very psychologically oriented people.

(c) very passive people.

(d) very impressionable people.

9. When you admit to a lover who's backing off that you want the relationship to continue, you are:

(a) trying too hard to keep someone who doesn't care about you.

(b) running away from the anger you naturally feel over the rebuff.

(c) risking your pride, but moving the relationship toward real intimacy.

(d) wasting your time.

10. If you do decide to make an admission like that, it's best to:

(a) back off for a few days and then get in touch to reiterate your feelings.

(b) back off and keep your feelings to yourself.

(c) stay in close touch and reiterate your feelings.

(d) lighten the mood by hiding your true feelings, at least for the moment.

STEP ONE: TALKING YOUR WAY TOWARD INTIMACY

Communicating in an intimate relationship is 10 percent relating facts, and 90 percent about relating feelings. Dale Carnegie said it well: "When dealing with people, remember you are not dealing with creatures of logic, but with creatures of emotion."

If a first date symbolizes mutual attraction, then the next few dates represent genuine two-way interest. When people decide to arrange time together a second and then a third time, they clearly like each other enough to keep up the pursuit. In other words, real communication is happening. True communication is a bonding of spirits through sharing and exchanging thoughts. We get into someone else's skin, we come to know how that person thinks and feels under varying circumstances, their likes, loves, and behaviors. It can only occur when there is a two-way street.

The act of communication involves talking, listening, responding, and acknowledgment. What people complain most about in their relationships is a lack of satisfactory communication. Yet it isn't just any one of those elements that makes for good communication; it is the amount of connecting at the level where we're in touch with the essence of the other individual.

Like so much else about courtship, the romantic journey from introduction to intimacy follows a fairly typical pattern. That's not to say your nervousness is exactly like everyone else's. Naturally, your basic temperament will determine how easily you can "move in" to your partner's life—both physically and emotionally. But whether it takes six intense hours, or sixteen slow-paced years, the process of getting to know someone is pretty predictable.

First there's conversation. By that I mean the exchange that takes place when two people use language to really understand each other, when they both speak of things that matter to them. These first genuine conversations between a man and woman— the ones in which they open up and risk being vulnerable—mark an important move toward intimacy because they change from casual acquaintances into friends.

Deciding when and how to make that move is a big issue when forming any close relationship. Sometimes it just happens. You meet someone and within minutes you find yourself talking more openly and honestly than you ever have with another human being. If you're lucky enough to find that kind of immediate connection you can be sure the person finds you as fascinating as you find him or her. True rapport is never a one-way street.

More often, though, you will have to work toward this sort of conversation. That means it probably won't happen on the first date. During those initial hours together, you're both likely to stick with silly dialogue about "What-do-you-do-at-your-job?-Where-are-you-from?-How-did-you-spend-your-last-vacation?" In this respect, most first dates are like job interviews. You're on the spot, nervous that you might utter the wrong response to any or all questions. No one likes to feel like being on the witness stand. No one appreciates being interviewed. Both tactics only put off people by putting on more pressure in an already challenging situation.

Instead of thinking that you're trying to hire or be hired by someone, view your date as an opportunity to develop a new friend. Despite the advice of pop psychologists, you don't need to "get it all out in the open" right off the bat. Everything really doesn't need to be laid out and resolved by the first date. So don't feel rushed into conversations you're not ready to tackle.

When you finally meet, don't be what I call a "Date Killer." Those are people who talk too much about everything negative—their ex; their poor health; how they don't have time to date; how they're almost always out of town; how other people they've dated haven't understood them. You don't have to be entirely positive about everything. But you also don't have to share all the worst aspects of your life on your early dates, for this only puts a big strain on a still-budding relationship. Remember, you're just getting started. You've got as much time as the two of you want.

Do consider these ten tips that I found enormously successful when I dated:

1. Don't make yourself your favorite topic. Bragging about yourself is not an aphrodisiac. It only makes you look like a show-off. Listen and pay close attention to how the other person talks and how much you listen. There should be an equal give and take. Talking too much is a sure sign that you're not listening.

2. Don't interrupt. Interruption tells the other person that you're not interested, that you're rude and self-centered, and it certainly doesn't make your date feel appreciated.

3. Tune into your date's interests; people like to feel that their life is interesting enough to warrant being heard.

4. Use humor whenever you can, but remember to stay away from sarcasm, sexual innuendos, ethnic slurs, being judgmental or threatening, or anything negative.

5. Be warm, friendly, positive, and nice as you can. Remember what Zig Ziglar said: "While it's nice to be important, it's more important to be nice."

6. Be sincere, honest, and avoid game playing.

7. Have lots of eye contact! And when a fabulous looking person walks by you, do *not* look at him or her (not even a tiny glance!). It's an immediate insult and turnoff to your date.

8. Listen twice as much as you speak.

9. Don't complain or whine; misery loves company, but company doesn't love misery.

10. There's no reason to discuss: exes (boy/girlfriends, spouses, or in-laws), awful childhood, dysfunctional family, political affiliation, or religious zeal. By the second date, things may have loosened up a little. Still, most discussions should probably continue to center on the immediate: a movie you just saw together, the decor of the restaurant, what you've heard about the kind of car he drives, whom you know in her office. Or just take notice of what's going on around you and comment upon it. Remember to keep it light and have fun. Don't feel pressure to open up about personal issues unless you are certain that it will be appreciated.

It's important to recognize that conversation works in different ways for men and women. Women usually feel comfortable sharing and exchanging thoughts, opinions, and ideas because that means "I feel comfortable enough with you to tell you just about anything." Men, on the other hand, don't feel comfortable sharing everything. Men are especially uncomfortable with sharing deeply personal information to someone not yet trusted. Men tend to protect their privacy, and they view this kind of exchange as "airing dirty laundry in public." They like to wait on that until after they feel safe and sure that their "secrets" will not be repeated. In this sense, women are more comfortable and experienced in doing what is necessary toward building intimacy. Men are more reactive.

Genuine and gut-level conversation should happen naturally by the third date. If you found your date interesting thus far and feel like investing more emotional energy, then your conversational content should now progress to a deeper level of intimacy—assuming of course, that you both feel the same way. Try dismissing the small talk we associate with early dating in favor of more and more revealing questions and answers. Singles report to me that it's probably too soon to talk about feelings toward having children. But perhaps you could ask about professional goals. Men tend to be more sensitive than women about seemingly innocent questions relating to work, career, or lifestyle. Questions of this sort may translate to him as "How much money do you *really* make?" They perceive that women have dollar signs in their eyes.

Women are especially sensitive to being viewed as sex objects. Women like sex, but if sex is on your mind, keep it off your lips. Consider asking her whether she envisions herself always working in her current field. Can she imagine other professional involvements ever taking hold? Has she ever thought about working freelance? Would she consider leaving town if a better job offer came along?

You might also think about open-ended discussions concerning personal values, family background, and quality of relationships. Does he see much of his family? Would he like to? What qualities were missing from his past relationships? Has she ever done any volunteer work? For what organizations? What motivated him to get involved? Where does she spend her holidays? Put simply, you could begin to ask your date to reveal a bit of personal information since relationships are about relating to one another. Finding a lasting love is based on knowledge, not assumptions, wishful thinking, or what you perceive as potential. Make sure that when your date tells you a story, you get the whole story. Your questions will only make you appear interested, and will definitely provide you with some insight into this person you find so attractive. Remember to pay attention to body language, and what's *not* being said.

If you've met someone you're *really* interested in, pay attention to the following ten tell-tale factors:

1. How he or she describes family backgrounds and ongoing relationships
2. Financial habits and decision-making style
3. Religious affiliation and its importance
4. Emotional style in which he or she describes past and present experiences
5. Communication style and how he or she relates to other people
6. Social style and etiquette
7. Past or present codependent relationships and behavior
8. Has he or she been a victim of violence and/or sexual abuse?
9. If you're a single parent, is there a real potential for blending your families?
10. Self-esteem

After this date, stop and carefully compare what you've learned about your date with what you need in a relationship. Just look back at what you wrote in Chapter 2 in "Notes for Myself" (that exercise you did about the qualities that you want most from a partner, and what you simply are not willing to tolerate in one). This will be a good basis for determining your compatibility quotient. You should only move forward in this relationship if there is more than sexual attraction, and more than partial compatibility. You want a combination of compatibility and sexual chemistry.

If you find that your careful evaluation of your date doesn't appear to meet your needs from your checklist, or doesn't even have partial compatibility, it's time to admit to yourself that the relationship is not going to work, say good-bye, and move on by diving back into the dating pool. There are too many available singles out there waiting to meet you. Don't settle for less than your greatest expectations. Remember what I said earlier: "great expectations yield great results."

For intimacy to grow, you will eventually need to talk about even more fundamental questions. You will need to share your individual thoughts about man's responsibility toward man; the moral and ethical questions, such as the right and wrong of euthanasia, feeding the world, caring for the homeless; the reality or fallacy of God, attitudes toward toxic-waste sites, rainforest defoliation, oil spills, or personal level of commitment to family and friends. Still, don't be in any great hurry. Religion and politics don't have to be discussed before you enjoy an evening together.

STEP TWO: SEXUALITY

As I begin this section of the book, I wonder how many readers have skimmed quickly through everything else and turned straight to this subheading. If you have, you're likely to be disappointed because I don't have foolproof advice to offer. I can't tell you how to get him in bed on the first date. (I'm sure that would not be a smart *or* healthy move.) I can't provide a set of sure-fire suggestions for how to turn her on beyond her wildest fantasies.

However, I am interested in where—and how—sex fits into courtships of the 1990s. For most of us, the idea of romantic love without sexual passion is not desirable. But it does exist. For instance, the Dani people of West New Guinea are virtually indifferent to sex. Weddings take place only once every four to six years. Yet there is almost no incidence of premarital sex among these tribal people. After marriage, Dani couples abstain from sexual contact for at least two years. After the birth of each child, they abstain for six more years.

So it would seem that sexuality, and the need to express it through lovemaking, are not universal facts of life. They're culturally determined behaviors. And as our Western society confronts a host of sexually transmitted diseases—AIDS being the most devastating of them—our attitudes about sex are bound to change.

In fact, they're already changing. Back in 1982, research found that almost 65 percent of all men and nearly 50 percent of all women had sex by the third date. Today, those statistics are dramatically lower. Experts tell us that both men and women are now having less "casual" sex and practicing safer sex techniques when they do decide to make love.

You might expect that this reluctance to jump from one love

affair to another would simplify courtship. Actually, it has further complicated the journey that modern couples make toward intimacy. Think about it: when many of today's singles learned their sexual style, interpersonal exchange between men and women was often reserved for after sex. First you made love. Then you asked her about her childhood. First he spent the weekend with you in your bedroom. Then you asked him if he believed in life after death.

To some extent, single men and women of the 1970s and early 1980s came to rely on sex as a way to get intimate. They mistakenly felt that sex meant early emotional connection. Lovemaking came before human closeness. Today, it often works the other way around. We proceed more responsibly—our lives depend upon it. You become socially, intellectually, and emotionally close. Then you think about going to sexual intimacy. Quite frankly, it makes a great deal more sense to approach personal, intimate relationships in this manner. Before we're able to totally let go of ourselves (which is what sex is all about) and allow ourselves to lose control, we must feel secure and safe enough with our partner.

This new attitude was reflected in a recent poll on opinions about romance and sexuality. Asked to score the relative appeal of various romantic adventures, 85 percent of the people surveyed rated a cozy weekend with a steady mate as most romantic. Surprised? In contrast, a weekend of sexual abandon with a new fling was rated as least romantic. This same research study found that over 80 percent of all Americans between the ages of thirty-five and forty-four define romance as "affection, caring, and the comfort of marital sexuality."

In short, it's a new mating era that calls for new social dating etiquette. People want more romance, less sexual activity with all but one partner, and an understanding that lovemaking without emotional commitment is not what it's all about.

Sex may not be as simple in your next relationship as it was in your past affairs. You may be several dates into the courtship, and still uncertain about whether it's too soon to make an advance. In general, my advice is to take it slow. Don't assume that a good-night kiss means an invitation to do anything more than call tomorrow. If you're as appealing to your date as he or she is to you, the opportunity will come again. And by waiting, you send a message that you're looking for something deeper than a short affair. If you're a man, this can have a powerfully positive effect on the woman. If you're a woman, this tells a man that you treat your body with respect and expect the same from him.

Don't get me wrong. I'm not advocating that you wait for weeks to touch your new flame. (A sweet, soft, and friendly touch is almost always received well.) But I am encouraging you to fully explore the enjoyment of touching—all by itself—before you slip out of your clothes and under the sheets. Kissing, once considered the means to an obvious end, is enjoying a great comeback. I think that's because it is the eternal symbol of romance, the ultimate celebration of attraction. That's what people are after now: less hard-core sex and more playful foreplay. One surprising recent survey found, for example, that fewer than one man out of every four would choose sex over romance. And, only one woman out of twenty would make that same choice.

As long as we're on the subject, remember that a good kiss is a gesture, not a strategic maneuver. As a result, it's always best when it's spontaneous. Have you ever been completely unprepared for a kiss and then, suddenly, it just happens? I have. And no amount of practiced sexual finesse can compare to the passion that comes with that first, unexpected touching of lips. Kiss not because you want to slide your hands where they have not been invited, but because you want to show that you care.

If your new romance is going to last, sex will definitely become a part of it. The feelings of sexual attraction push courtship forward. When it does, be prepared for your relationship to change. It's inevitable because you've now introduced a new element. Acting on those sexual feelings alters the courtship forever. Before two people sleep together, the exact nature of their relationship is unclear. After they make love or connect sexually, there's no doubt in anyone's mind anymore: they're lovers. Uncommitted lovers, perhaps, but lovers nonetheless. And lovers play a defined role in each other's lives—a role that involves feelings, hopes, vulnerability, and expectations. One bit of advice I'd like you to consider: be careful not to allow your emotions to overrun your rational mind and become sexually involved with someone based solely upon sexual attraction. As in all relationships, you must act responsibly and weigh the possible consequences, not impulsively. It's okay to have sexual feelings for someone whom you have just started to date, but you need also to believe you have the power to choose whether or not to act on your sexual urges.

Step Three: Retreat and Return

One of the great myths of our time is that having sex brings people closer together. It doesn't. In fact, it often pushes them apart. It serves to introduce the third step toward intimacy: retreat and (we hope) return.

I recently talked with a man from Chicago, and was reminded of how miserable people can be if they believe the myth. He called my office in response to a national television interview in which I discussed this unnerving retreat pattern. "I thought you were crazy," he said, "until it happened to me."

Warren and Jocelyn met almost a year ago, at a professional conference. She lives in Boston, so the relationship developed slowly. Still, they were instantly attracted, and nurtured the romance via three-day weekends every month. From his perspective, she did the pursuing. "I knew I liked her a lot, but I never pushed," he explained. "I never pressured her about becoming lovers. She was always the one who wanted more involvement, more commitment."

The weekend before he called me, Warren had gone to spend one of their long weekends with her in Massachusetts. "When I arrived late Friday night, I took a taxi to her home. The whole place was dimly lit with candles. She was wearing this top that kept slipping off her shoulder. I mean, it was obvious that she was seducing me. And my response was to jump at the chance."

The retreat came quickly. "Even by the next morning, things had changed. I could feel it. Suddenly, Jocelyn was backing off and had cooled toward me, acting like the relationship was something to sandwich in between the important parts of her life. I was bewildered and tried to prolong our time together. I suggested that we at least go out for brunch. But she said she couldn't; she had to do a few hours' work at the office and made me feel unwanted. That was pretty odd considering that I was only going to be in town for two days!"

Warren flew home that afternoon, and waited for her to call. He was very confused. When he and I talked, it had been five days, and that call still hadn't come. "I thought making love would add to our relationship," he said. "Instead, I guess it ended it."

This is a classic example of romantic retreat. During the pursuit phase of their courtship, Jocelyn assertively pushed for intimacy. She wrote love letters, called long distance at least twice a week, cooked for Warren whenever they were together, and sent clear signals that she wanted more physical contact. Then, when she had finally drawn him close, she took a sudden and giant step back.

Actually, there's nothing unusual about what happened between Warren and Jocelyn. Most lovers go through this awkward dance of intimacy phase. Most couples enjoy the thrill of a new affair for at least a short time before one of the two partners gets nervous. But eventually the withdrawal comes. With Warren and Jocelyn it happened immediately. In a sense, it's like an emergency brake for the emerging relationship. It's a mechanism to slow things down while both people decide their next move.

The retreat poses a challenge to each of the lovers because it signals a redistribution of power within the affair. Curiously, it's almost always the pursuer who backs off. A man chases a woman, finally seduces her, and then runs away. In doing that, he emerges as the new power force in the relationship, the one who can call the shots and set the limits. And the woman—who just days earlier could spark happiness or heartache with just a single word—is suddenly powerless. It's classic. The retreat phase of a relationship is the escape hatch and a time when both he and she must decide if that exchange is desirable. Both people must give up some personal freedom in order to get commitment.

For the short term, it's harder to be the person being shunned. Only an ability to assume that role with secure, self-confidence, and knowledge that this is a predictable stage can make it possible for the retreat period to end and for the necessary return to take place. So let's review the four basic response options from which this person can choose.

Behavior Option Number One: Ignore the Retreat

This is certainly the path of least resistance. Your new lover cools, and while you feel hurt, you act like nothing's changed. Occasionally, this approach works. The retreat is short-lived, and within a matter of days (or weeks) the return takes place. The affair seems back on track.

If you opt for this course of action, expect the retreat to recur. Emotional withdrawal comes from a natural and profound fear of entrapment. We all have a tendency to want what we can't have. So when a long-held goal is attained, many of us wonder if the prize is really worth what we paid for it. Reason will tell your lover that you are wonderful. Still, a powerful internal voice will keep asking the same question: "Is this worth the loss of my freedom?" That same inner voice may simultaneously ask, "What more opportunities and newfound freedoms have come to me because I'm in this committed relationship?"

Behavior Option Number Two: Analyze the Retreat for Your Partner

In our age of plentiful pop psychology, this is an increasingly popular response. A lover withdraws and instead of feeling the hurt, you analyze his behavior, categorize it, and attempt to trivialize it. You sit him down and explain his behavior to him. You tell him what he's feeling, what he's doing, why he's doing it, and how he ought to move beyond it. You may end up sounding patronizing and condescending.

This tactic can also work. Sometimes. It's most effective when the retreating partner is extremely passive or not in tune with his or her feelings. These people actually want you to tell them what they're feeling and why.

Men are more prone to being emotionally closed than women. Raised to be somewhat awkward and ignorant with matters of the heart, they think it's acceptably masculine to be with a woman who can translate their behavior into understandable logical language. The dynamic works, too—as long as she's willing to carry the full emotional burden of the relationship.

Behavior Option Number Three: Get Angry and Strike Back

An eye for an eye; that's the heart of this approach. Your partner turns attention away from you, and you react and decide to become angry. You decide to fight back. Feelings get hurt and you want the other person to experience the pain you're going through . . . or worse! You demand to know how in the hell she got the idea that you were some pair of old shoes, comfortable but not very special. You feel used and confused. If she tells you she's busy tonight, you decide to be equally busy tomorrow night. If he plans to see his kids this weekend, you make arrangements to visit your folks next weekend.

This approach boils down to a frantic game of one-upsmanship. It's whether you win or lose that counts, not how you play the game. That's hardly a recipe for happiness.

Behavior Option Number Four: Tell Your Partner That You Want the Retreat to End, and Then Back Off

This is the riskiest of all your options. It demands that you swallow your pride and tell the truth: you want the relationship to continue. Then you must bow to your partner's power and ask if that desire is mutual. In short, you have to sidestep the other three options. You've got to acknowledge and admit that the retreat is happening; give your lover the space, time, and right to interpret his or her own behavior; and not get mad at him for needing this.

Generally, the first question you ask if you follow this approach is "What's wrong?" Inevitably, the answer is "Nothing." This could mean one of two things: Either your partner is experiencing uncomfortable feelings, but really doesn't understand what's happening, hence the "Nothing!" response. Or your partner does want to cool things in retreat and doesn't want to discuss thoughts or feelings because that would initiate communication and possibly bring you closer together. Still, you feel it's important to clarify the basis for this withdrawal. You need to clearly state that "the relationship" exists for you and is important to you and ask for feedback with a response from your partner. Ask if it exists for your partner and whether it is important. How long does your partner want to take to evaluate it?

Lots of relationships go astray at this point due to differing communication styles, expectations, and emotional openness. Remember the communication basics: communication isn't about *your* talking, *your* getting your point across, *your* being understood. Effective communication is about *our* understanding; it's not a one-way avenue. Open communication is also receptive, which means your partner needs to be actively listening and responding. And both of you need to acknowledge the content and meaning.

Once you've posed these basic questions and gotten resolution, you have to do the hardest thing of all: back off. Be patient. Put the relationship on hold, too. This is the most difficult because we tend to want something more when we cannot have it. When we're denied something desirable we are prone to fantasize and obsess about having it. We find ourselves not being able to get it off our mind. By backing off you must stop calling, stop being so available, stop talking with mutual friends about the problem, and stop bending over backwards to make your lover happy. Recognize how difficult this part is. My suggestion is to be tough and discipline yourself. Every time your lover enters your thoughts, force them away by visualizing something else, perhaps something clearly positive in your life as a replacement. In the beginning, it will likely occur frequently. However, by forcing yourself each time to say "Go away!" you'll train your mind to move away from this negative situation. In this way, not only will your lover enter your thoughts less frequently; actively taking control and substituting positive thoughts will actually empower you!

Remember, you aren't the problem. Your partner's fear of commitment is the problem. Your fears in this area were acted out during the pursuit phase of your courtship, when you couldn't decide whether or not to really get involved. During that phase, your lover was pushing full steam ahead. Now, suddenly, things have changed. The test of true love is freedom of choice. You've got to be willing to allow him or her the freedom without guilt to make this choice. Your partner must now decide about committing to the relationship and recognize that it's something more than a temporary goal or prize.

When you willingly back off, you take the real chance that retreat may never lead to a reunion. Some affairs are short-lived because they don't get past this final step toward intimacy. Some singles begin many relationships, but never get beyond this point. They get stuck forever in retreat. There are many psychological explanations for this, but simply put, some people are only after the hot pursuit and the excitement and thrill of a relationship roller-coaster ride. After the initial thrill is gone, they move on to the next thrill ride. Others have unresolved issues going on from childhood. They have such low self-esteem and neediness that is unsatisfied that they subconsciously decide they're not worth it. So they unwillingly sabotage themselves and forever walk away licking their wounds. Still others never learned conflict resolution and cannot seem to sustain a mature adult relationship, but project blame onto others. Another type recognizes that it just wasn't meant to be. Something intangible was missing within the parameters of the relationship and sex was just the final blow.

Both of you have to feel positive about your relationship for it to continue. If it's one-sided, it will not work. If you're the one who wants the relationship but have been the rejected one, you'll feel like you constantly have to work selling yourself and the relationship to the other person. So this rejection is really a favor in disguise.

Nobody ever said that love was fair or easy. And when it comes to intimacy and sex, the game gets even tougher. Few rules apply. If you get a partner into bed but wake up the next morning to a cold shoulder, you hardly feel victorious. By the same token, if you wait too long to commit, your partner may come to see the courtship as fruitless and give up. Turn rejection around. It's difficult to figure out why someone has rejected us. The important thing to learn is not to dwell on the negative but to move on. To some extent, we all see what we want to see, both in ourselves and in others. That's why I hear so frequently from singles that so many of their promising partners never turn out the way they thought they would. It doesn't really matter why they rejected you (unless you're always getting rejected; then perhaps you need to examine deeply why this continually occurs to you).

Remember, it's not your fault you were rejected. Try not to personalize it and beat yourself up. Go easy on yourself. Negative thinking never leads to positive action. Change your mind and you will change your luck. Turn this into an opportunity to move forward. Now is the time to reflect on "Notes for Myself" that you wrote as an exercise in Chapter 2. These will help remind you of how much you have to offer to someone else, and how terrific you really are. Smart people learn from failures. They turn something that they once felt negative into a positive opportunity.

Rejection is an equal-opportunity annoyance. Remember that not all the good ones are taken. You are right for someone. In order to find that person you must get out there and give yourself decent exposure!

PUT IT INTO PRACTICE

If genuine conversation is at the heart of intimacy, then you should work on your ability to tell people what you think and feel. The way you do that on a first date is very different from the way you do it after several dates—and different again from the way you express yourself once you've become someone's lover.

So pour yourself a cup of coffee or a glass of wine, and sit down. I want you to give three separate "performances" when there's nobody in your home to hear you. Each will be a one-person show. Just you, talking out loud. I want you to answer the question:

"How did you like school when you were a kid?"

Answer three times. The first time, imagine that you've been asked the question by someone you like on your first date. Second, imagine that it's the same person asking you, but now you've been seeing each other for almost a dozen dates. And the third time, picture yourself in bed after sexual intimacy with this person. You've made love and are close together, sharing pillow talk the way that only lovers do.

Of course, the easiest of your answers will be the first. It will probably be the shortest, too. But what about your second time? How much of yourself are you willing to share with someone you've known but do not yet know well enough to trust fully with your deepest, innermost thoughts? And how about with a lover? Are you as willing to share your personal memories and feelings as you are in bed?

There are no good or bad responses. I simply want you to practice the art of open communication—a little open, a bit more open, and a lot open. They're all appropriate at the proper time and in the proper place. Start talking to everyone. Don't limit yourself. Just get out there and take the initiative with others. Consider this: acquaintances can become friends, and friends have friends whom they can introduce you to. Remember to practice. Practice. Practice. Practice makes perfect. Repetition and familiarity give you the confidence to succeed.

ANSWERS TO THE QUIZ

1. b
2. c
3. d
4. c
5. a
6. b
7. d
8. c
9. c
10. a

7 The Workaholic's Lost Love Life

"You sometimes work overtime at work, right?
Why not occasionally work 'overtime' on your
relationship?"
—ANONYMOUS

*H*ave you ever heard a single person say: "I am *soooo* busy at work! I just can't find the time to date." If you were to push them for various what-*ifs* ("What would you do *if* you met someone really wonderful?") they would likely answer: "*Wellllll, if* I met the right person, I'd make the time."

My response to that is: Make the time *now*. You can never re-create lost time and opportunities. And friend . . . you're not getting any younger! Don't wait for love to happen, make it happen. Love is about living, not just earning a living.

It's no small feat to balance our professional, social, and emotional needs. If we put an unreasonably disproportionate share of our energies into our career, we may very well lose contact with other equally important aspects of our life. Although a certain amount of sacrifice of our personal life may be necessary, we have a choice as to just how much we're willing to sacrifice. Just as we plan our career fastidiously, we must remember that our emotional health is dependent upon our planning for personal activities as well. When we constantly work, we don't allow ourselves to reach within ourselves and hear our own inner voice. Hence, we don't let ourselves get to know ourselves well enough.

I know quite a few friends and business associates whose commitment to a job has seriously interfered with their romantic lives. They spend so much time building their careers that there's nothing left over for love or romance. I don't think my social circle is particularly unusual, either. In fact, according to some sources, the basic human need for love and companionship actually has given way to an even stronger passion for professional success. There's evidence for this idea all around us. For example, one of the nation's largest adult education centers recently reported that its longtime most popular course, "How to Find a Lover," has been replaced by "How to Start Your Own Business." This appears to be an unhealthy sign of our times, as we all must find a healthy balance between work and play.

Even the most compulsive job junkies know that there's more to happiness than a job. When these same people are asked to rate the truly important things in life, invariably they put personal relationships and family ties at the top of their list. In one *Psychology Today* study, "being successful at work" earned a shabby fifth place among college students' life goals. So if it appears that career mania has taken hold of us, it's not because we consider emotional commitment to be unimportant. And, oddly enough, those who hide deepest in their work are often those who most want to find a mate. It may sound ridiculous, but it makes sense in a strange sort of way. Stop for a moment to consider how very empty life feels when you're alone. Rather than confront that emptiness, a lot of us choose to work overtime— even doubletime—to escape it. And that overtime brings us rewards that further encourage us to escape this way.

What's more, our jobs promise us the chance to reap what we sow. In today's world, it can sometimes seem impossible to find someone. No matter how warm, talented, wealthy, or well-connected you are, there's the possibility of never meeting any-body "right." Still, one thing is certain: if you work hard enough, you will succeed . . . at work. That's the myth, anyway. And, quite literally, millions of Americans have bought into it. In an other-wise uncertain world, work and its tangible rewards seem ab-solutely reliable. Why not apply the same principle to your personal growth? If you work hard enough you will succeed . . . with dating and relationships.

My system also reflects that hard work will bring success when you apply it to your personal life. In fact, it's essential that you don't just work at improving your social life, but that you work smarter!

By the way, we can lay some of the blame for our work fixa-tion on our parents and grandparents because they managed to redefine the whole meaning of professional achievement. For most of our grandfathers, success was a steady job during the Depression and postwar era. Anything beyond that was gravy. By the 1960s, the head of a household faced a tougher challenge. A college education and semiprofessional job ensured a comfort-able, middle-class lifestyle. Real success meant a law degree from Berkeley or Yale, medical credentials from Johns Hopkins or Harvard, millions made from real estate or from other entrepre-neurial ventures.

Well, welcome to the nineties. Today's job market is even more demanding; a postgraduate degree and professional career are just the basics. To even hope for things like your own house, a luxury car, private school for your kids, and a once-a-year vaca-tion, you've got to be ambitious, willing to work long hours, bright, well-educated, well-connected, and well-placed in a re-spected profession. In this environment, real success is nothing less than national prominence in your field and your first million by age thirty-five.

With these high expectations motivating them, and an un-certain economy to keep them on their toes, it's understandable that work is a genuine addiction for countless ambitious singles. It's also understandable—but not acceptable—that their com-pulsive habit takes a huge bite out of the personal life they never have time to build for themselves.

HOOKED ON THE HABIT

There's a fine line between the healthy drive to do well and a neurotic need to overachieve. Have you crossed it? Do you work to support your lifestyle? Or have you built a lifestyle around your obsession with work? Almost as important, do you repeatedly get involved with members of the Working Dead? If so, your love life is in trouble. It's sad but true: you cannot have it all. Romance and riches, passion and promotions, the bedroom and the boardroom, Little League and Junior League—they don't often come all wrapped up in one package. So take a moment to go through the following quiz. Discover your own ability to distinguish between career commitment and work addiction.

1. The average workaholic spends how many hours per week on work?
   (a) 40 office hours and 10 take-home hours
   (b) 50 office hours and 10 take-home hours
   (c) 60 office hours and untold take-home hours
   (d) More than 60 hours, not including weekend office time
2. A workaholic's biggest "high" is:
   (a) the impressive economic rewards that come from all the effort.
   (b) the social respect that comes from all the effort.
   (c) the metabolic rush that comes from all the effort.
   (d) the self-respect that comes from a job well done.
3. When job junkies realize that their habit has cost them a happy private life, they typically respond by:
   (a) working less—unless their sense of failure subsides.
   (b) tackling their failure as another job to be done well.
   (c) ignoring the thought; it interferes with job performance.
   (d) working even harder. It helps them escape a sense of failure.
4. Most workaholics view a close personal relationship as:
   (a) very important; it's another area of life in which to excel.
   (b) important, but not as rewarding as their work.

(c)   rather unimportant; it takes too much time away from work.

(d)   wonderful for other people but not right for them.

5. If it means sacrificing quality, workplace shortcuts strike the workaholic as:

(a)   a lazy alternative to methodical effort.

(b)   a great way to get more things done faster.

(c)   a shrewd "cheat" that should never be publicly admitted.

(d)   profoundly unprofessional.

6. Workaholics look at their achievements and usually feel like:

(a)   winners! They worked hard and they got what they deserve.

(b)   losers! They let success cheat them out of romantic happiness.

(c)   impostors! They fooled everyone into believing they're special.

(d)   fools! The success has cost far too much.

7. The biggest reason why workaholics are so bad at intimacy is:

(a)   they put more energy into career than into relationships.

(b)   they are satisfied only with perfection, and their own feelings never seem good enough to qualify as "true love."

(c)   they are satisfied only with perfection, and they never meet anybody who seems good enough for any length of time.

(d)   they can't stop working at a relationship long enough to enjoy it.

8. Successful single women worry that their professional status will threaten potential partners. In reality, most men:

(a)   are insecure around a woman's competence and power.

(b)   want to date women who are as accomplished as they are.

(c)   don't care about a woman's professional standing as long as she makes them feel masculine.

(d)   like to stand in the shadow of a woman they truly respect.

9. For most workaholics, socializing means:
   (a) a little time off with just one close friend or lover.
   (b) a huge bash where they can get lost in a sea of strangers.
   (c) a quiet day at home, communicating with friends via fax machines.
   (d) out-of-office time with clients, coworkers or competitors.

10. Workaholics who are trying to reactivate a love life should:
    (a) date only people from outside their job environment—people who see them as persons separate from their work.
    (b) date people from work but also people they meet outside work.
    (c) date only people connected to their jobs—people with whom they have something important in common.
    (d) get to know themselves better before dating anyone.

IF I'M DOING SOMETHING SO WRONG, WHY IS EVERYONE APPLAUDING?

I'd like to tell you a story about a young man who was on his way up. By the time he was fourteen, and while most of his friends thought about winning Friday night's football game, or passing their next geometry test, he spent his time trying to change the world into a better place to live. He oriented his life toward becoming a civil liberties lawyer and congressman. Later he was voted president of his college sophomore class. And even before graduation, he was invited to teach courses in both communications and journalism at one of the country's top ten universities.

He started his own business when he was twenty-six years old. By the time he was thirty, he had built it into a multimillion-dollar national venture. He worked all the time, plowed all his money back into his business, and didn't know what the word "vacation" meant. Between corporate board meetings, charitable activities, and cross-country speaking engagements, he mastered polo and compiled an extensive library of classical and blues music. Sandwiched between these, he managed to marry, have children, make friends, and remain close to his parents (despite occasional conflicts). He was, in a word, a superachiever. He thought he could have it all without sacrificing or compromising anything.

I can speak in expert detail about this man—about his ambitions and his fears, about his outward presentation and his inner self. I know him quite well, because I am that man. So when I write about career addiction and the high price you pay for it, I speak from experience. I spent too many years defining myself by my work. Fortunately, I have learned from my mistakes and changed my paradigm from micro-managing and macro-addiction to delegating more responsibility and working smarter. I now know the necessity of time off and rejuvenation. I figured out that it's just as critical to put resources into my personal relationships as into my career.

Like most workaholics, I did not develop my focus on being Superman during adulthood. I was hooked on it even as a child. And like many smart kids, my behavior was reinforced since I grew into the kind of young adult that everyone admires. I was loaded with high self-esteem. I was responsible, confident, achievement-oriented, and felt comfortable taking charge of almost any situation. I was passionate about everything I did, and I did everything with 100 percent gusto. I loved what I did so much that my business life literally blended into my personal life. This took its toll in many countless small but significant aspects of my personal life. I'm certain that I must have bored many of my closest friends with all my shop talk because I didn't know how to turn it off when I left the office. In fact, as an entrepreneur even when I left the office, my mind never stopped thinking about improving the business.

Looking back, I can see that by the time I was a teenager, I was already putting far too much achievement-oriented pressure on myself. When I was old enough to get a job, I simply transferred my behavior from academic mastery to my career goals. I was rewarded for it, too. The feedback that I got was that people admired and envied my achievements. With all that admiration coming my way, I figured I must be doing things right.

Ultimately, that's what's so addictive about the workaholic's habit. It is the most accepted and encouraged of all addictions. Because work is associated with solidity and responsibility, everybody figures you can't do too much of it. Job junkies may live on coffee to keep them up, antacids to settle their stomachs, and aspirin to stop their headaches. But their misery is relieved by encouraging slaps on the back, fat bonuses, and gold plaques for their office walls.

Most people incur telltale signs that their body is under undue stress. Personally, since I never got sick, never had stomach aches, never had insomnia, and always felt great, I wasn't aware how work-addicted I was. My positive physical condition helped mask my addiction. (Does a fish know it's in water?) At that time, if cornered on the subject I would have undoubtedly professed that my personal life was given as much attention and as much intellectual, spiritual, and emotional energy as my professional life.

Unfortunately, I was wrong. I felt I had a full relationship with my wife, small children, and dearest friends. But they got second best. Since there's only so much time in any day, I never had enough wind-down time to pause and really reflect on what was going on in this part of my life. My concentration was on doing, accomplishing, and planning. What did they (and I) actually miss from my lessened attention? Although I cannot ever really know for certain, I can only speculate about how much more I would have been able to enjoy my children's early years. My wife definitely would have appreciated more of my time and energy around the house. That time is gone and can never be made up again. And, as one might expect, I divorced after nine years of marriage.

Another monumental characteristic that I failed to notice was how much my business manner and persona spilled over into my personal life. Like so many hard-driving entrepreneurs, I took home with me the same "I'm-in-charge-let's-do-it-my-way-I-know-best" attitude. The decisive, not very tolerant, and rather impatient pace that often makes a workaholic successful in business doesn't produce the same results at home. And as anyone who's been in a marriage can tell you: That's no way to run a railroad . . . unless, of course, you plan on railroading your mate out of town or out of the relationship.

Workaholics have difficulty recognizing this. They are almost blind, deaf, and definitely dumb to the insidiousness of how their business demeanor affects their home life. Phone calls from the office? No problem. Messages and faxes while on vacation? No problem. Yet interrupt the business days with calls from home? No way! Or at least "Not now" or "Hurry up!"

When you're single, workaholism is an especially deceiving trap. You don't have plans for the evening anyway, so why not stay those extra hours at the office? Besides, focusing on work will distract you from the loneliness you might otherwise feel at home. I mean, who wants to flop on the sofa and watch television programs about picture-perfect couples working their way through modern relationships? Work will help you forget. It will entertain you. And you are rewarded for it by money, status, and results. Most important, it will offer you a silent companion for the night.

Of course, after a few months (or years) of this sublimation, you'll probably find yourself even more isolated than when you began. Now your life lacks not just a loving mate, but friends and family as well. Why? Because you've lost those people to the highest-bidding employer or client.

Yet how do you react to this increased loneliness? In perfect workaholic form, you roll up your sleeves and dig even deeper into your job. Without realizing it, you start expecting your career to protect you from more than just the unwanted solitude that comes from being undesirably single. You also expect it to lessen the guilt you feel over all that you've put aside in the name of professional advancement. You expect it to dull the anger you feel at still being alone despite your impressive achievements. And you expect it to put a bandage on your confusion about how to end the vicious cycle that you've created for yourself.

Obviously, workaholics aren't very good at establishing the foundations of relationships. They're even worse at maintaining them. Still, they often try very hard to be good at both. This is simply because they don't take the time and effort that is necessary for the rituals of courtship. Since they think they can have it all, being desirable and well-mated are extremely important to them. After all, these are two more areas of life in which they feel they must succeed.

As a young single workaholic recently bemoaned to me, it's just not enough to be a business success anymore. Overachievers feel a need to be both. "I've set certain objectives for myself," one woman explained, "and I would let myself down if I failed to meet them." What were those objectives? I asked her. "First and foremost," she said, "I envision myself as someone who will be a wonderful wife. I want to give my mate everything he wants or dreams. I want to be a gourmet cook, a gracious hostess, a tasteful decorator, a good corporate wife, and a seductive lover." As if that was not enough, she went on: "I also think I'll be a terrific lawyer, writer of powerful articles about the community and environment, and local political activist. I don't expect to battle undue stress or strain because I really love what I do and I do what I love. Eventually, I also want to have a family and involve myself in carpooling and fundraising for school, but I don't want that to prevent me from being a devoted daughter, sister, and friend to the people who love and need me." Finally, with a chuckle, she added, "Like all women, of course, I also plan to exercise regularly, be healthy and beautiful, and never show my age!"

You may think I made that up, but I didn't. That's an actual quote from a real person. Is she unusual? Sadly, she's not. Instead, she's a perfect reflection of what can happen to our best and our brightest. They can get locked in a prison of unrealistic and self-defeating and self-imposed expectations.

TELLTALE SIGNS OF A PERFECTIONIST

Healthy or hung up, we've all burned the midnight oil a time or two. Pushing yourself beyond reasonable limits is part and parcel of being a professional in the nineties. It's a sign of our pressured times.

Nevertheless, there is a very real difference between a committed professional and a workaholic. That difference has to do with balance. How well do we integrate work into a well-rounded existence? Healthy people give about as much time and thought to their work as to other major activities in their lives. For workaholics, career cannot be separated from all other activities in life. They aren't able to see their job as just one aspect of who they are. For them, what they do defines who they are.

Although the complete psychological profile of a work addict is too complex for me to cover here, there are five key characteristics shared by virtually all overachievers. Usually, one or two of them will dominate, but to qualify as a card-carrying member of the compulsive rank and file, you need to regularly display all five qualities. Let's see if you or someone close to you qualifies for this growing club.

One: Workaholics Have a Compulsive Need to Stay Busy.

Have you ever seen a master juggler able to keep several balls flying gracefully through the air at once? Well, that's the workaholic's dream; only the balls aren't small rubber toys. They're major professional and social commitments. When you're work-addicted, you live in a constant state of anxiety. Haunted by a never-ending sense of urgency, you spend most of your time rushing against the clock, trying to accomplish all the things you've promised yourself you'll do. Of course, you spend any leftover time feeling that you've got nothing to do.

Lots of workaholics conduct two or three activities simultaneously. They'll talk on the phone, update their calendar, eat lunch, and think about what to say at the next day's sales meeting—all at the same time. When they travel in their car, workaholics will almost never shut off the radio; they crave the constant input that they get from the news station, books on tape, or some other information source. The faster they can shower, dress, get the kids to day care and clean the house, the more time they have left for additional work, and the better they feel. Because workaholics are goal-oriented, saving time is crucial, hence work addicts look for shortcuts. Even if it means sacrificing quality, they want to produce more than anyone else faster than anyone else. And, for the perfectionist workaholic, the stress is increased considerably because of the strains of what cutting corners might mean for quality.

What also distinguishes workaholics is that to them free time is a waste of time. They don't know how to spend time not doing something productive, recognizable, or measurable.

Compared to a workaholic's crazy pace, the rest of the world operates on turtle time. So compulsive overachievers often end up impatient with everyone around them. Once they give or receive an assignment, the meter begins running. If the task is not completed fast enough they're dissatisfied.

Two: Workaholics Need to Control Just About Everything.

Never hold your breath and wait for a work addict to ask for help. It's not going to happen. They prefer to do everything themselves. To them it's more efficient for them to handle the job themselves. Because they work so hard, they're often in supervisory positions, but they have great difficulty when it comes to delegating. Workaholics don't want to give up the control long enough to delegate. Besides, they're convinced that nobody else can do what needs to be done as well or as fast as they can.

All of this points to the obvious: workaholics are often not considered good at teamwork. If negotiation and compromise are required, they're on edge. So they're not good at being just one part of a group decision. They would much rather deal with the exhaustion and burnout that come from living life like a one-man band. Remember, work makes them feel secure, especially amidst adversity. It's the one thing they've learned to count on and control.

Work addicts don't like as much change as you might think because they're not terribly flexible people. They feel uneasy in unpredictable situations. Time off with nothing planned is unsettling to them, and their idea of a nightmare. So they build in to every assignment as much work as possible. When a project nears completion, they'll often decide to expand it—all in the effort to keep the work ball rolling.

• • •

Three: Workaholics Are Satisfied Only with Perfection.

No matter how hard you try, you'll hardly ever please a work addict. After all, that would be an admission of your competence, and nobody is as capable as they are. Usually, their criticism turns to petty details. Rather than attack the big picture, they'll complain about small things: the one wrong figure in an otherwise perfect financial report, or the socks that don't exactly match your new suit.

Of course, workaholics are no less judgmental about themselves. They do not permit mistakes. They maintain incredibly high standards for themselves, and they assess others by these same unrealistic criteria.

Four: Workaholics Secretly Feel Like "Impostors."

Despite all the public praise that comes their way, work addicts secretly worry that they don't deserve success. They don't feel like the bright, creative, dynamic people they are thought to be by the rest of the world. Instead, they feel like phonies who have somehow managed to get away with far more than they've actually earned. Deep down they figure that their success comes not as the result of true talent but because they kept their nose closer to the grindstone than anybody else. Or maybe just because they got lucky. Workaholics also battle against what they fear to be inevitable: exposure. They're convinced that every new assignment, every additional commitment may be the one that will prove them mediocre. So they push themselves to the outermost limit over absolutely everything, hoping to sneak past still one more test of specialness. Then, when their efforts bear fruit, they're even more convinced that only superhuman effort can earn them the label of "exceptional." We all know that hard work is an important part of achievement. But for workaholics, it's the only part. They never learn that innate ability, competence, and talent also play a major part in their success.

Five: Workaholics Have Difficulty with Intimate Relationships.

Why are so many work addicts single, divorced, or in constant conflict with their partner? In part, because they put more thought and time into the least important aspect of their careers than into the most significant elements of their relationships. Highly successful people relentlessly pursue their goals. They know that perseverance is the key to success. What they haven't done successfully is to put this same kind of energy into pursuing and sustaining a mate.

But there's a far more profound reason why compulsive over-achievers don't do well with intimacy. They firmly believe that they cannot rely on anyone. They live in a pretty small universe. It holds them, and a whole bunch of their inferiors. They carry this keen sense of isolation into each of their relationships. In the beginning, it can disguise itself. Sometimes it makes them appear a mysterious loner: other times, a dynamic leader. But eventually, the mask falls away, and the workaholic can be seen accurately—cold and unable to make a commitment between equals.

There's another factor at play in all this. Because they constantly strive for perfection, compulsive overachievers have a hard time accepting that their feelings might qualify as "real love." The first bad date or the slightest disagreement makes them doubt everything about the relationship. If their affection is not total all the time, it appears to them to be "flawed." That flaw quickly is magnified far out of critical proportion, and the work addict begins to question whether this affair or that new crush is worth the effort.

It's ironic that workaholics strive for perfection in their work environment, yet they actually settle for mediocrity. They do not live life as fully or "perfectly" as they can because they bury themselves in their workaholism: *that* they can control. Love has no guarantees and is entirely risky, so they insulate and protect themselves from it.

SUPERWOMAN: A NEW KIND OF OVERACHIEVER

For the majority of today's women, career achievement is not one of several options. It's the only option. There are more than 50 million women in the U.S. labor force today. Together, they earn $500 billion a year, and take home almost one-third the nation's pay. As more of them opt to marry later, they choose to support themselves through work. That means women of the nineties are professionally up against men, day in and day out. And men have been raised to respect and respond to aggressive competition.

Even more important, most modern women have a new attitude and commitment toward their work. More of them than ever before are seriously after a successful and noteworthy career. They want (and plan) to leave their mark in fields once reserved for men. They are not taking jobs for economic survival only. They're taking them for a solid sense of purpose and personal pride.

All of this creates a new social reality for women, a reality in which workaholism looms just around the corner. For better or worse, women are now the true equals of men when it comes to a risk of job addiction, heart disease, stroke, chemical dependency, and workplace wipeout.

Women also have to confront expectations for what makes a successful private life. While our sense for what special women should accomplish at work has changed dramatically, our ideas about what worthy women should achieve at home have not. They must try to excel in both their careers and their personal lives. Feeling capable and confident in our personal and professional lives is important, but that means crossing traditional boundaries and merging both our feminine and masculine sides. Women need to project strength professionally, and at the same time nurture relationships. When it comes to dating, professional single women may find it a real challenge to drop the professional aura, and relate to men in social settings differently than they do at work.

There is, of course, a new ethic about what it takes to be a real man these days, too. A "real" man of the nineties should be a

"New Man." You know him. He's the guy who can still be loving and attentive to your needs after a twelve-hour workday on Wall Street. He can coach Little League, make dinner, understand your feelings, romance and seduce you in creative ways, and still rake in a sizable income every year.

But in reality, we don't judge men as harshly as women for falling short of this outrageous ideal. Most men continue to judge themselves and each other by criteria that relate to work, money, and professional status. Men will frequently describe themselves (or other men) as "successful" even if their personal lives are terrible flops. Women, on the other hand, will almost never refer to themselves (or other women) as "successful" if their personal lives are in shambles. Most professional single women tell me they didn't anticipate the sacrifice to personal, social, and sexual needs that their career demands from them. Women seem to pay a higher price than men. It seems that it is nearly impossible to have it all.

Single women worry that in gaining professional status they may become threatening to the men they hope to attract. In fact, according to one study, most single women in successful jobs feel that they are simultaneously attractive and intimidating to men. The sad truth is that many men are deeply threatened by a woman's competence, intelligence, success, and power. They wonder: if she doesn't need me for status, money, or protection, then does she really need me? Yes, of course she does. This is significant especially if she's in a higher status job than he is. She is choosing to love him for his emotional side, not for the status or material objects he can bring to her. These men should feel lucky to know they have a woman who loves them for who they are, and not for what they can provide financially.

THE AT-HOME WORKAHOLIC: A NEW BREED

When we try to get a mental picture of the average workaholic, many of us conjure up images of a frenzied career woman, tapping her pen on an expensive leather appointment book while motioning to her secretary to take a letter. Or we see a harried businessman, working until the wee hours of the morning trying to come up with that perfect proposal to win over a new client.

What we usually don't think of is the harried home office worker. You know, the one with one hand on the computer, fax, or copier and the other on the vacuum cleaner. This new breed of workaholic is the Super Person of the nineties—the one who wears every professional hat at once. After all, when you work at home, you're the CEO, the receptionist, the CFO, the secretary, and the janitor—all wrapped up in one person. It's true that some people may have increased freedom. But freedom to do what? Probably to work longer hours than ever before and to assume all the worry yourself. That doesn't leave much time (or energy) for dating or any other element of a social life.

I don't mean to belittle the freelance professionals of the world. Actually, I'm like most other office-bound workers of America. I admire their initiative and envy their independence. Nevertheless, as this segment of the singles population grows (and research indicates that it definitely is growing), the dangers of getting too hung up on work are obvious.

When you do it all yourself, there's nobody there to tell you that you're doing too much. Freelance, home-based workers are very isolated. Without even knowing it, they can slip from dedicated to addicted. They can totally lose sight of themselves. And who's there to point them in the direction of the closest mirror?

PRESCRIPTIONS FOR A ROMANTIC REVIVAL

If romance and career make such strange bedfellows, what's a poor workaholic to do? The truth is, if you're hooked you've got only two choices. Either you can pair up with another job junkie and hope that love will blossom during quick calls between power lunches and corporate cocktail parties. Or you can make an effort to put your profession into a new perspective.

It's easier said than done, of course. But work abusers really can learn to fill their lives with things other than career assignments and volunteer overtime. In fact, many psychologists have argued that the only way for workaholics to escape their basic fear of isolation is to stop letting their jobs substitute for what's really missing from their lives: self-awareness and intimacy. It comes back to my original premise: to find and get love, you've got to get realistic.

The danger is that when workaholics find out they need to make changes in their lives, they respond like the true compulsives that they are: they go to work on the problem. They sign up for a dance class, or take up tennis. Then they proceed to schedule into their lives this new element of balance. They mark it into their bulging date book, and hurry to complete it. In effect, they turn it into still one more responsibility, one more way to practice their problem.

I know from personal experience that the nastiest word in a work addict's vocabulary is "No." Thinking this negative thought is bad enough. Hearing it is worse. Saying it is just about impossible. Naturally, life being what it is, "No" holds the key to a romantic comeback for job junkies everywhere. To guide their efforts, I've developed the "Workaholic's No-Can-Do" list. It's not long—just four life pressures that compulsive overachievers must give up if love is ever going to replace success as life's sweetest pleasure.

Rule Number One: No Seven-Day Work Weeks.

A recent questionnaire was sent to fifty nationally recognized overachievers. Basically, it asked them how they manage to keep it all going. When the answers came back (from twenty-six professionals who had made time to respond), they suggested that success is not just a jungle. It's also an endurance test.

The average respondent works between fifty-five and sixty hours a week, not including take-home assignments. One respondent works seventy to eighty hours a week. Another claims to put in eighty to ninety. And one famous seventy-three-year-old workaholic puts in ten hours a day during the week and eight hours a day on weekends! Most get to their desk between 7:30 and 8:30 every day, and average less than six hours of sleep per night. As for socializing, most respondents explained that almost all their social life is work-related. An evening out is usually dinner with a client. A typical vacation is the half day or overnight that falls between the end of an out-of-town business conference and the flight back home.

Sound familiar? Well, with that kind of schedule, it's no wonder you're still looking for a mate. You're not making time for romance to happen. So cut back the hours by working smarter! A forty-hour week is nothing to be ashamed of. It would be great if you could leave all the problems behind each day at 5:00 P.M. But if you're a true addict, that will be impossible, at least at first. So just concentrate on leaving. Worry if you must. But don't spend more than fifty-five hours each week doing work-related activities.

Rule Number Two: No Business Calls After 7:00 P.M.

Between office phone systems that allow you up to a dozen incoming calls at one time, cellular car phones, home answering machines, high-powered cordless phones, and fax equipment—the modern workaholic can stay in absolute constant contact with colleagues and competitors. (And who knows what even more advanced "stay-in-instant-touch" technological tools are just about to hit us?)

Fight the urge to reach out repeatedly and touch someone. Learn to cut the cord. Remember, delegation is a skill you need to master. So begin right now. Let your partners and staff know that you are unreachable after 7:00 P.M. every evening. That still allows you 120 minutes of phone time after normal office hours have ended. If you can't handle the matter within that time frame, leave it for tomorrow. Or let somebody else take over. Let the telephone answering machine screen your calls at home; and keep the volume down so you can't hear what's being said.

When you've mastered these basic techniques, you're ready for the big test. Stay at a mountain lodge or seaside hotel that doesn't have phones in its rooms. (It's much more romantic, anyway.) When you survive the experience, think back to earlier days, when an hour away from office contact would have felt like time in San Quentin.

Rule Number Three: No Escape From Daily Quiet Time.

For workaholics, leisure is not only rare; it borders on the immoral. But medical experts tell us that relaxation, mental or physical, is not wasted time; it's rejuvenating time. In fact, scientific research has shown that it can relieve stress and increase intellectual stamina. A casual stroll helps circulate blood, improve muscle tone, and burn off tension. In the process, it makes you better able to think your way through all kinds of dilemmas. Sitting for even fifteen minutes, doing absolutely nothing, will gently focus the mind inward—to a review of what's most important and what brings the greatest rewards.

Expect to experience some withdrawal at first. When you try this quiet set-aside time, you may initially confront boredom and restlessness. Being quiet and passive is difficult because you have come to see both activities as wasted time. What's more, you're not used to paying much attention to yourself. So your mind and body will naturally resist. Don't give up, though. Within a week, you'll see a significant improvement. As you get better at handling quiet, increase the amount of it you give yourself until you're up to one hour a day.

Rule Number Four: No Dating Business Contacts.

This is probably the hardest rule of all. If it's any comfort, be aware that you won't have to follow it forever. Still, in the beginning, it's important for you to see your love life as entirely separate from work. That means you can't date coworkers, professional colleagues, or clients.

If you want to meet people, you'll have to start a real social life. You'll have to see friends, go to parties, visit a gym, maybe even join a dating service. And with the cutbacks you're making in available work hours, you'll probably become more tuned into dating in a way you have not for a long time. You'll begin to see the big hole in your life that a mate could fulfill, a hole you used to cram full of job-related tasks and responsibilities.

Eventually, of course, you can reconsider this rule. Once you've learned how to meet people outside work, you may look up from your desk to discover that the love of your life sits right across the office hallway. But until you can live beyond the square footage of your office, you should not look for love within its narrow work stations.

Put It into Practice

Making your career a part of your life (as opposed to all there is to your life) is simply a matter of balance. The question is, how big a part of your life should work be? Can you keep it in its place?

Find out by making a calendar for yourself. But instead of scheduling in all the professional commitments that you have, block off time each day for nonwork-related activities. Decide in advance how much of every day you want to hand over to a personal life. One hour? Two? Can you spare only fifteen minutes? You decide. And, of course, be aware that the more time you give to a private life, the more it will give to you.

If you're confused about what to schedule in for yourself, why not start with some of the restful solitude that this chapter described. And how about time for other activities? A movie? Some much-needed exercise? The trip to your neighborhood library that you've been promising yourself? You decide, and then mark them down.

I'm not expecting you to fill your entire week with this stuff. However, I do want you to set aside at least *some* personal time every day. Make an appointment with yourself. And this is crucial: once you've scheduled in a leisure activity, don't forget about it or replace it with other "more pressing" obligations. See these plans as real commitments.

When the week is over, take a look at how you did. How faithful were you to your schedule? Did you live up to the commitments you made to yourself? Or did you (once again) put your own best interests aside in favor of your job? If you did, then you've got to try again the very next week. A personal life won't just fall into your lap. You have to build it, just like you build your career. Most job counselors say that it takes a five-year plan to accomplish even one major professional goal. I promise that it won't take that long to build a private life. But it won't happen overnight. Rome wasn't built in a day. Romance won't be, either. So start today and pace yourself, one week at a time.

ANSWERS TO THE QUIZ

1. c
2. b
3. d
4. a
5. b
6. c
7. b
8. a
9. d
10. a

8 Single . . . Again

"It's not whether you get knocked down.
It's whether you get up."
—VINCE LOMBARDI

I believe that even though your past relationship didn't work out, you *are* a better person for having loved. Whatever the reason for your now being single, there's no doubt that you have learned a great deal from your previous marriage. What's now important is how you apply what you have experienced to your future relationships.

While it may take two people to make a couple, we get divorced or go through the tragedy of widowhood all by ourselves. That's the hardest part of separation either by choice or chance; it leaves you all alone. You have to rebuild a new, independent life. The excitement that brought you together is long gone. The mutual interests and values that made you hold on now seem more imagined than real. So, if you're like the majority of separated men and women, you can no longer turn to that special someone for emotional support, that person you've relied on for so long.

The challenge of breaking the bonds that tied you to your old life, while at the same time weaving together the threads of a new one, confronts everyone who divorces. You have to rework your relationship with your ex, your children, and your friends. You need to redefine yourself for nearly everyone who knows you. Most important, you must re-create a new sexual, emotional, and social identity for yourself. You are no longer one-half of an identifiable couple. You're suddenly a single person operating in a mating-oriented and couples-conscious society. Like tens of millions of other people around the world, you find yourself torn between two poles. On the one end is your "failed" past. On the other is your uncertain future. One thing you can count on is that men and women suffer pretty much the same way. Divorced or newly single people I have spoken with have said to me that they usually assume they have "failed," and many feel they have to defend their decision to divorce.

Divorced women frequently voice the same lament. They feel that others judge them harshly. For many, their support network of friends tends to disappear just when they need it the most. They hear, "You expected too much from him!" Or "You just didn't try hard enough!" Or "You weren't committed enough to make it through the tough times!" This all translates into: "It's all *your* fault that your relationship didn't succeed."

While no two breakups are the same, and each has its own unique set of circumstances, there are common denominators. For example, whom do you turn to for guidance to solve your problems? Where do you find a mentor to help you during this time when your life becomes undeniably altered? How do you learn to cope with all the new responsibilities life now demands from you?

This is not an easy task, yet more people than ever before are deciding to tackle it. The United States has one of the highest divorce rates in the industrialized world. Every year, over 2 million people get divorced in this country. Three out of every four couples getting married today will eventually separate. Of those who do, two-thirds will divorce within the first year.

By the same token, the average length of marriage today is almost the same as it was a century ago. It's just that divorce has replaced death as the most common form of separation. What's more, remarriage is more popular than it's ever been. Only one out of every eight people who separates will stay permanently single. The rest will recouple, usually in marriage, within three to seven years. Unfortunately, with each additional try at marital success, they statistically increase their chances at eventual divorce.

But the numbers don't seem to stop many of us. Having known the innumerable and incomparable pleasures of intimacy, human beings relentlessly opt to try again. It seems, at least in matters of the heart, that hope really does conquer experience. That's a good thing, because, as a famous philosopher once said, "To fear love is to fear life, and those who fear life are already three parts dead."

TESTING YOUR "DIVORCE I.Q."

Like other emotional crises, divorce is often best understood after the fact. If you've passed through it, take a few minutes to measure your sense of what actually happened. Did you come face-to-face with all the consequences of the breakup? Or did you sail along on the surface, afraid to look at what it really meant—about you and your ability to choose a partner?

Whether you've gone through a marital bust or not, test yourself to see if you have a realistic picture of life on the other side of divorce. Looking at the facts now may prevent you from living them out in your own life later on.

1. When you're newly divorced, a loss of close friends indicates that:
   (a) you're unconsciously rejecting those who care most about you.
   (b) you're making your life a war in which everyone must take a side.

(c) you're going through a normal separation from your old life.

(d) you chose to be friends with the wrong people.

2. If your ex-spouse constantly complained that you were a slob, your first move after divorce might well be to:

(a) buy a whole new wardrobe and paint your entire apartment.

(b) throw all your clothes on the floor and stack dirty dishes for a month.

(c) interpret your "sloppiness" as a reflection of self-loathing.

(d) view those complaints as a coward's way of saying "I don't love you anymore."

3. Most divorced men and women have a first sexual encounter within:

(a) one month of their separation date.

(b) three months of their separation date.

(c) six months of their separation date.

(d) one year of their separation date.

4. What percentage of divorced men admit to having had extramarital affairs?

(a) Over 70 percent.

(b) Almost exactly 50 percent.

(c) About 20 percent.

(d) Less than 10 percent.

5. What percentage of divorced women say they had a lover before their separation?

(a) Over 70 percent.

(b) Almost exactly 50 percent.

(c) About 20 percent.

(d) Less than 10 percent.

6. When a middle-aged divorced man chooses to date a twenty-four-year-old woman, it's usually because he wants to be with someone who will:

(a) help him feel young again.

(b) make other married men envy him.

(c) admire his worldly sophistication.

(d) match his own level of emotional maturity.

7. For the best shot at long-term happiness, a divorced person should begin looking for another serious relationship:
   (a) immediately. The sooner you start, the sooner you find someone.
   (b) as soon as s/he is ready. Two or three years is usually best.
   (c) only after s/he has learned to focus on personal development.
   (d) when friends and relatives suggest it. Their approval will make the process easier.

8. How does the average woman's standard of living change after divorce?
   (a) It usually goes up about 15 percent.
   (b) It usually goes down nearly 25 percent.
   (c) It usually drops by over 70 percent.
   (d) It usually stays about the same, provided she protects herself in the divorce.

9. How much should kids be told about their parents' divorce?
   (a) As much as they can understand; children deserve to know.
   (b) Questions should be answered, but not until children ask them.
   (c) As little as possible; children should not be asked to grapple with divorce.
   (d) However much will allow them to see both parents as good people.

10. If you get involved with the right person, a postdivorce affair will:
    (a) rouse the vulnerability that worked against you last time.
    (b) allow you to sever ties to the past marriage, once and for all.
    (c) only bring you happiness that is unrelated to your previous marriage.
    (d) help you improve your relationship with your ex-spouse.

STARTING OVER

Most people get divorced when they're between the ages of thirty and sixty, the most vital period of their lives. Their careers are in high gear. They're raising their families. They' re steeped in financial responsibility. Like the furious center of a cyclone, divorce blows everything aside to become the main focus of life. Being introspective and reflective is a positive move. But don't use it as an excuse for not rejoining life.

For all the grief and loss that come with divorce or the death of a loved one, the sadness is not a deadly disease. You may be too old for romantic myths, but you're still too young to give up. So, like it or not, you're forced to pick up the pieces and move on with your life. And remember, all good things must start somewhere. One door closes, but another opens. It's up to you to decide whether you're going to stare at the closed door or open it and go in. Don't just expect something good to happen—you can't depend on luck or anyone else to get you through it. Fate is what you make of it.

Too often, divorced people fail to give themselves credit for the strength it takes to survive the termination of a marriage. Divorce means finding a new residence for at least one partner. Many men change jobs during or shortly after a divorce, and for the first time they must learn hands-on parenting skills. Many women have to rebalance their traditional mothering role against additional commitments outside the home. Divorce for these women may mean planning a new career, living on a lower income, juggling domestic and professional responsibilities, managing children, and making time for a new social life. Each of these accomplishments says a lot about a person's ability to weather the hard realities of adulthood. It's important to remember that the relationship that's just ended was both good and bad. Life is both good and bad, and everything in between. After a loss, people tend to dwell on the darker side of life and long for serendipity. It's useful to remember that life is never perfect. It includes both perfection and imperfection.

As you emerge from the shock of divorce, you also tend to suffer unexpected anger over your "public divorce." In your private divorce, you faced your ex-spouse, your past, and yourself. But that's only half the battle. You must also face the world you used to live in: the friends, family, and acquaintances that you built up as a married couple. And while this may be the Grand Era of Divorce, most people are still very uncomfortable with a breakup. They don't know what to do or whose side to take. What's more, your separation reminds them that marriages don't always work out. That's frightening.

Quite often, a major result of divorce is the loss of friends. During this period you're going through a tough-enough time emotionally, and you figured your friends would want to rally around you. Instead, you've probably found that a lot of them have slowly slipped away. People react differently to the survivors of death or divorce. My advice to you is don't take it personally. Don't hold it against yourself if they react to you in ways that disappoint, surprise, or downright annoy you. And now you find yourself without many friendly shoulders to cry on, either; your support network has disappeared. It's possible that your old married friends only know how to relate to you as one-half of a couple. They feel that you no longer fit into their social schedule. Many divorcees tell me that they feel their friends have deserted them. Some say they're even viewed as a threat. You're also likely to be short of Friday and Saturday companions. Who will go with you to dinner or the theater? Who will introduce you to exciting romantic prospects? Who will go shopping with you for a sexy outfit to wear on the first date you've had in ten years?

It's very possible that nobody will. Your friends are all busy trying to get through their own daily routines. They may consider your attempts at a new love life interesting phone conversation. However, they may not have the time or desire to get involved in the small triumphs and defeats of your courtships. It's also possible that they will see support for you as a betrayal of your ex-spouse. The result is that they'll sympathize halfheartedly with you or not at all. That means you're going to have to start from scratch. You'll need to form new friendships as well as find new lovers.

It's okay to need comfort and support from others who've been through similar experiences. Invite new people into your life. Seek out others who have survived a similar loss or change in their lives, and develop new interests. Look around for the various groups that cater to the newly single individual. Check your newspapers, local magazines, or bulletin boards for who they are, and where they meet.

You may discover as you set about creating a new social circle, that you're following directions suggested by your ex. If he always complained that you didn't dress trendily enough, you may find yourself buying new clothes and becoming more fashion-conscious. If she nagged that you were too cheap, you may decide to let the dollars flow; or you may join a health club, lose some weight, stop smoking, change your hairstyle, learn to dance, take a vacation, or go to a spa. This is normal behavior and it may even be a positive step in the right direction. (Even the worst ex couldn't have been wrong about everything. Your ex probably knew you better than most anyone.) But beware the tendency to overidentify with the past. Be prepared to start experimenting with new behaviors, new styles, activities, friends, new ideas to old ways, and new ways to fulfill daily needs.

One of the signs that you're ready to start looking for new relationships is the ability to separate from the old you. You'd think that, fresh from a divorce, we'd all love nothing more than to put our own interests and pleasures first. It doesn't always work that way, though. Your lives were so enmeshed that it may be difficult to separate the "you" from the "we" of yesteryear. You can't pursue your own individual tastes and preferences until you know what they are. Many of us stay in unhappy marriages because we don't want to go through that process of looking at ourselves. Self-examination can be scary. There are many professionals who help others heal and grow. Seek professional help if necessary. It's sometimes the best jump-start to get your life going in the right direction. Appreciate your new personal growth. Expect to discover within yourself a different you, a stronger you, a more enlightened you, and certainly a more independent you.

Postbreakup dating is usually not easy. In fact it can be truly petrifying for many. You may feel totally unprepared, inadequate, tongue-tied, nervous, gawky, insecure, afraid, angry, guilty, depressed, and all the while you're expected to wear a smile. Hopefully, you'll be comforted that you are armed with the reassurance that you are not the only one out there going through this! There's no reason for you to allow yourself to feel all this pressure. It's all in your mind.

Some people choose to date as many people as possible once they are newly single. Others take a different tack and go out only with those who they "know" are quality. Whatever you choose, the important thing to remember is that dating gives you the opportunity to start your new life. You might even experience guilt about feeling joyful after the loss of a loved one, or the ending of a long-term relationship. But please recognize that you're not being disloyal by moving on with your life.

Research has shown that many people may experience one or all of the following after the end of a relationship through death or divorce: changed sleep patterns, reduced energy level, poor concentration, poor nutritional habits, suicidal thoughts, or overindulging in destructive or addictive behaviors, such as overeating or drinking, drugs, increased smoking, or promiscuous sex.

Sex After Your Marriage Is Over

Sexuality is as important to our lives as nourishment and rest. It can be frightening to suddenly return to the singles sexual world after a long-term relationship. According to all the experts, it really is going to happen—and faster that you might expect. Most divorced men and women begin having sex with someone new within six months of their original separation date. The common view is that divorced people are anxious to explore their sexuality because they've had a sexual partner in their lives for a long time. The myth is that once you've had available sex, you want to have more.

But research shows us that most marriages ending in divorce die a slow and painful death. And sex, along with virtually every other aspect of the relationship, practically disappears before the end finally comes. In fact, a large number of people interviewed for one survey reported that they had not had sex with their ex-spouse for between three and five years preceding divorce.

That's not to say divorced people don't want to be sexually active. They do. But not because they've been so used to wild sex at home. Usually—if it has existed at all—their sex life took place outside of their marriage. According to California Children of Divorce Project, 71 percent of all divorced men admitted to having had extramarital affairs. Slightly less than 20 percent of all divorced women said they had a lover before their breakup. So it would seem that, at the start, divorced men would be much more sexually confident than divorced women.

The evidence, however, suggests that many men who engaged in harmless flirtations or even sexual affairs during their marriages see flirtations in a whole new light after their divorce. Once the shield of marriage is stripped away, the same behavior takes on a whole new meaning. Now a come-on is supposed to really mean something. It's not just for fun and excitement anymore; it's the first step in genuine courtship or pursuit. That makes it a kind of commitment. For many newly divorced men, the "C" word (commitment) is too threatening. So even those who played the lover-boy role during their married years while they were married may get scared and skittish when they're actually "available."

Because they're initially gun-shy of another serious involvement, many middle-aged men will start out by being attracted to and dating inappropriate or younger women who make them feel fun and powerful. According to many psychologists, this is unconscious behavior. From an objective point of view, they're trying to prove their masculinity and desirability or pretend they're younger by association than they really are. In truth, they may just be looking for someone during this time whose emotional level matches their own. Perhaps at the unconscious level their brains are allowing them be with a playmate, but not with someone appropriate at this time because they need to learn from their past before they can truly involve themselves in a significant new relationship. As they gradually gain confidence and lick their wounds, they're likely to feel more like dating and relating to women better suited to their long-term emotional, spiritual, physical, and sexual needs. Studies indicate that mature men want consistency, stability, femininity, dependability, flexibility, lots of fun, and a love of life in long-term relationships with women.

Many divorced women, on the other hand, report that their separation marked a fantastic sexual awakening. After several years' effort at a relationship that's finally over, they feel free. Research does suggest that, initially, some women have trouble coming to terms with their sexuality. While they know they're no longer virgins or lusty teenagers, they have little or no other frame of reference to fall back on. Recent studies continue to show that women get more enjoyment from physical touch and closeness rather than actual sexual intercourse.

Often as a first step toward sexual freedom, lots of women (and some men) will go back to a "first love." Instead of pursuing new relationships, they'll call a boyfriend or lover from their past and try to warm up the old flame. Their hope, of course, is to return to some more emotionally familiar past, and to correct old mistakes with someone they know. It can also feel safer than meeting someone out in the dating world. These affairs rarely last. The comfort to be found in them is soon undermined by the problems and dissatisfactions that led to their collapse the first time around. Still, these short-lived romances offer women a chance to feel wanted and desirable again.

One word of caution: there's usually some shock at seeing someone you've only fantasized about for several years. People change. Time takes its toll. The shapely woman with the thick dark hair has become heavier, grayer, and wrinkled. That man with the great build and easy smile is now pot-bellied and sour-faced. You can never go home again. In addition, values once shared can be long gone.

Professional women who are newly single may find it difficult to drop their professional personas and relate to men socially and sexually in a different way. Many of these women may find themselves attracted to younger, unstable men with charismatic, boyish qualities who make them feel feminine, fun, and desired.

If you're just returning to the singles dating arena, your sexual problems may be challenging. You may find a decrease in sexual desire or an inability to perform.

There is nothing wrong with being either more sexually reserved or more adventurous after your divorce. The real danger is in choosing to be one or the other for too long. Many pop psychologists argue that divorced people should wait several years before committing to a new relationship. Don't become involved in an all-consuming passionate romance. Allow the healing process and soul-searching to take place before you involve someone else's emotions. Sexuality and vulnerability go hand in hand. If you do not allow the heart to heal completely, you may find yourself emotionally oversensitive or overneedy. The message is that we should nurture our own emotional well-being. It may be better to tend to our own development as human beings. We should learn to be our own best friend. To quote Oscar Wilde: "To love oneself is the beginning of a lifelong romance." If we take the time to tend to our own development and nurture our own well-being, we then become more secure within. This enables ourselves to be more giving to others. The more open we are, the more we can enjoy our sexual relationships.

Be aware of the rebound affair. You may be prone to rushing into a relationship prematurely in order to fulfill the emptiness inside you. Until your emotional healing is completed, you may find yourself doing this repeatedly because the lure of falling madly in love quickly after a trauma makes us initially feel terrific—it numbs our pain and replaces it with pleasure. Eventually, though, you will recognize that this "new love" wasn't at all what you perceived.

I have also found, in the course of working with thousands of divorced people, that many go through a number of affairs before they find the right partner. They know the value of dating different types of people. They recognize that before involving themselves in a long-term commitment again their choices will be made with a higher degree of wisdom and experience. Nonetheless, studies have shown that many of them make a long-term commitment within two to three years from their divorce or loss by death.

The whole point of this book is to show you that finding a

mate is an achievable challenge, but a challenge nonetheless. It's not a predetermined reality that you will easily find your perfect soulmate. The sooner you want to take on the challenge, the sooner you will find someone right for you to love who will love you back.

Kids' Stuff

No aspect of divorce causes more uncertainty, insecurity, and worry than the parents' concern over the effect of divorce on their children. Being a parent, as Sigmund Freud once remarked, is an impossible profession even under the best of circumstances. And divorce is certainly not the best of circumstances. What's more, the need to put your ex-spouse and your married life behind you is opposed to the need to create the very best life experience for your children. Through your children you will always be tied to your ex-spouse, like it or not! The child-rearing-related battles that went on when the two of you were married will probably continue if you have shared physical and/or legal custody.

The burden of the custodial parent is well-recognized. Commonly, it's the mother, and on the average, she suffers a 73 percent drop in her standard of living while her ex-husband experiences a 42 percent improvement in his. The custodial parent has to struggle day in and day out with the children's negative emotions. And because the children depend on the custodial parent as their source of security, she or he usually has to deal with their unpleasant behavior and reaction to the doubt in their lives. Children of divorce seem to need higher amounts of love, nurturing, and undivided attention because of the mass upheaval in their lives. However, this is the time when their parents have less time to give and less of themselves, as well, than before. They're struggling to take on more responsibility and divide it in the same time every day. As the new head of household you find you need more energy and time for successful parenting, and your resources have already been stretched as far as you can go. You wonder how you're going to make time for earning a living, going back to school, parenting your children, connecting with friends and family, looking for someone to date, dating, and still have some time left over to indulge in exercise, hobbies, or simply rest. Which part usually suffers? Unfortunately, they all suffer! The amount of physical and emotional stamina required to "do it all" is enormous. If she's like the majority of divorced women, the newly single mother may have to face for the first time entering or reentering the workforce to help support her family, and dealing with late (or completely missed) child-support payments. These situations may be a source of real anger and distress for single moms. They're suddenly cast into the role of mother, father, and primary breadwinner.

Meanwhile, the noncustodial parent, traditionally the father, sometimes called "Weekend Dad" or "Disneyland Dad," becomes a kind of Santa Claus, Mickey Mouse, and Mr. Entertainment all wrapped up in one package. Lots of divorced men settle for being offstage parents wheeled in for crises, holidays, and weddings. (Not exactly the parental image either one of them ever wanted or envisioned for themselves.) As a single father I've learned to resist the urge to overload my children with material objects, clothing, books, expensive activities, or music to compensate for my guilt over my divorce. These things will not make up for sixty-hour work weeks, busy travel schedules, or other adult pressures that take up time. Of course, these feelings apply to moms who are also battling with the same feelings of guilt. To many ex-wives, the dad is the "lucky" partner, free from the daily responsibilities of day care, carpooling, doctor visits, homework, feeding, clothing, bathing, and entertaining, having only to send a monthly check and show up on time to pick up the kids.

To most of society, a father battles with being labeled the "other" parent. He is required to prove that he is a decent father, but not expected to mind being separated from his children. To outsiders he is viewed as a parent of convenience. Those who are insensitive and ignorant to what it feels like to be separated by circumstances from one's children cannot even imagine how he's feeling. He feels left out and powerless, and thus resentful. What exacerbates his feeling is that he is a man accustomed to being powerful and in control of his life at work. Suddenly he no longer has the same authority in his children's lives that he thought he had before. If he and the children's mother are battling (which is not unusual), their communication has broken down. This causes even more feelings of impotence regarding his children's lives. Compounding this scenario, he grows even angrier when he feels that he is working harder than ever to make ends meet, been displaced from his household, sees less of his kids, and has even less influence in their lives.

Given these sad realities, it's little wonder that so many divorced parents become bitter and money-obsessed. Neither is it surprising that children of divorce so often become weapons and pawns in the battle played out between parents. In the very real human tragedy it often becomes a merciless game of vengeance and oneupsmanship where everyone loses out. There's *no* winner. Unfortunately, the kids bear the brunt of it because they're so easy to exploit. Kids never stop loving their two parents no matter how much stress, abuse, or hurt you put them through. They frequently feel the pressure (imagined or real) that they must choose one parent over the other.

What single parents must also recognize is that their "angels" are deliberately going to attempt to manipulate both parents! They can be extremely skillful at it—better than we parents give them credit for. Watch out—they have the ability and creativity to make an already precarious situation even more so by playing one parent against the other. Oneupsmanship, loyalty issues, and guilt are all part of the picture. Kids are especially good at using inconsistent parental discipline to their advantage.

Experts say that children do not need their mother and father to live together. What they do need is for them to live peacefully apart. After all, it's not their fault that the two of you cannot live together. They're not being divorced. In the pit of divorce anger and hurt, many people wonder how much to tell their kids. Obviously, children need some information. Otherwise, their imaginations will work overtime to fill in the blanks. The conclusions they draw are often far worse than the truth. They tend to internalize the problems and place the blame on themselves. Nevertheless, I think too many loving parents decide to explain too much, complain too much, and, ultimately, depend too much on their youngsters. To escape their own temporary loneliness and pain, they allow themselves to receive the bulk of their emotional support from their children. These children end up taking on the inappropriate adult role of their parents' keeper; i.e., therapist, friend, sexual adviser, babysitter, or housekeeper. Kids should not have to feel responsible for the adults' responsibilities. Kids need to be kids. Some parents force their children to play an ally in a war they're too young (and ill-equipped) to fight.

Of course, a healthy balance point is desirable and with the best intentions should not be so difficult to achieve. The only tricks are to tell the whole truth—not just your side of it and what's age-appropriate. You have to resist the urge to place blame. And, above all, encourage self-expression in your children. Give them permission to voice their fears, concerns, and opinions about what they're feeling. Spending time listening to your children gives them the "safe" place they need to vent their confused emotions. It allows you to know as a parent what worries and needs they have, and enlightens you as to the pressures they're feeling.

The trouble is, what seems simple in theory can require superhuman effort in real life. When Dad really is a jerk who doesn't come through with his time, commitments, or financial support, it's hard not to present a completely negative picture to the kids. When either parent decides to act out their negative feelings toward the ex by unreasonably limiting holiday visits or phone calls, being uncooperative, or not informing each other of school or other important activities, it's not easy to appear fair and understanding.

With so many children sharing time with both parents, they have the additional burden of shuttling between two homes (or is it two "houses"). It's difficult for them to feel comfortable and at peace unless both parents are effective coparents in every sense of the word. Kids have to deal with the problems of transporting homework, clothes, toys, and other personal items back and forth. So long as the parents fight, then it's inevitable that the kids' valuable stuff will fall through the cracks. This will definitely spark new and intense problems. ("Why didn't you remember to bring your homework and toys with you?!")

Discipline is a complicated task for single parents. They may be struggling with guilt over not being there every night and/or not being as readily available as their kids were previously accustomed to. They may have to work and have someone else raise their children. They're dealing with increased fatigue due to taking on increased responsibilities. All these factors will lead to a shorter emotional fuse, and less objectivity when it comes to consistent parental discipline.

Experts warn us that in order to grow up liking and believing in themselves, kids need to love and trust both their parents. Part of how we define who we are as kids is how we view our parents. If we see them as not okay, we're apt to assume that about ourselves.

Single . . . with Children

Not only does the single parent have to deal with the emotional problems that come with children of divorce, but he or she must also face the prospect of returning to the dating life again. And that can be with or without the initial moral support of children.

This usually makes things harder on the single parent. In addition to dealing with the kids and their emotional well-being, the single parent often must hold down a decent job to support those children. And, like the at-home workaholic, most single parents feel a great deal of pressure all of the time. Life is so much more complicated now. Who needs the additional stress of dealing with a new companion and all that that energy requires?

It's not easy, and the single parent needs a very special kind of understanding from any potential partner. You're not just dating the parent, you're also dating their kids. That's something to be aware of as you embark on a relationship with anyone who has kids. Are you willing to take on that challenge? If not, it's wise to end things sooner rather than later.

The most interesting news of the nineties shows us that there is a real rise in the number of single fathers. As career choices for women become more common, single-father households have increased 34 percent in the last five years, to 1.2 million. That's a lot of Mr. Moms! And just like divorced mothers, these guys typically put their kids first, even before their own romantic goals.

Still, most single parents do date and, eventually, commit again. As they pass through the various phases of that journey—from initial divorce to remarriage—they all struggle with the same problem: what should be said to the children?

How do you explain your need to date in a calm, nonthreatening manner to your kids? They may seem reluctant and unsupportive of your need for adult companionship. Kids can be especially adept at sabotaging your dating efforts. School projects may suddenly appear, temper tantrums can occur, sibling rivalry may flare, and all kinds of physical ailments may hit them just when you're trying to leave the house to go out. But if you don't get out and date, you're allowing your kids to run your household and you! You must find a way to maintain a balance in your life.

First, you must always work to reassure your children that they are an important, cherished, and valuable part of your life and that their needs are a first priority and will be taken care of. You must let them know that their security will not be threatened by your dating. Make certain that you set aside special "dates" for you and your children, so that they feel more comfortable about your spending special time with someone else. Help them to understand that both of you have needs and should be able to respect and support each other's friendships with others.

It's also important to take things at a *slowww* pace. Don't parade men (or women) in and out of your house every week. It's up to you to be a good role model for your children. Show your kids that you take the same care in choosing a new relationship as you'd expect them to demonstrate. Albert Schweitzer once said, "Example is not the main thing in influencing others, it's the only thing." It's wise to insulate or protect children from new people in your life until you determine whether or not they will be potentially long-term in your life. There's absolutely no reason to expose your children to *all your dates*! Offer to meet your date away from your home. Although this may be more work and inconvenience for you, it makes your children's lives less confusing and complicated.

Be a good example to them sexually. Consider how you would want them to behave as teenagers. As their role model, you must show them acceptable sexual values and practices by your own actions, as they will not readily distinguish why you have different rights than they do. Practice what you *do*, not just what you say. Be discreet about your experiences, and responsible about your actions. If you have adolescents or teenagers, let them know that you are being selective about your partners and using careful protection.

Eventually you'll find someone special enough to want to introduce to your children. It's important to prepare your children in advance. They'll feel more involved and secure. Go slowly and make the first dates with all of you relatively short. Remember, just because you're excited about your new relationship doesn't mean your kids will be, or should be expected to be. Don't shove your new heartthrob on your children. This is not the time to be all over your date and act like a teenager yourself. Always make sure that you continue to give your children lots of your undivided attention.

Boys and girls have differing perspectives toward your new significant other. In the single-parent household, boys think of themselves as the new head of the household and will feel threatened by the new boyfriend. Girls may try to compete with you for your date's attention. They have a tendency to flirt and monopolize the conversation. Both boys and girls might even act unduly unruly in order to drive you crazy, and to drive your new love away.

Conversely, what I've experienced as a single dad is different that what most single moms say. I found that boys will try to be especially nice to the woman to gain the female date's acceptance, or show great resentment at any woman whom they perceive as trying to replace Mom. Girls will likely feel possessive, jealous, and left out, as if they're being replaced as his partner and will try to compete for Dad's time and attention in front of the date.

Because children are vulnerable you must pay special attention to their needs during this time. Children don't want to feel like you care more about your new significant other than you do about them. Although it's natural for all children to feel like they don't get enough of you for themselves, only you know in your heart if you've given them meaningful time and attention.

If you want to avoid problems, reassure your children of your love and dedication for them by your actions, and not just your words. Just saying "I love you!" again and again, or affectionately calling your children by funny/endearing names but not *acting* lovingly, won't cut it! Remember that you must always fulfill your parental obligations without your children feeling that they're a burden to you.

THE "OTHER SIDE" OF DIVORCE

You don't have to get a divorce of your own to know the difficulties involved in trying love a second (or third) time. Sometimes you get involved with someone who's going or been through a divorce. Let's face it: the myth of falling in love and living happily ever after (with ease, tranquillity, riches, great sex, etc.) is as much wishful thinking in a second serious relationship as it was in a first one.

Another myth is that as the new lover you can help your mate cut all ties to a previous marriage. If that bond formed children, then those ties will always bind the now-divorced couple. You may have divorced, but your ex is still the parent of your kids. The truth is that for most divorced people who recouple (including those who form successful new relationships), the "divorce process" continues long after new romantic ties are formed. So, even if you're not the one who brings extra emotional baggage into the affair, you'll probably be forced to carry some of it around. All the anger and hurt that your mate experiences as a result of a past divorce or significant relationship will affect your new relationship and life in very real ways.

If children are involved, the problems are even more complex. During the excitement of your new courtship, you'll have to sacrifice at least some of the time you'd like to spend with your new lover to spend loving time alone with your kids. With only so many hours in a week, some of them must go to the kids, especially during the first years of divorce. And if the affair eventually becomes serious, you may find yourself suddenly cast in the role of stepparent and archrival. This can happen whether you marry or not. If you're involved with their custodial parent, you'll have to juggle the daily difficulties of child rearing right along with your divorced partner.

If you're seeing the noncustodial parent, you'll need to survive your mate's deep sense of loss and almost unavoidable feelings of guilt. Even more important, you'll have to settle for less of your partner's heart than you might want. Like all people in the heat of love, you want to be the center of attention. That's normal. However, when you're involved with a person who has children, you have to realize that the parent's commitment to his or her children will often take priority. That's hard to cope with for most people, especially if they aren't parents themselves.

Since so many of today' s families contain at least one child who lives with only one parent, there's the increased difficulty in blending two such families. It's natural for kids to feel that they need to compete with your lover's kids for both parents' attention. Sometimes they feel the "other" ones get better treatment and more attention. Help them to avoid feeling competitive with one another for parental attention by spending individual time with your children.

Divorced people make up more than one out of every five single Americans. That means the chances of dating someone who's been married before are very high—and with that fact come ex-spouses and children. What's more, the number of romantic arrangements involving divorced men and women is almost limitless. Just for starters, there can be two divorced people, neither of whom have children, trying to make love work. There can also be one divorced person without kids trying to form a relationship with someone who's never been married. Or two divorced people, one with kids and the other without them. Or two divorced people, both with kids. Then you have to consider the tremendous variation in custody arrangements that exist today. And the number of remarriages that result in still more children—making "family blending" extremely complex. It takes a lot of strength and security to deal with a new relationship where ex-spouses and children are involved.

"The Brady Bunch" was an idealized television family. It wasn't based on the real-life complexities and problems that occur when you blend families. Statistics show that the divorce rate is highest with second families that involve blending families, and that divorce usually takes place within the first three years of marriage. Pretty scary!

To survive in such a mixed-up environment, it's wise to follow a few basic rules. First of all, support your partner, but don't take on problems that aren't really yours. If an ex-wife puts up one obstacle after another when he tries to speak with his kids on the phone, or refuses to see his kids on the weekend, let him work it through himself. She's his former spouse, not yours. He will appreciate your understanding, support, and patience at these times. If your girlfriend's ex-husband never sends his child-support payments on time, let it be her problem to handle; she'll appreciate a sympathetic ear to vent to. Aim to show support and love, but don't try to fix somebody else's life unless you're invited to help problem-solve. Unsolicited advice is rarely appreciated. Don't get in the middle. It's a no-win situation if you do. Be supportive, yet not directly involved.

A second good rule of thumb is to act like a stepparent if that's what you are. You may ultimately become a good buddy, or even a trusted friend to your partner's kids. But you'll never be their other parent. And don't try to be. Studies show that it may take up to two years to get your stepchildren's trust and respect. Granted, there aren't many positive images out there on which to model yourself. From our earliest childhood, we all memorize fairy-tale legends of wicked stepmothers and cruel stepfathers. But those stories don't have to set the limits of the relationship you'll have with one another. With lots of effort and creativity, you can define what works best for all of you. Remember, though, it's your mate who fell in love with you. The children didn't. Don't expect them to. It is reasonable for you to expect them to act responsibly and to show respect toward your mate.

Third, have a solid sense of your own level of comfort, acceptable and intolerable "can-do's" and "can't-do's." In my opinion, you should not try to impose your standards on your partner's children in his household. Values, morals, and ethics are something we all deserve to inherit from our parents. Nevertheless, as a new lover on the scene, you shouldn't have to change your own comfort level and beliefs just to make your mate or his kids feel good. Even more important, when you're on your turf, they must be responsible for respecting your rules. For example, if a badly behaved eight-year-old balks because she cannot jump on your bed and declares that "Mom lets me do it at her home," you have every right to reply, "Then do it at *her* home. I have different rules around here, and they are . . ." But if she is not respecting acceptable boundaries by clearly set limits, you should let your mate handle the actual discipline techniques.

The time will come when you and your partner will need to set some long-range strategy to handle discipline, especially if both of you are single parents. It's likely that you may have differing styles of discipline and expectations. A common mistake new mates make is in the area of discipline. Kids under the best of conditions don't like to be corrected. So face it, kids won't like any new or more discipline. The kids will resent both of you for it. It's best to stay out of the situation as much as possible. You will be tempted to get involved especially if you see them abusing or showing disrespect for your partner. You will feel the need to protect them. It's up to you and your mate to determine in advance and away from the children how you are going to handle these kinds of issues. It's absolutely essential that the kids view you both as a team that cannot be divided and conquered.

Perhaps the hardest and most important rule concerns money. You must find a way not to feel victimized by the financial burdens you see your partner carry as a result of the divorce. When a marriage dissolves, money is the way through which control issues, disappointments, fears, and anger get expressed.

In fact, I think it's fair to say that money is the final leftover of the relationship. As a result, the dollars that you see flow out of your life and into that ex-spouse's pocket are loaded with negative feeling. As one professional friend of mine complained to me about her lover's teenage son, "That kid has more cash flow than I do! I work to support Gary so he can support his son. It's crazy!" Maybe. But remember, as the adult you are responsible for the decisions you make. You should know the parameters of the relationship and what you are taking on when you get involved with someone who has kids. A stepparent—as in all relationships—needs to know that there's a certain amount of juggling that will continually need to be handled. As with all endeavors, I suggest giving this your very best effort. Your mate will be grateful for your open-mindedness, objectivity, patience, and unconditional love.

Finally, you have to accept at least the possibility that it may never work out. Sometimes we want so much for the connections to be right that we refuse to admit defeat. Like it or not, you may have to realize that nothing will help. When all the effort that you've invested in the partnership falls short, causes you more harm than good, and more negative energy is being expended than positive, it's time to do some serious evaluation. Perhaps the children really won't ever accept or like you. If that's true, then go back to the first rule: don't take on problems that aren't yours. It's their problem and not you. Just as you must take responsibility for choosing to love somebody who's been married and/or has children, your partner must assume responsibility for loving you. That goes whether your lover's kids like you or not. If your lover can't assume that responsibility, then the real problem has to do with the lover, not the children. So, while ending a relationship that involves kids is not the easiest, in some cases it might be the wisest.

DIVORCED LOVERS: A SPECIAL BREED

People who have been through a divorce—first or secondhand—do have substantial advantages in making love work. They have a very real frame of reference when it comes to the commitment, energy, and rewards that always come up when people dare to be intimate. They know all about relationships that don't work, and they have a special knowledge of the deadly power plays that can ruin even a promising relationship. They have learned from past errors, and they now know how to focus on resolving conflicts. They have a stronger sense of commitment to their partner and relationship. They're committed to learning more about what makes relationships last, and they have found support systems that they can reach for when the going gets tough.

That's why people who are happily recoupled are a very special breed. Like decorated war heroes, they've been tested. Like the legendary phoenix, the bird that rises out of the ashes, they've been down and learned to fly again. They've learned to appreciate life and loved ones. They're living proof that love really can be better the second time around.

Put It into Practice

As you weigh your options after divorce, it's important to see that with the pain come some positive things in your life. Divorce is certainly more like the War of the Roses than a bed of roses. But it does free you to begin to see yourself in a new light. Every ending is also the opportunity for a new beginning.

The first action you should take is to write down in your notebook all the positive changes that have happened since your marriage ended. Make a list and be specific. For example, maybe you enjoy the chance to finally have a bedroom that doesn't look like an English country garden. Or the chance to have one that does. Do you like eating in peace, able at last to read what you want without being called an inconsiderate bookworm? How about all the stuff that you don't feel obligated to enjoy anymore? Family functions, business parties, home improvements, foreign films, baseball games, sushi dinners. The possibilities are endless.

There are also positive feelings that you might want to add to your list. Write down even the positive "baby steps" you've made. Everything counts. Like the pride you felt when you got your first job in eight years. Or the ego boost that comes from flirting with someone you find attractive. If you feel good about being able to go out and spend some time by yourself, or find yourself happily thinking about being with someone new, write that down. That's positive.

Once you begin to see that there are some benefits to life alone, that you have had positive feelings since your separation, you will begin to have the inner confidence to go out and try to find a new companion. It's time to start dating. In order to meet someone new, you must feel you are ready for the experience. Your list of positive things and good feelings about yourself will support you as you go back out into the dating world.

I recommend that you keep adding to the list and, on the days when you're feeling down about the divorce, take the list out and read it over. Even say to yourself, "I'm going to be all right. I'm going to get through this." The list is a technique to use when you are feeling overwhelmed or think that you are a failure for having "lost" at marriage.

If you have children, there's another list you should start: a list of all the positives that you can teach your children about dating and relating. It's important for them to know that when you're happy you're more able to be a better parent. They need to know that what's good for you will also be good for them. But you can't just pull all the good things out of thin air. Use this list as a place to develop your script. What do you want them to know about your new dating life? That dating makes you feel better about yourself and better about everything else (including them)? That you want them to see you as busy and happy and fulfilled so that they can go ahead with their lives without worries about your being alone and unhappy?

Think through the message you want to send, and practice the words for sending it. Then, the next time the dating issue comes up at home, you can remember these notebook entries. You won't have to fumble to express your reasons for dating. You'll be well-rehearsed with lines that you can believe in because they come from your own head and heart.

Answers to the Quiz

1. c
2. a
3. c
4. a
5. c
6. d
7. b
8. c
9. d
10. c

9 Love in the Golden Age: Senior Singles

"Age does not protect you from love. But love, to
some extent, protects you from age."
—JEANNE MOREAU

I was at a party in Argentina recently where
I met a terrific older woman named Sylvia. She must have been
between sixty and seventy with silver hair. She was very attractive and kept herself in good shape. When I told her that I was in
the relationship business, she threw her head back in laughter
and said, "Boy, could I ever use your services!"

"But what's a wonderful woman like you doing single?" I
asked.

"That's what I want to know," she teased. "I guess there just
aren't enough old guys out there who can still remember a
phone number long enough to use it."

We both laughed, but I wasn't willing to just let this one go.
So I pursued the subject a little longer. "Isn't there anyone you
know who might be able to introduce you to someone?"

And then came the inevitable closing line to a conversation I have with single seniors all the time: "Ah, honey," she said with a voice now much less zestful, "I was just kidding. I'm too old for all that. It's a little late in the game for me, don't you think?"

More often than not older men and women want to joke about finding a partner, but they're afraid to really take the actions that would make it happen. They all too frequently feel less than desirable. Many of the women have resigned themselves to spending the rest of their life alone. That's unfortunate because they secretly desire romance just as much as younger singles. And despite popular myths, they make sensitive, sexy, and invigorating lovers.

In today's world, most of us are old a whole lot longer than we're young. For millions of Americans, the second half of a full love life doesn't even begin until the age of sixty. So it's a little ridiculous to think that people should close the door on that aspect of their lives just because their birth certificate entitles them to Social Security benefits.

What's more, old age isn't what it used to be. Older people are staying younger than ever. When I was a kid, most people in their sixties liked to sit on park benches gossiping or playing cards. Today, with so many people waiting longer to make important life decisions, many sixty-year-olds have not yet finished paying for their kids' college educations. They still have to make at least another seven years' worth of mortgage payments on their house. They may even be completing a second university degree, or starting the business they've wanted since they were in their forties.

In other words, being sixty today is a lot like being fifty (or even forty-five) just a generation ago. Sixty-year-old people have the opportunity to be more professionally, socially, intellectually, and sexually active then ever before. So isn't it time that our perceptions of them caught up to reality?

FACTS AND FANTASIES

How's your knowledge of the senior singles scene? If you're a younger reader, that question probably seems a bit theoretical or irrelevant. When the Golden Age is still far off, we all tend to ignore the issues that surround it. But remember, even if this book helps you find a fulfilling relationship tomorrow, the chances are good that you will eventually be single again. It will happen either by death or a divorce decree. The point is it should be comforting to know that there are many exciting choices if and when that occurs. What may seem irrelevant today may be extremely important later on.

For senior readers, the question is far more pressing. When it comes to matters of the heart, I generally find that age does not bring wisdom. The more mature singles that I meet are no more enlightened about their situation than younger people looking for a mate. If anything, age usually puts you out of circulation. As a result, you're out of step with modern realities. So go ahead and test yourself. See if you can tell what's fact and what's fantasy about livin' and lovin' after age sixty.

1. If we all woke up tomorrow to found that every single man sixty-five or older had been paired with a woman about his own age, how many senior women would still be left unattached?
    a) None. There are actually more single men than women after age sixty-five.
    b) Just a few. There are about the same number of single men and women in this age group.
    c) A lot. There just aren't enough eligible senior men to go around.
    d) Nobody knows. Virtually no research has been conducted on senior singles.
2. Most single seniors worry that a new romance may:
    a) cast doubt on the value of the life they lived before it began.
    b) use up what little energy they still have left for living.
    c) drive a wedge between them and their children and grandchildren.
    d) create a foolish public image for them.
3. Research suggests that, two years after the death of his wife, a man over sixty is likely to be:

    a) living alone in the house he shared with his mate, slowly adjusting to his new life.

    b) living alone in a new residence, feeling unhappy and unhealthy.

    c) living happily with a friend or relative.

    d) living unhappily with a new spouse.

4. Being "properly introduced" is:

    a) most important to older women. It makes them feel safer about the idea of a date.

    b) most important to older men. It gives them more confidence about asking for a date.

    c) equally important to older men and women. Both hesitate to date without it.

    d) not very important to seniors. They're too mature for such formalities.

5. This need for a proper introduction:

    a) helps them establish good ground rules for an active dating life.

    b) helps them meet some people but limits their chances of meeting truly exciting prospects.

    c) has little impact on who they meet because introductions can always be arranged.

    d) hurts their chances of dating because proper introductions are getting harder to come by.

6. When seniors reenter the dating market, the issue that confuses them most is:

    a) when and where to have sex.

    b) how to act around the opposite sex now that there's been a sexual revolution.

    c) when and how to introduce their new partner to relatives and close friends.

    d) whether or not to discuss their past relationship(s).

7. Older single men generally think that a woman should pay for the date:

    a) sometimes on the spur of the moment because it's nice to be surprised by generosity.

    b) only when she's done the inviting.

    c) if and only if she can truly afford it.

    d)   only when it's been expressly agreed upon in advance.
8. People often think that widows are better than divorced singles at making a romantic commitment. That assumption is:
    a)   pretty simplistic. Never getting a divorce doesn't necessarily make you a good mate.
    b)   usually valid. Long marriages do testify to a person's determination to make it work.
    c)   often false. The past has actually taught divorced singles how to make wiser commitments.
    d)   an overgeneralization. Widows and divorced singles are equally good at commitment.
9. What single men want most in a woman ior
    a)   vitality, a well-groomed appearance, and a thin body—in that order.
    b)   a well-groomed appearance, vitality, and a thin body—in that order.
    c)   a thin body, a well-groomed appearance, and vitality—in that order.
    d)   inner qualities that have nothing to do with appearance or energy.
10. What single women want most in a man is:
    a)   varied interests, tenderness, and money—in that order.
    b)   tenderness, money, and varied interests—in that order.
    c)   money, varied interests, and tenderness—in that order.
    d)   inner qualities that have nothing to do with finances or hobbies.

SIXTY-FIVE AND STILL COUNTING

America is aging. And women are aging more successfully than men. That means it's a man's marketplace for single seniors. According to a University of California/San Francisco study, there are only sixty-eight men for every one hundred women aged sixty-five or older. Bluntly put, about one out of every three older women would be left without a partner if all available singles were paired off overnight.

Older women realize the imbalance. They can see for themselves that they outnumber single men their age. Still, a lot of other people don't. Instead, they figure that older women are "just too picky" or "way too shy" or "still mourning." These stereotypes didn't emerge out of nowhere. Some older women are guilty of these behaviors, and it does hurt them in the dating market. Nevertheless, there are millions of women who don't fit these descriptions and yet they're single. Why? Because there aren't enough eligible men to go around.

If you're a man, that's good news. If you're a woman, it should wake you up to the harsh reality: you've got to stop waiting for something good to just happen by fate. Just like younger single women, you've got to take control because the competition is stiff.

That's hard to swallow, I know, especially because women of that generation were raised to be sweetly submissive and perfectly passive. But it's your only option if you want a guy. By the way, I know this direction can bring up one fear expressed by older single women. They worry a lot that, in dating, they may appear less than "dignified." At the ripe old age of, say, sixty-four, women figure they should have it all together. They should know exactly what it takes to communicate that they're both a lady and have needs. They want to show that they're competent and know their own mind. They want to act their age.

In today's single seniors' environment, ladies are given permission to act their age and know their own mind by deciding what they want and then going after it. I'm not suggesting that you should transform yourself into a modern Mata Hari. But I do encourage you to be exactly who you are as publicly as you can. You don't need to become someone else. You just need to let a lot more people know you're comfortable within your own skin and aren't looking for anyone else's approval.

Most seniors whom I've met through Great Expectations feel that they've earned this privilege to get what they want out of their life. They are less encumbered in needing others' approval. They do what they want to do and what makes them feel comfortable. They seem more relaxed about dating than the previous generation of senior singles. This is because they have fewer expectations and are less insecure than younger singles. They've not put themselves under the same pressure as younger singles to find the perfect mate. What they're looking for is a loving new friend with whom they can be comfortable and intimate.

Another fear that gets expressed by single women (and men, though to a lesser degree) is the worry over how their children will perceive their romantic adventures. Research tells us that if you have kids, after initial surprise they'll probably love your newfound love life. Psychologists who study parent-child dynamics find that among the deepest concerns faced by grown children is the worry over a parent "being alone." And, if you're happy, they should be happy for you.

The truth is, your singleness actually causes your kids some concern. They worry about your safety. They worry about your ability to successfully manage your life alone. They worry about your happiness. Experts maintain that if they can see you out there having fun and dating, it helps alleviate some of their concern. They no longer have to feel solely responsible for your entertainment and well-being.

Senior women and men worry that a new romance would somehow cast doubt on whatever life they used to lead. For those whose mates have died, there's usually the fear that a later-in-life relationship might denigrate the earlier marriage. They somehow feel disloyal to their deceased loved one. For the older divorced singles, there's often a fear that a new affair will make their divorce seem like a frivolous way to get free rather than a courageous escape from a truly bad situation.

Again, these issues matter most to the people who dwell on them. Your past is of very little importance to most people, frankly. It would probably be a gentler world if people did care more about each other. But in the mad rush to just stay on top of things, most of us barely have enough time to think about our own behavior, let alone worry about our neighbors. Nobody has time to notice much of what you're doing. So my best advice to any single senior is this: It is not what we think about who did what, or what others think about us. It's only what we think about ourselves! Take action because it's what you want to do, not what you think someone else would want you to do.

• • •

Single by Death vs. Single by Decree

Who has an easier time adjusting to the modern singles world? Those who dug their way out of their relationship with a painful divorce? Or those who have buried a mate they loved until the very end?

This is a much-debated topic among senior singles and the researchers who study them. My experience has shown me that it's hard to generalize. I think the question also tends to separate people who actually have an awful lot in common. No matter how you become single in later life, it's certain that your life is going to change dramatically. And for most of us change is difficult. Changes actually occur all the time throughout our lives despite anything we do to the contrary. My advice is to accept the prospect of change because that's the only way you can move ahead.

According to a social readjustment scale worked out by experts at the University of Washington Medical School, it's darn right unhealthy. They found in fact that the more your life changes in a two-year period, the more likely you are to get sick. And the more dramatic the change, the more serious your illness is likely to be.

Their scale gives points to various life changes. Death of a mate, for example, earns one hundred points. Divorce earns seventy-five points. A change in your financial status is worth forty points. Moving is worth twenty points. So is a change in your social life.

Think about it. Two years after the death of her husband, a woman will probably have moved, experienced an altered financial outlook, be expected to take on new responsibilities, and begin a new social life. That alone earns her 180 readjustment points. With that many points, researchers argue that she has nearly a 50 percent chance of becoming ill. If she became single through divorce, her total score would be over 150 points. That takes her chances for illness down only a bit, to about 35 percent.

So instead of focusing on the differences between divorced and widowed people, let's look at how they are the same since they're both dealing with a loss. After all, divorce is a kind of death, and even more than the death of a loved or cherished spouse, it robs you of many happy memories, unfulfilled expectations, hopes, and dreams. Both the widowed and the divorced are forced to be alone, often for the first time in their lives. And they're forced to take care of themselves for the first time. Most senior men who have been married for many years are all thumbs at cooking, cleaning, and even the fundamentals of running their own social life. Senior women who suddenly find themselves alone are almost as out of sorts because they've spent their whole life taking care of somebody who's now out of the picture and are forced to take on insurance, money management, establishing credit, and even earning a living.

The point of all this is fairly simple: there's an unspoken value system that operates within our culture. It says that widows are generally nicer, sweeter people than their divorced counterparts, and they have a more wholesome attitude toward love and commitment. How simplistic and stereotypical! Divorcees are just people who went through a divorce—for whatever reason.

As you venture into the singles scene, don't let these prejudices blur your vision or limit your options. A nice person is probably a nice person is probably a nice person. No matter how he or she got into the dating market. No matter how long a past relationship lasted.

My, How Things Have Changed!

When senior singles finally decide to reenter the dating market, they're often faced with some major surprises, and while they anticipate changes, they are surprised when things just aren't the way they used to be! The whole concept of courtship is very different from what it was when they dated before they married. The experience of their single youth, sometimes decades prior, has not prepared them for today's social reality.

Remember many people of this generation never really dated much before; they married their high school sweetheart or soldier boy next door.

Be prepared to take some silly and awkward steps along the

way to happiness. Unexpected roads are waiting to be traveled. Comfort yourself with the knowledge that only one of two things will happen when the mistakes occur. Either you'll make mistakes in front of someone who's been thrust into the singles scene as recently as you have. In that case, your mistakes probably won't even be noticed. Or you'll goof in front of a more experienced senior single. In that case, your naïveté will probably be the most refreshing thing to come along in quite a while. It doesn't matter how many times you goof, all you need is one success.

I do have a few basic rules for you to keep in mind.

Rule Number One: Don't Think There's Special Honor in Staying Single.

I've already touched on this, but it deserves repeating. I find in talking with a lot of single seniors that people have a misguided notion about old-age loneliness. It's seen as some sort of medal of honor. It signals their loyalty to a deceased spouse. Or it validates their right to have divorced a lousy mate.

Well, forget it and stop that! You're only being a martyr! As a fascinating and accomplished older man once said to me: lonely is selfish. There are so many seniors out there who want (and need) someone wonderful to share the rest of their lives with. They're being denied the opportunity to meet and get to know you. Who are you to deny them the chance to discover all that's wonderful in you? (Well put, don't you think?) Certainly, death or divorce put you through a period of anger, grief, sadness, and withdrawal. That's part of the normal grieving process. It's also normal to come on out the other side of that sadness, ready and eager to love again. So when you're even a little ready, get out there. Your future becomes what you make it.

Rule Number Two: Don't Expect It to Come as Easily as It Used to.

In today's dating market, nobody can sit back and wait for desirable prospects to make their intentions known. This is a fact of life for all singles, but it's seniors who find it hardest to accept. I think that's because when you were young, it all came a lot easier. Especially if you were the prettiest girl in class, you always got all the dates you could handle. If you were the high school quarterback, you couldn't get around to all the girls who wanted to date you.

Today, even the best-looking, best-dressed, best-educated, and best-built singles have to compete in the open marketplace. So don't be shocked when you discreetly leak the word that you might be interested and nobody responds. You've got to take the initiative and translate even mild interest into a clearly stated invitation. He who hesitates is left behind. Go for it! What do you have to lose?

Rule Number Three: Don't Wait for a "Proper" Introduction.

This, too, applies to all singles, no matter their age. But it's older men and women who most resent the fact. In a survey of hundreds of single seniors by Adeline McConnell and Beverly Anderson for their book *Single After 50*, they found that a vast majority of women would not give out their phone number to a man they had not formally met. A smaller majority (but a majority nevertheless) of men said that they would feel uncomfortable asking for a date with a woman they had not been introduced to in at least an informal way.

Formal introductions are great, but in the nineties, they don't guarantee a thing. Frankly, I suspect they never did. It's just that people expected that they would. To repeat what I said earlier, limited expectations yield limited results. The truth is, you are as likely to meet someone wonderful in the supermarket as you are at a relative's holiday party. And in either setting you're likely to meet only because you make it your business to walk up and introduce yourself. Learn to judge people yourself instead of trusting in someone else's assessment of them. After all, somebody else's idea of a good date or relationship potential may not coincide with yours. This only limits your possibilities. You wouldn't want others to choose your clothing, hair care items, or meals, would you? If you like somebody, give it a try—formally introduced or not. By the same token, protect yourself by playing it smart. Don't invite a first date to come to your home, and don't go to his or hers. Meet your date somewhere where there are other people around.

Rule Number Four: Remember What Senior Men Want Most.

According to the *Single After 50* survey, older men still care a lot more about what's outside than they do about what's inside. When asked what they want most in a woman, McConnell and Anderson found that a majority of single senior men rate "thinness" first. Second, they want her to be "well-groomed." And their third most desired quality is "vitality." Next, they want someone attentive to their needs, a good listener, and a woman who is flexible enough to fit into their lives.

When pressed to be more specific, these men usually say that a desirable woman doesn't necessarily need to have a perfect size-eight figure. However, they do want her to have a healthy and attractive body. So it seems that boys will be boys even when they celebrate their sixtieth (or even their eightieth) birthday. Sex appeal remains an important priority more to older guys than to older women.

Rule Number Five: Remember What Senior Women Want Most.

If senior men want thin and well-groomed vitality, according to McConnell and Anderson, senior women's concerns are quite different from men's. First, women say, they want a man who's "interesting." Asked to explain more specifically what that means, they reply that they want a partner who is healthy, has varied interests, and remains open to new ideas.

Their second priority is "tenderness and consideration." Often after many years of dutiful service to a man who took a lot more than he gave, single senior women want to be pampered and treated as if they're special. They want someone to comfort them and treat them with respect.

Third, these women seek money in their mate. They don't necessarily want exceptional wealth, but financial stability is extremely important. They don't want to go through a struggle all over again. Often, older women worry that a new relationship may jeopardize whatever nest egg they have secured for themselves. They want assurance that any potential partner will be able to fully support himself, now and for the long haul.

Rule Number Six: Always Reciprocate.

Many seniors get into the habit of accepting hospitality without returning it. This is especially true of older men who are uncomfortable entertaining alone after their wife's death. This occurs primarily because their wife was the one who did all the social planning. It also happens a lot among seniors who have never been married and, therefore, tend not to have done a great deal of entertaining.

If you accept a dinner invitation, you need to reciprocate. You don't necessarily need to have your friends to your home. You can take them out. Or you can find some other activity that's happening around town and call to invite them. If money is an issue, there are plenty of free community festivals and park fairs to choose from.

The bottom line is: you don't want to let your social life stay active simply because your friends and relatives "feel bad" for you. After your mate's death or after a divorce, people who care about you will probably extend a loving hand. Usually, that's not out of pity. It's out of true caring. You can either keep that caring alive by re-creating two-way expressions of friendship, or you can feel so sorry for yourself that you wear out your welcome.

Rule Number Seven: Don't Think Every Date Leads to a Relationship.

This rule should work two ways. It should warn you not to get too caught up with somebody just because you went to a Thanksgiving dinner at her daughter's home. Likewise, it should comfort you with the knowledge that a date doesn't mean you're ready to share your apartment space. A date between two seniors means exactly what it means for any two people of any age: they both have enough interest in each other to spend a little more time exploring mutual chemistry and companionship.

You may feel that after you've been single for a long time, after you've learned to be single again after many years of marriage, it's time for you. It can be quite pleasant to keep some parts of your life completely off-limits to everyone. Maybe it's gardening that you've made all your own. Or a nightly walk around your neighborhood. When older people begin dating, they often worry that they have to give up these rituals of privacy. They shouldn't. You have every right to maintain the best elements of the life you've made for yourself. And so does the new person you're seeing. So mutual respect in this area is critical.

The New Man-Woman Thing

Of all the changes to hit the dating scene over the past fifty years, the shift in appropriate male-female behavior is probably the most dramatic. No wonder it's the one that most confuses seniors as they try to reenter the mating market. Just remember that good manners are always good manners. Following the Golden Rule is always smart. Men aren't sure what's considered gentlemanly. For example, is it still polite to open the car door for a date? Or is this the mark of a male chauvinist? Is "colorful" language still insulting to a lady? Or does it suggest equality? Women are just as baffled. Will their sexual timidity be thought attractive or prudish? Does their offer to cook dinner make them appear gracious or old-fashioned?

Most surveys find that, among older singles, there's not much desire for new sex roles. Both older men and women seem to like traditional values. They feel most comfortable with partners who behave on dates pretty much as they did when they were single the first time around. Many women want the same dating etiquette as they had when younger. So don't feel the need to change. Do what feels comfortable to you. It would probably work against you if you did.

In no area does this hold more true than in issues of sex. I have actually been a bit surprised myself to discover that older guys are not much more eager to hit the sack on a first date (or a second) than are older gals. Once sex becomes a part of the relationship, men are often the more aggressive. Until then, however, most seniors, men—just like women—say they want to take it slow.

There are two big exceptions to this honor-the-old-rules guideline. The first concerns who should do the asking. I'll bet that when you were in your twenties, it was considered racy for a woman to request the first date. Research tells us that today older men love it! You don't have to make a terribly formal invitation. For example, a woman can simply remark to a gentleman that there's a movie she'd like to see. And she can suggest that perhaps they might make a plan to see it together next weekend.

The other important change in attitudes centers on who should do the paying. Again, in times past men always paid. Today, they don't want to—at least not all the time. Older men report that they want a dating partner who will share the cost of a casual (or serious) relationship. They do not, however, like to be surprised by her generosity. In fact, they find it a real turnoff because it leaves them unsure about how to respond. If you were the person to ask for the date, then it's your responsibility to pay for all the dating activities. So, senior ladies, you should make it clear in advance that this dinner will be your treat, or that the concert tickets will be on you. Also, don't underestimate the value of a dinner at home or a picnic basket filled with homemade food. Just because he always takes you out to eat doesn't mean you must take him to a restaurant. Who wouldn't prefer a fabulous homemade brunch to what's available at even the nicest dining room?

IT'S NOT HOW OLD YOU ARE; IT'S HOW YOU ARE OLD

Will a new love eventually take the place of one you've lost? Can a romance later in life make up for the one you never found when you were young? No, of course not. The pain you bring to a new love affair is just like the happiness you bring to it. It stays with you. So don't look for your new partner to take away all the sadness. That's part of your emotional baggage. It's yours to carry around for as long as you need it. It's yours to put down when you feel ready to leave it behind.

Still, love between two older people is not the slow shuffle through life that we often imagine. It can be just as sexy, just as dramatic, just as consuming, just as infuriating as love at any other time of life. Don't expect to settle for "just companionship" once you get to be sixty. Or eighty. Or even 100. You deserve something a lot more exciting than that. And you can have it if you just get real. Remember, it's your life and you deserve what's right for you.

Put It into Practice

One of the biggest obstacles to senior romance is the tendency among older people to stop planning for the future. They see their lives as basically completed, and they peacefully decide to wait for the final years to pass. That's negative thinking, and that kind of mind-set never leads to positive change. Change your mind and you'll change your luck. Take risks in order to create new opportunities to meet people. Formulate a plan and follow it.

So if you consider yourself a senior reader, I want you to make yourself a calendar. On a sheet in your notebook, write down tomorrow's date. Now skip two lines and write down the date it will be in exactly two weeks. Skip four lines and write the date it will be in one month. Six lines below, write the date three months from now. Six lines below that, fill in the date it will be six months from now. And six lines below that, write the date exactly one year from tomorrow.

Now, fill in your calendar. You can make some simple plans for tomorrow. For example, you might decide to call your brother and go for a drive to the beach, or to the movies, or to the park. As you move forward in time, make your calendar a bit more exciting. Maybe you'll plan a downtown shopping excursion for two weeks from now. Then a small dinner party at your home for a month from now.

For the date three months from now, you should be willing to jot down some really adventurous plans. Set some goals. Think about the current risks facing you and the challenges you expect to face. For instance, you can write in that you will have already joined a seniors support group and will have attended at least one meeting. That will give you enough lead time to find out about the groups in your area and to choose the one that best suits your interests. Maybe "a real date" would not be too outrageous a plan for six months from now. Next step will be to provide yourself the opportunity to meet other available single people. Remember to stay open-minded; one door of your life may have closed, but you have the keys to open new doors.

Next, make some long-range goals for yourself. What about your calendar entry for a year from now? Well, marriage might be a bit much. How about this: by a year from tomorrow, you can vow to be referring to yourself as "single" instead of "divorced" or "widowed." With that change a whole new and wonderful phase in your life will begin. One last thought: Steven Covey, the author of *Seven Habits of Highly Effective People*, described love as a verb. Love is a choice of thought, then action. If we choose to love, then we love.

ANSWERS TO THE QUIZ

1. c
2. a
3. b
4. c
5. d
6. b
7. d
8. a
9. c
10. a

10 Men Talk: Their Wants, Their Needs

"No man really becomes a fool until he stops asking questions."
—ANONYMOUS

*A*sk almost any single man what he wants most in life and he'll say without missing a beat: the perfect woman. But ask him to narrow what he specifically means by that, and the conversation is likely to go in a million different directions.

Men are great at fantasizing. (In fact, I know some women who say it's our best-honed skill.) Sometimes men want the free-spirited world traveler. Other times, they want an old-fashioned doting sweetheart who'll have dinner waiting each evening, someone who'll offer a sympathetic ear as he complains about the injustices of the world and will encourage her mate to keep going in the face of it all. Other times, men like to imagine life with a passionate and lusty tigress whose drive could exhaust them on a regular basis. Most of the time, though, men envision the perfect dream woman who looks like a magazine centerfold and combines all the best qualities he loved in his mother. I'm talking about the sensitive confidante, dressed in a silk slip, who can verbally spar with him over a delicious meal that she's prepared. The woman who's cooked up for adventure after a full day's work at her office, and with energy left over to fill their nights with sensual abandon and delight.

Does she really exist? Well, yes and no. The truth is, most single men have spent the past twenty years tossed by the pressures of women's liberation, postfeminism, the working woman, and safer sex. Despite the women's movement and the emphasis on female/male equality, the fact remains that we are different. While we believe we are smarter now in the nineties, we still fall into the same traps. For example, young boys and girls are taught different socialization skills. Boys learn to be independent, whereas girls learn that it's okay to be dependent. Boys learn to compete, while girls learn to cooperate. Boys learn to problem-solve alone and are encouraged to do it themselves. Hence they frequently have difficulty exposing their conflicts to others. They'd rather fix it themselves, and they tend to feel like failures if they cannot. They're not comfortable feeling out of control and helpless. Men fear the unknown.

Men focus on status. They are constantly practicing one-upsmanship mind games, questioning where they fit into the financial and social hierarchy. They learn to compete with each other, to respect themselves. As boys they're taught to associate success with respect. As men they associate success with love; when they're successful, they will be loved.

From early on we're treated differently with differing expectations. Growing up is an arduous, demanding, complicating, confusing, and painful process. Male and female approaches to life differ. There are so many different ideals to balance and compare.

Boys are taught to put feelings aside in order to achieve. They connect feelings with weakness. Since their lives have been confined to burying their feelings in order to achieve, they're uncomfortable with now having to answer the woman's request to be both successful and able to share feelings. In fact, men don't seem to understand why women feel the need to share "*soooo* much" with another. They feel threatened, for example, when female friends exchange their mates' "dirty laundry." ("How could you share *that* with her? It's our business!") They feel violated because they believe that personal matters are no one else's business. He feels that his manhood has been attacked because she has violated and betrayed his trust, and invalidated his status in the house as chief problem-solver. Women approach life differently; to them, sharing is a natural and comfortable way to help brainstorm and solve problems. However, in this situation, both will likely end up feeling rejected, because neither gave the other what they really wanted. Each treated the other as he or she wished to be treated, rather than giving the other what he or she needed. Perhaps for healthier male/female relating, each must give the other the opposite of what he or she personally wants.

With this example in mind, it's easy to understand how men and women have different approaches to life and confusion when it comes to attending to the other's needs. They look at relationships differently. Men seem to struggle with being consistently close with others, while women tend to have a tough time separating from others. So while men learn to be introverted and self-dependent, women learn to reach out to others. While men learn to be strong and self-contained, women place great value on relationships and sharing. What's important is trying to figure out what combination of style, values, and personality is right for the two of you.

In order to find out what we want in someone else, we first need to discover who we are all by ourselves. In other words, before we can be one-half of a successful relationship, we should have reached a certain level of self-knowledge. If we want to build healthy, intimate relationships, we must begin by working on ourselves first. It's not what we do for a living. Not what car we drive. Not our golf score, or our condo address. We need to know who we are as human beings: our individual strengths and weaknesses, our fears and true ambitions. We must learn to connect with the deeply held inner self that is (more often than not) a mystery to us.

As men, how do we approach this mind-expanding mission? Traditionally, and somewhat interestingly, men have turned to women for help in these murky waters. For example, the John Wayne–type husbands of the fifties and sixties thought it was the manly thing to do to keep it secret that they had any feelings at all. They buried their own feelings. After several years of marriage and after more than a few drinks, they sometimes let their guard down in front of their wives, but only behind closed doors. But in the light of day, any secrets were safely kept between them.

Then came the liberated men of the seventies and early eighties, who often behaved as if their feelings existed only between their legs and who often confused sex with relating and connecting to another. Still, hard as things were for those guys, it's even more complicated for men today. The reason is that men have been told to be in touch with their feelings. But they don't have a role model/mentor to turn to for advice and counsel on the subject.

When you get right down to it, the perfect woman for each man is probably the one who could help him understand and accept himself. But the reality is that they aren't going to appear magically, ready and willing to help him examine his inner self. Instead, men are on their own. They've got to learn for themselves first who they are. After that, they have to learn what women want, and how to give it to them. A strenuous endeavor? Yes! But with some real heartfelt effort, men should be able to bridge the distance between their heads and their hearts.

A MAN'S TEST

As men and women stand on the brink of a new millennium, it seems a good time to test your sense of what both men and women expect and want from men. Do you think that most men actually want to know themselves? Or are they content with their current sense of self? Another nagging question concerns the role that men have always played in the ritual of courtship and seduction. Are men really willing to abandon their old roles?

Or is the nineties man just the same old guy using a new line? Take this test for yourself and see how well you understand today's man.

1. Most men have responded to the rapid changes in their social role by becoming:
   (a) withdrawn and defensive.
   (b) clever at mouthing trendy phrases but nothing more.
   (c) angry.
   (d) confused and vulnerable.
2. The tired old image of the male meant that, first and foremost, he had to be:
   (a) James Bond: strong, capable but still sweet.
   (b) Rambo: driven to succeed no matter the cost.
   (c) Batman: mysterious and in control.
   (d) the Roadrunner: one crazy, unthought step ahead of whoever pursued him.
3. The positive traits of being masculine are:
   (a) loud bragging combined with hot aggression.
   (b) mystery combined with emotional control.
   (c) quiet strength combined with an ability to be direct.
   (d) intellectual strength combined with acute emotional awareness.
4. The negative side of the out-of-date masculine image is that it:
   (a) shuts down feelings and emotions to the point of numbness.
   (b) denies men the ability to listen as well as they speak.
   (c) forces men to be harsher than they really feel.
   (d) boxes men in emotionally.
5. Most important and above all, women want men to:
   (a) offer them unconditional love and security.
   (b) laugh more and complain less.
   (c) talk and listen more.
   (d) always overpower but never abuse them.
6. If women could have their way, they would also like the nineties male to:
   (a) willingly make emotional commitments.

    (b)   learn how to really satisfy their sexual needs.
    (c)   let go of control and let them make more decisions.
    (d)   laugh less and cry more.

7. In a recent survey, 98 percent of all women said what they want most from men is more:
    (a)   honesty.
    (b)   respect.
    (c)   two-way conversation.
    (d)   sexual contact.

8. To avoid talking about their feelings, most men will change the subject to:
    (a)   their work.
    (b)   current events.
    (c)   sports.
    (d)   anything at all.

9. Most single men have a powerful aversion to:
    (a)   aggressive women.
    (b)   passive women.
    (c)   their own feelings.
    (d)   dramatic displays of female emotion.

10. An important step in attracting and keeping women is:
    (a)   expressing your feelings.
    (b)   being true to yourself regardless of the consequences.
    (c)   possessing self-confidence in yourself as a lover.
    (d)   improving your financial position.

THE OLD VS. NEW IMAGE

Change is inevitable. All across society and in very intimate ways, the nineties have brought unmistakable change into people's daily lives. Think about it: the balance of power has shifted, not only among nations but also between the sexes.

Aside from a few Neanderthal throwbacks, men do realize that they aren't the big red roosters anymore. However, they aren't too sure how to define themselves. They're confused about what set of rules, social nuances, mores, and etiquette to follow. It all seems so undefined; after all, these are the adults of the "Me Generation," the original "Whatever-feels-good-do-it!" generation. So most men spend a fair share of their time trying to balance how they were raised to be, how the media portrays them as being, and what they perceive women want from them.

In the middle of all this is an often unspoken knowledge that men aren't defining their own identity. They're busily trying to shed an old skin for a new one that feels designed to fit the needs and wants of the opposite sex rather than their own. Most men respond to this identity crisis with confusion and defensive silence. Most take a wait-and-watch attitude, figuring that the less they say, the less ammunition they give to pushy and demanding women. Others react by tossing a few trendy phrases into basically the same old come-on. They assume that some fresh frosting can ice the same old cake and nobody will be the worse for indulging in a bite or two. Then, too, some men find themselves in a quiet rage over the fact that the old known traditional ways are gone. Many men also think that no matter what they do, women inevitably wind up unhappy anyway.

Of course, all these reactions are self-defeating because they're passive; they're *re*-active instead of being *pro*-active. In that sense, they're classically male—the stereotypical strong-but-silent male. We're forced to keep all the unease, disrespect, and anger pent up inside. Men seem to constantly battle with image. They need to be perceived as secure and with self-assured confidence. They can't really confide in other men either because in the eternal male battle for one-upsmanship they've managed to isolate themselves from one another. They tend to believe that sharing these thoughts with the women they're interested in will make them look less confident, less strong, and less secure. They're so worried about self-image that they short-change themselves by not opening up. There aren't many men who are willing to admit how insecure they are, especially when it comes to their careers, for example. Men tend to fear that their all-important career could be yanked out from them at any moment.

So why would men continue to adopt these uneasy postures? Partly, I think, because they allow men to maintain what they think of as control. Granted, the feelings they hold inside may be negative. In fact, they may sometimes be incredibly heavy. Unfortunately, they're theirs. In a world where men are raised to defeat and conquer, control is the prime directive. It makes sure the man is in a position of strength and power.

Many men find it difficult to accept help from others. They've been taught to be independent. Let's take a look at how men go about problem-solving. For example, you're driving around with your partner looking for a particular address. You're lost. Asking for directions for a man can be an excruciatingly degrading experience. It's been my experience that women, when lost, have no trouble asking for help, while men, on the other hand, will go out of their way *not* to! They'd rather drive miles out of their way and lose valuable time, perhaps along the way frustrating their female partner, than stop to ask someone to help them. They'd rather do it themselves than need the assistance of someone else. For men, this is yet another way of how they achieve "strength." To them any other way chips away at their competence, hence confidence. Remember, boys compete, girls cooperate.

Lots of times we hurt ourselves with the very best of intentions in mind. Let's take a look at the following male/female scenario: When individual problems occur, women's natural tendency would be to help, because to women this signifies commitment and involvement. They, in turn, like to be helped, comforted, and to have someone's ear to bounce ideas off of. Men tend to withdraw and need to have their "space" respected when sorting through issues. To them any sort of idea exchange could be interpreted as "smothering." So what does all this mean to male/female interactions? She feels abandoned when he gives her space; he feels smothered and threatened by her doting on him. What's most important to bear in mind are the differences working within the gender parameters.

Just as important, most men (for good reason) mourn the loss of the old male mystique. And in their grief, they go back and forth between denial and rage against the new reality. Remember, not everything about the old masculine ethic was bad. Roles were clearly defined and we knew what was expected of us. It told us that men were the breadwinners, protectors, independent, in charge, heroic, strong, and admired. That's a hard self-image to bury. And being told that it comes across as dominating, narcissistic, selfish, pushy, and juvenile doesn't make the loss any easier.

What does make it easier is a good, hard look at the other side of the old image. Hollywood moviemakers may have created James Bond, hard as armor on the outside but also tender. But most men were brought up to be more like Rambo: determined to win—no matter what. Usually, that means totally throwing away their feelings. After all, it would be pretty hard to rise above everybody if you stopped to consider how the battle hurt them.

But perhaps you're saying James Bond was a hero of the sixties. Haven't our expectations of masculinity completely changed? One recent survey shows that our most admired symbol of modern manliness is the research scientist. He can tune out the world and focus just on his work. His needs for companionship are met by his computer, his microscope, or his test tubes. His commitment to an impersonal ideal never changes.

That image, it seems to me, is a lot like Bond. It may exclude the sexual weakness of the spy's otherwise hard shell. Otherwise, it's just the same. The new ideal suggests that only the complete denial of our feelings will allow for competence and success, which is really the old ideal! It certainly rules out tears and laughter. In fact, it forbids any possibility of going with the natural and often unexpected flow of things. The researcher is a serious man, a driven man, and a man who keeps his own counsel. How different is he, really, from the ridiculous macho relic from some distant past?

Today's single man must sort through the traits of the old male mystique to decide for himself what should be kept and what should be discarded. He must look at the myth, claim what he really wants to keep from it, and discover for himself the parts of it that are a lie. Only in this way can he become his own real man.

Above all, every man must take this inventory for himself. Gentle criticism from a still-infatuated lover won't lead to real change. It will only create another mask for a man to wear until the next lover asks for still another side of who or what he is.

Threatening demands from a woman on her way out of his life will only worsen the defenses he might have already put up. It is part of the old male ethic to let women do all the emotional work. The new ethic gives men both the responsibility and the right to handle such tasks for themselves.

WHAT ARE WOMEN LOOKING FOR?

No man should try to remake himself into the image of what women say they want. For one thing, that kind of false front can produce only a shadow self, never a real human being. For another thing, women are as confused as men about what they want. If you set about altering yourself to suit them, prepare yourself for a lifetime of costume and character changes.

Most women, when asked what they seek most in a man, will say "strength." They are looking for someone who is able to find and maintain his place in their world. When I lecture on this topic, the men in the audience almost always assume that having a place in their world means being professionally accomplished and respected. Frankly, I don't think that's the central issue. The bottom line is that women want to meet men who can establish a solid place for themselves within a relationship. They also want men to care enough to stand their ground when that place is challenged.

Not in any special order, women want a man who:

- communicates openly and is willing to be emotionally vulnerable
- is honest and genuine
- projects a positive image
- has high self-esteem
- has chemistry
- is respectful and considerate
- is humorous
- is playful
- is tactful and courteous
- has social graces

- has good personal hygiene
- doesn't rush sex
- is flexible
- is motivated and likes his job
- has a nonaddictive personality
- is open to self-improvement

Ask women what they like least in men and you're likely to hear them bemoan the fact that there are so many "wimps" among today's single males. They complain that men don't have the guts to discuss emotions at all or they express their feelings through whiny, touchy-feely babblings about what they can't do or can't offer. Women want a man with enough conviction to care enough to stand their ground when challenged. Women—like men—appreciate decisiveness. We all like people who are confident and stand firm. And within the confines of a relationship, women admire the man who takes action. They want a man who knows what he feels and can express it without coming unglued.

According to many recent surveys, reports, and studies, today's women also want men to acknowledge the worthiness of female values. And they want men to begin working traditionally feminine qualities into their own behavior. The most desirable of these qualities, say women, is the ability to open up and honestly talk about things. Men with this ability are called evolved or enlightened.

For males who are single and looking for a long-term relationship, it's important to recognize that women expect an emotional contract. They want this to be willingly entered into by both parties. Research reveals that most women think men hold back their emotions and are too quick to distance themselves from the situation at hand. Fully 98 percent of the women surveyed in one study said they were not getting and would like more verbal closeness from the men they date. They would like the men in their lives "to talk more about their own personal thoughts, feelings, plans, and questions, and to ask them about theirs."

Women want the two of you to be a team. As every team

player knows, communication is the key ingredient to a team's success. Winning depends on the level of communication between team members and it's what women want in an emotional partnership.

This same survey also found that 83 percent of all women claim to be the first to initiate any kind of "deep talk." They say that they want to discuss mutual feelings, but that men prefer to talk about activities; i.e., work, sporting events and other interests of theirs. A majority of women—71 percent in this study—believe that the men in their lives are afraid of showing emotion. They are emotion-withdrawn. And in another research project, four out of five women said they would not marry the same man again. Why? Because of his inability to face feelings.

Still, I think most men like to keep alive the perception that women always want to talk about emotions. A more accurate analysis is that they want to talk about how people behave. They want to talk about what happens to each of you as individuals. They don't want to talk about objective facts or even objective problems. For instance, the average woman would prefer to discuss the dreams you both had last night than about the new addition that's being built onto your house. She'd rather you sank into the living-room chair and expressed how difficult you find it to get along with a particular coworker than have you complain about escalating bills and household expenses.

For most men, though, talking about behavior cuts too close to the quick. It gets too close to looking at their feelings and that feels threatening. Men are so distant from their emotions that anything personal triggers anxiety. So they immediately and often unconsciously move the discussion into areas that make them feel in control and more comfortable. The most popular subject is work. Men love to talk about their career. Unfortunately, they rarely want to look at the subtle and sometimes even obvious feelings that affect their work life. Men like, instead, to keep things on the surface because that doesn't threaten their mask of detached objectivity. Don't hold this against them. Learn instead to work with a man, to help him rise above his upbringing.

Remember: men aren't born with this deep and abiding

aversion to feeling. It's socially bred. They're trained—by women as well as men—to believe that getting in touch with their feelings could result in unmanly and weak behavior. After years of that conditioning, I think they forget the initial threat and remember just the scary possibility that emotion might unleash the intangible, something that would allow them to lose control of themselves and the world around them.

Finally, just as men mourn some of the elements of the old male mystique, women (even liberated women) are grieving over what they've lost along the way toward personal and social freedom. Within the privacy of a close relationship, women want these losses to be acknowledged. At one time, men were simply taken to be the dominant power within a romantic partnership. The truth behind that was often sexist abuse. But it was also protection from the brutality of the real world. Single women of the nineties have no muscle man behind whom to hide. Long separated from the security of their parents' home, they are earning their own money, and figuring out how to spend and invest it wisely. Whether it's fun or frightening, they have to make their own decisions. Just like men, they are in the middle of a major social change. Like men, they sometimes wonder if they've left the best things behind in pursuit of an evolving new image, whatever that may be.

Give Women What They Want

We've come a long way since books about men and women focused on sexual technique. We're also well past the era of the "sensuous man," when men giving women what they wanted meant either the feathery flick or the velvet buzz saw. Today, men realize that their partners expect them to be aware of and able to express their own inner feelings. What's more, women are looking for men who know when to stop talking about themselves and start listening with sincere attention and concern.

Still, a majority of the men I know will willingly admit that there's a big difference between understanding what women want and knowing how to give it. Obviously, I don't have room here to provide an in-depth recipe for the perfect behavior style. Frankly, I'm still learning what it is myself. But I can tell you what women have told me—countless times and in various ways. If you want to make a positive impression upon a woman, you've got to open up emotionally; you've got to communicate your feelings sincerely—both the good and the bad, positive and negative, beautiful and ugly. The era of silent and mysterious sex appeal is over. The "Mum Man" is out. The "strong and silent" type is irrelevant. Today's single woman wants 100 percent of a man, imperfections and all.

To translate this almost impossible ideal into practical rules of behavior, I've developed a simple five-step program that can help transform you from the old macho image into a new, more sensitive (but still masculine) nineties male. The new and improved you will have a much better chance of getting what you want . . . and really need.

Step One: Admit That You Have Feelings.

This first step is the key to becoming a man who attracts women. As boys, people told us to keep our emotions in check. In fact, quiet strength is one of the defining traits of the old male image. We were raised on the myth of the Marlboro Man—never confused and never overwhelmed.

When you recognize and admit that you have feelings (and that emotions are a positive part of your life) you will get to know yourself better. And self-awareness is a positive end in itself. As a key extra, though, you will carry yourself with the clear air of a man who knows, likes, and respects himself. Women like that because it means strength, self-assurance, and positive esteem. And to women, strength signifies safety and security.

Be careful, in the middle of all this, that you avoid the emotional self-involvement that was fashionable during the eighties. Eventually, it took most of its victims through doomed relationships of self-absorption. Learn from your female counterparts to accept and appreciate that side of yourself. By better self-knowledge you become more intimate with yourself, and are better equipped to relate to others.

Step Two: Express Your Feelings.

Once you've admitted to yourself that you have feelings, it's time to let other people in on the secret. You'll probably want to start out slow, sharing very basic and somewhat safe emotions with someone you know but who isn't terribly important to you. For example, you might tell a coworker that you are tired and distracted. For a man who has made it a rule not to expose himself in any way, it can be a major admission just to say "I feel like taking a walk" instead of "I have to run out for a minute."

As you gain confidence, you can begin talking about more intimate feelings. For example, you can say to a good friend: "I feel great today. Everything's wonderful." Or you could confide just the opposite: "I feel lousy. Nothing seems right." Once you've broached the issue, and depending upon the person you're with, you might feel secure enough to try explaining why you feel that way. Chances are that this effort will call on you to express even more feelings. In the beginning, you may be awkward. Like someone learning to speak a new language, you'll stutter and stammer and grope for the right words. Laying out your emotional state is a step toward freedom. But remember, it takes practice and work. So give yourself time. Your feelings are special and they are important . . . to you, that is. But they aren't likely to interest anybody else too much on a first or second date. So don't relate too much too soon. Don't think you have to become the guy who feels moved to share his deepest fears and hopes with every woman he meets. Be careful not to become a self-absorbed, neurotic whiner. Let her ask or give some sign that she wants more details. Everyone likes surprises. Leave some mystery about you.

Step Three: Make a List of All the People You Have Feelings For and Have Never Told.

It sounds crazy, I know, but it's important. Like most men, you've probably battered, bruised, and even buried some important relationships through sheer emotional neglect, and that's a sort of abuse. If you want to change your future, you've got to make some effort to rectify the past.

As you make your list (and I mean actually using your note-book and pen to write down the names of real people), decide if there are family members, friends, or even colleagues who de-serve to be told that you want to change. If you still care about some of them, you should make contact and let them know how you feel. Don't worry, it doesn't signify weakness to do this—it takes strength and courage.

Step Four: Cultivate the Art of Deep Talking.

By now, you are ready for the most important step in this pro-gram. That is, you should pursue deeply personal exchanges, in particular with a woman you care about.

All the time you've spent telling yourself that you have feel-ings, talking about them, acting on them will now begin to re-turn big dividends. Sharing your feelings, your true feelings, is a courageous step. Women may say that men in general are afraid of emotion, but as long as you are personally trying to express what you feel, you will not be counted among the emotionally numb. You are beginning to talk about personal thoughts and feelings. You're finding ways to communicate not only the facts about your day, but the feelings that result from them. You've moved beyond a willingness to answer direct questions about your past, toward a genuine desire to share your emotional rec-ollections of that past. Perhaps, most important, you are coming to accept your right to bad feelings—like anger, hurt, betrayal and jealousy—without the old-fashioned male obligation to do something about them. Emotions don't always need to be han-dled. Sometimes it's perfectly satisfying just to experience them.

Step Five: Take a Personal Inventory of Your Feelings on a Regular Basis.

Do you know what a lot of women tell me about men and their feelings? They say that men "feel" and "sense" their emotions just before they think they're going to make love. And then, right after sex, all the feelings magically disappear. "Men always tell me how deeply misunderstood they are," a female friend recently told me, "when they think they're going to score." But she added that "By the next morning, they make their meaning very clear: 'No Trespassing.' "

Her judgment is a little harsh, but I think it says a lot about the way in which many men have the ability to express feelings because they know it will bring the end result: it attracts women. If you're willing to make the effort honestly to get in touch with yourself, then have the self-respect to continually maintain the awareness of who you are. Continue to admit and accept that at least some of your behavior comes out of what you feel, and not out of what you think. In the same way, learn to recognize that other people have emotional lives and that they, too, need to discuss them. As a result, this enables you to create a closer, more loving relationship with people you care about.

FOUR TYPES OF MEN THAT AUTOMATICALLY TURN WOMEN OFF

If you've found the perfect woman for you, how can you be sure you won't chase her away by being the wrong kind of guy?

For easy reference, I've listed here the four main types of men that receive an automatic thumbs-down from women:

1. The Know-It-All
   This type of man is usually found at parties "working" the room with his tired tales of being the best at just about everything. He keeps everyone (especially women) at arm's length by constantly pointing things out, or uttering such off-putting phrases as "Let me tell you something. I know how to fix the economy in one weekend." This kind of bravado is almost acceptable among men, but most women feel threatened and turned off by a man who claims to "have it all figured out."
2. The "Me-Tarzan, You-Jane" Man
   Women of the nineties don't like to feel strong-armed into romance. They don't need men to be gorilla-strong for them

anymore—they've got their own careers and their own ways of living. What today's woman wants is a man who is her equal, not King Kong to her Fay Wray. Moreover, a woman feels offended (and even insulted) if two men pick a fight over her. It makes her feel like a piece of property instead of a viable human being with feelings and opinions of her own.

3. The Man's Man

This is the guy who would never even think of giving up his Friday nights out with "the guys," and would most likely laugh at a woman who suggested he come over for breakfast instead of going fishing for the day. Why is this such a turnoff for women? It makes them feel that they take second place to your male friends, and thus sends the message that maybe they're not too important in your life—that they're simply there in between outings with the guys.

That's not to say that women can't tolerate occasional outings with your male friends. A dose of being apart can only add to a healthy relationship, and most women are aware of this fact. It's just that when a woman is in a close relationship with someone, she prefers being *the priority*—not an outside activity or second best. Everyone has the need to be desired.

4. The Wimpy Pushover Type

The opposite of the Man's Man is the soft-spoken, "anything you say, dear" type often described by women as the "wimpy" man. This type of man is so terrified of losing what he perceives might be his only chance at romance that he agrees to almost everything and lets his woman run the entire show. Women like balance in a relationship; they don't like to feel like they're carrying a man around on a leash.

FINDING THE PERFECT WOMAN

I began this chapter by talking about the elusive "perfect woman." Does she exist?

Yes, she does. But she's different for every man. The patiently sweet helpmate who's capable of keeping one man through a lifetime of defeats and triumphs would be the model of boredom and suffocation for another. The career-minded partner who can look her mate in the eye to challenge his weakness and support his strength will offer some men great happiness. But this same woman would be the mistress of true misery for others. Like beauty, perfection is in the eye of the beholder.

For men of the nineties, romantic and sexual bliss demands an honest and unblinking self-examination, and the sooner the better. Knowing yourself is no longer a passing fad or a luxury reserved for the wealthy. It's now a necessity for us all because it unlocks the door to that fabulous combination of womanly virtue and vice that will make you happy to be a man.

And how do you attract this perfect woman—once you know who she is? All the research, interviews, and surveys point to a similar answer: you've got to get in touch with your feelings. And, as frightening as it can be, express them.

PUT IT INTO PRACTICE

Okay, so women want you to share your feelings. They want you to talk *with* them—not *to* them—about your life in a way that tells them something real about who you are. To do that, you're going to have to get good at talking about yourself (and everything else) in a new and more revealing way. Give yourself a break, though; don't expect it to happen overnight. It's a process, and if you're smart you'll take the long view.

For now, I want you to make a one-page entry in your notebook. Title the page "Revealing Myself." On the top half of the page, write the name of the last man with whom you had a conversation, and next to his name, explain what that conversation was about. What did you say? What did he say? Try to be as specific as you can. Then, on the lower half of the page, write the name of the last woman with whom you had a conversation. Next to it fill in information about what you discussed. Try to capture not just the facts and figures that were exchanged, but the mood and temperament that you both brought to the discussion.

When you're done, sit back and reflect on what you've written. First of all, how far back into your past did you have to reach in order to list a conversation with a man? How long ago was your last discussion with a woman? For many men, it's difficult to even remember the last real conversation they had with a woman. (Now that says something rather important, don't you think?) Look at your entries for what was said by both of you about feelings. Did your comments reveal anything truly personal about who you are? Were you more open when you spoke with the man? Or with the woman? What information might you have added to each discussion to have allowed for more interpersonal exchange?

I would encourage you to repeat this exercise every now and then. Don't make it a once-a-week thing because then you'll get in the habit of being especially revealing the day before you know you're going to make a journal entry. But every now and again go through the process. I hope that as the weeks pass into months and the months move you toward a year, you will see the nature of your conversations with everyone beginning to shift—away from the impersonal and toward the kind of appropriate openness that women want so much. We men need that openness, too.

ANSWERS TO THE QUIZ

1. a
2. b
3. c
4. d
5. c
6. a
7. c
8. a
9. c
10. a

11 *For Women Only*

"Our world has changed. It's no longer a question of 'Does she or doesn't she?' We all know she wants to, is about to, or does."
—*The Sensuous Woman*

*M*ost women have trouble with men. They have difficulty understanding men. That's usually because they believe two great myths. The first (and most deadly) is that deep down, men and women are alike. But the hard fact remains we are basically very different. Sure, I know men who suffer from the same delusion. But it's women who buy into it with real gusto. I can't even count the number of single women who are willing to go on the record with statements like "Except for the obvious anatomical differences and socialized sex roles, we are all alike." Not true. Forget it!

The second myth grows out of the first. It's what women frequently tell themselves when their hearts get broken. This myth promises that when hurtful differences arise between a man and woman, they can be talked through and overcome. They can be brought to the emotional bargaining table and worked out. Guys often feel overwhelmed by women's social skills. Women think that all a man has to do is listen and support them, because that's what they would do to help their man feel better. But men approach life's challenges differently, and they aren't as able as women when it comes to this intercommunication. Again: get real.

Neither of these myths has anything to do with the reality of romance or partnership. They sound great, and they've become the basis for innumerable seminars on making love work. But they don't hold up against real life. Like it or not, men and women are not the same. We are very, very different. It's almost irrelevant whether our differences are the result of biology or environment. The point is, they exist, and they affect every aspect of courtship and intimacy. Many experts advise that the ability to resolve these differences is *the* most important challenge for relationships.

Likewise, many of the issues that come between men and women are not negotiable. The battle between the sexes is eternal. Even as men of the nineties sincerely attempt to change—to gain an emotional intelligence that they've always lacked—new tensions surface. In my opinion, there can never be a final peace between men and women. But there can be a joyful, shared journey though life's peaks and valleys.

Traditionally, women were reared to be housewives. Now, women have other doors open to them. They can choose home, work, or both options. Women today are better educated and expect more out of life than did their mothers. A mother took the backseat to her husband's career and lived vicariously through his successes; she was at his disposal more often than not. Gender roles were well-defined. The old paradigm about relationships was based primarily on gender and traditional roles. We need to form a new paradigm for the next century based on equality in individual aptitudes.

I have to admit that women are the wiser sex when it comes to relationships. I also believe that women don't recognize just how much power they have over men. In terms of social skills, they're years ahead of men; they're much more evolved. They're the keepers of the flame. It took me almost twenty years of professional work with singles to learn that one simple fact. Even the most emotionally closed-down woman can figure out what's good and bad for a love affair faster and more accurately than the average man. Within the universe of feelings, women rule.

Think of the women you know who are successful in their relationships with men. These women usually have high esteem. They know what they need to feel good, and they expect (and get) it. They are good communicators—they speak their minds and voice complaints, even demands, but they also accept their man. These women balance their criticism with praise.

The problem is that despite their ability to understand men, women don't often accept them. Faced with who a man really is—with his imperfect nature and emotional fumbling—women frequently shake their heads and complain about the burden they bear. In the process, they put down male efforts at sensitivity and zealously manage to keep their power. Too often, that power becomes a choke hold on the feelings that govern a relationship. It seems that men respond favorably to women who are hard to please. That's because they want her more when she's unavailable, and they then feel lucky to get her. Men like a challenge. Women: this is not a double standard because you tend to reject men who are too "nice," label it as "weakness," and call us "wimps." Men and women need to learn to accept their differences and negotiate new ways to relate to each other, new ways that work uniquely for them.

WOMAN-WISE

Not every misconception about males and females works against women. We all benefit and suffer because of our gender. So as you join the millions of other single Americans who are trying to sort through the mishmash of sexism, feminism, and individualism, test yourself Can you distinguish between the myths of modern romance and its realities? Do you have a good sense of how men and women are different? And how they're alike?

1. For most women, a truly romantic and sexually exciting relationship would involve:
   (a) a lot of independence. It's a sexist myth that women seek deep emotional attachment.
   (b) almost equal amounts of closeness and autonomy. Ultimately, it's balance that makes women happy.
   (c) a deep and lasting sense of two-way commitment. Women feel best when they have this kind of security.
   (d) more passion and commitment from their man than from themselves. Every woman wants adoration.

2. In general, men feel most romantic and sexually aroused when their relationships involve:
   (a) a deep and verbalized closeness that we used to think only women wanted.
   (b) a fifty-fifty balance between attachment and independence. If it's too close, men feel trapped. If it's too free, they get insecure.
   (c) as much freedom as they decide they want. When the woman decides, a man gets threatened and nervous.
   (d) freedom for them but commitment from her. Every man wants it all.

3. A lot of men have trouble committing, and when they begin to pull back emotionally, most women decide to:
   (a) go on the offensive and make their demands clear.
   (b) cool it for a while and see if things heat up again.
   (c) talk things through and resolve them.
   (d) try harder and give more.

4. The harder a woman tries to make a man happy:
   (a) the sooner he'll relax, feel secure, and let down his defenses.
   (b) the more outrageous his needs will become.
   (c) the greater his confusion over how to reciprocate.
   (d) the less he'll value what she has to offer.

5. Men have always been most attracted to women who are:
   (a) sexually appealing and assertive.
   (b) sweet and gentle.
   (c) vivacious, self-confident, and playful.
   (d) mysterious and aloof.

6. Men also seem to have a great need to:
    (a)   dominate women sexually.
    (b)   take advantage of a woman's kindness.
    (c)   squelch a woman's exuberance.
    (d)   take credit for a woman's specialness.
7. When a woman says she wants her mate to be more sensitive, she probably really means that she wants him to:
    (a)   express more concern for her, but for nobody else.
    (b)   care more about everyone in his life.
    (c)   talk about feelings, but still behave like a "real man."
    (d)   talk sweetly but remain emotionally controlled.
8. When a truly sensitive man opens up to his mate, he's most likely to talk about his:
    (a)   childhood and parents.
    (b)   friends and hobbies.
    (c)   work.
    (d)   fears.
9. The worst way to let a man know you don't like what he's doing is to:
    (a)   tell him directly. Men can't handle criticism from a female equal.
    (b)   criticize his behavior, but offer no alternative. That doesn't allow him to do anything right.
    (c)   rant and rave against his stupidity. That makes him feel unmanly around you.
    (d)   gently ask him to change. Men aren't subtle enough for that.
10. To improve their love lives, most women should:
    (a)   behave in more constructive ways, even if it initially feels phony.
    (b)   behave the way they feel because that's emotionally honest.
    (c)   work toward more appropriate feelings about men and expect their behavior to gradually match those feelings.
    (d)   respect men enough to ask them what they want, and offer it.

A Man's Dessert Is a Woman's Poison

So how, exactly, are men and women different? Entire books
have been written on this subject. One clue lies in a bit of recent
research trivia. According to national circulation figures, the
most popular magazine among American men is *Playboy*. The
most popular among women is *Better Homes & Gardens*.

Granted, this data won't support a full-blown theory about
gender differences, but it does point out the very basic gap between what the two sexes really want. It suggests that while men
fantasize about unlimited access to many sexy partners, women
fantasize about domestic security and commitment. While this
sounds awfully stereotypical, men and women need different
types and degrees of emotional involvement in order to be happy
and fulfilled. One survey found that 85 percent of successful professional single women choose to remain single if they cannot
marry up the social ladder.

Experts tell us that in order to understand the ways in which
men and women go after romantic satisfaction, we must imagine
the human desire for closeness as a continuum. At one end is total attachment; at the other is complete separateness. Most
women, they argue, are happiest when they feel very attached—
pretty far toward the end of the attachment scale. Men, on the
other hand, are most comfortable and most romantically
aroused when they feel about halfway between attached and independent. If some men sense that they're getting extremely attached, they feel trapped. When they spend too much time
alone, they worry about isolation.

Clearly, there's a built-in conflict between what men and
women want. The bonding zone most comfortable for women is
one that makes men feel smothered. For some men, commitment means the loss of freedom. For some women, it means
they've found security.

The result is that, once inside a relationship, a lot of women
believe that their partners fear commitment and shy away from
closeness. Experience has taught them that men are alternately
drawn to and then turned off by a truly loving bond between two
people. Just when they begin to feel the closeness building, the

guy beats a speedy retreat. Most important, women see our on-again off-again behavior as a sign of weakness and instability.

What women take for weakness is just a basic part of most men's normal romantic character. Men want autonomy. Women want the security of the commitment. That's the reality. In fact, if they're honest, most men will tell you that their whole sense of masculinity is tied up with their ability to excel and be acknowledged as an individual. Women focus their personal relationships on building intimacy. They value making friends with closeness, while men focus on winning the game. Girls grew up with the "Cinderella Complex"—that it's okay to be dependent. Girls learn to cooperate. They get together to connect with one another and to share; from an early age they learn to be intimate and to seek support and assistance from others. They're also taught to compromise at all costs to preserve a relationship.

Men don't understand why women feel the need to share so much with others. After all, boys grew up learning to be independent, to go at things solo. That doesn't mean they want to be alone forever. But it does mean that the manliness men seek is a feeling they get from things rather than their personal relationships. To further enhance a relationship, men need help from their female significant other in learning communication skills. Listen closely to each other as though your life depended on it. That means paying attention to what's being said. Learn what it takes to understand how your partner experiences life. Make yourself approachable, available, and patient. Show respect for your partner's thoughts and feelings. Keep the tone of your voice warm, friendly, and positive. Tackle the problem, not your partner. Learn to overlook the little things, and pick your issues wisely. Don't make mountains out of molehills. Learn to acknowledge your partner's feelings even if they conflict with your own. When men feel understood, they run (!) toward commitment.

Even when this fact of male nature is explained, women are less than accepting. In fact, women resent this whole notion of inescapable sex differences. They really hate it. Perhaps that's the reason that, without even knowing it, they often add to a man's emotional armor. I've seen this dynamic function many times. The most recent reenactment took place not long ago at my auto dealer's service shop. I had taken my car in for a maintenance check and was stopping by to pick it up. I went to the office to pay my bill, but the woman behind the desk was on the phone. She asked me to wait a minute, which I agreed to do, and as I stood there I heard her side of a short and extremely uncomfortable conversation.

"Did you get my note yet?" I heard her ask. "I remembered that you said once how much you like Hawaii, so, the picture on the front reminded me of you." Then, in the unmistakable voice of someone in love, she said, "I miss you." There was a long pause. Then she said, simply and with almost no life in her voice, "Okay, then I guess I'll talk with you later." And she hung up. It was obvious that she had been cut off and thus cut down. Trying to show some compassion, I reminded her of that old adage: you always hurt the one you love. "Yeah, well I guess I should be used to it by now. I've been in love with this guy for a year and a half and he runs from hot to cold at least once every other week."

This woman's only conscious goal was to hold on to her lover's affection. Yet without meaning to she had pushed him away. I suspect they repeat these little dramas on a fairly regular basis. Every time she feels him retreating, she tries a little harder to build a connection, to tighten the bond that to him becomes an albatross, a stranglehold.

Is she doing anything "wrong"? Absolutely not. She is, however, working against herself. She's assuming that he wants the same thing she wants. But he doesn't, and the more she tries to convince him, the less interested he will be in her. At least emotionally, she's doing all the work. As long as she's willing to do that, there's very little motivation for him to do anything. Worst of all, her constant willingness to give without getting back condones his emotional selfishness. She's rewarding the behavior that hurts her. She's hard at work, serving as her own worst enemy.

On the positive side, women seem better able to learn from rejection. Where men will almost always retreat when they're rejected and take it very personally instead of looking at it objectively, women tend to discuss such problems with their friends to hash it out. This sharing process enables women to gain a helpful and healthy new perspective. As a result, they get lots of new ideas about what to do differently the next time they initiate something. Although rejection is difficult for anyone, women seem to have an ability to bounce back from it and use it positively. Men don't. In my view, that is yet another reason to support my theory that women are the stronger sex.

What Men Want in a Woman

This is a very controversial subject because women believe that what men really want is a wild centerfold who will also play the role of "mother" when called upon. However, men are not such narrow or shallow people. Not in any special order, men want a woman who:

- is attractive
- is a good listener
- is spontaneous, lively, and playful
- has the right chemistry
- has a sense of humor
- is an interesting conversationalist
- is kind, respectful, and considerate
- is patient and available for their needs
- is intelligent
- has good mothering abilities (or potential)
- has high self-esteem
- has athletic ability
- has a nonaddictive personality

Learn to Play by the (Smart) Rules

For most women, the first step toward a happier love life is a new perspective. You've got to accept that the sexes want different things from a relationship. While you're at it, you might as well resign yourself to living with those differences for the long haul.

Thirty years into a fulfilling, faithful marriage, you and your husband are still going to be different. You're still going to want a strong two-way commitment. And that's still going to make him somewhat uncomfortable, but with strong communication skills you, too, should be able to reasonably weather the storms.

Once you've accepted the realities, decide to change your whole courtship approach. For starters, you've got to figure out how much freedom a man really wants and needs. Since overdoing it in the giving department won't keep a guy interested, you've also got to find new ways to excite him. Most important, you must learn to see and accept men for who they are instead of what they are not. Men are not like women Men think, feel, and behave in ways that are appropriate to our gender, not to yours.

Women like to be courted. They love it when a man pursues a woman in a gentlemanly manner, getting to know her on dates, and treats her like a prize, not a possession to be won. Women want to be swept off their feet. That's what worked for me in my relationship. It's not just flowers, candy, and romantic music. (In fact it can easily be something offbeat like cactus, a rainforest stick, a friendship bracelet, tickets to a jazz festival, and singing—even off-key—some favorite songs together.)

Unlike their male counterparts, women are captivated by romance. Sex and love are intertwined with women—women easily tend to overlook their mate's warts and "see the prince within."

I think you'll stay on track if you follow these four simple rules:

Rule Number One: Don't Suffocate Him.

You need to let go—of his time and his passion. Put bluntly, you have to leave him alone. Instead of making yourself constantly available, let him want to see you badly enough to do the asking. (After all, "absence makes the heart grow fonder.") Don't send him little baskets of cookies or cute cards or balloons or anything else that proves you care. Don't make cozy dinners for him, or keep them warm until he gets home from working late. Don't wash his clothes, babysit for his kids, clean his house, type his papers, cut his hair, paint his kitchen, talk to his ex-wife, or host his parents. In fact, don't do anything for him—until he asks you to do it. Later on, a few months down the line, you can safely surprise him with these signs of your affection. But, especially in the beginning, don't overdo it.

Sounds inviting, right? I predict that it will be one of the hardest things you've ever done! Just as men are raised to be brave and stoic little soldiers, women are brought up to be sweet and tireless helpers. Chances are, you'll have to overcome everything your mother taught you about men in order to let him do even half the trying. But remember: nobody wants what can be gotten for free. Your new motto should be: do less/expect more. By refusing to martyr yourself, you let him know that you want him to contribute something valuable to the relationship. You also send him a clear message that you respect yourself. That makes it easier for him to respect you.

Rule Number Two: Be Vibrant and Interesting!

Vivacious enthusiasm and spontaneity are probably the two traits men desire most in a woman. Yet, from the dawn of time, guys have tried to suppress and control these very qualities. The woman who is vital, sexual, and who has an unshakable sense of herself is always the woman we find most attractive. But she's also the woman we find most intimidating. Why? Because we worry about our ability to give her what we imagine she wants from a man.

Over and over again, women tell me that they think men are afraid of strong, effective, and self-confident women. Yes, they are! Women like that seem to be more than men can handle. They're almost too attractive. That makes men insecure.

To help the man out a little, take the initiative! Let him know when you're interested. If it suits your personal style, ask him out. He'll like it. In fact, he'll probably find it a refreshing first because, despite all the talk about the so-called sexual revolution, survey after survey indicates that most men have never been asked out by a woman. And the vast majority say they would welcome the invitation.

Of course, if you ask, there's the chance that you'll get rejected. Frankly, I think that risk will do you good. It will let you stand in the man's shoes for a change. You can see what we guys experience every time we ask a woman out. I think it may give you a whole new appreciation for the bravery it takes to make the initial approach. Even more important, the invitation takes on symbolic significance. This entire book is based on a simple but typically ignored fact: if you want to find somebody to love, you've got to do something actively about initiating the search. You must stop relying on fate, friends, the gym, and the office. Your "support group" is not responsible for *your* life. *You* are! So take responsibility, no matter how frightening that seems.

One other important suggestion: be more of a playmate and less of a mom. Popular wisdom has it that a man needs the love of a tender and accommodating woman who will create peace and tranquillity in his life. Wrong! Most men are overly preoccupied with their work, and the best antidote for their troubles is play. They want to have fun! Men need and want a lover who is unafraid to ask, to compete, to be herself, to express her emotions and assert her desires. Provide mental stimulation and show interest and enthusiasm about the world around you. It's contagious and men like to be with a woman who has her own interest in life.

Rule Number Three: Accept a Man for Being a Man.

This also means: "Don't try to change your mate!" Learn to accept him for the person he is. We can only change ourselves. Don't expect too much too soon. Especially in the beginning of a relationship, men are awkward at expressing feelings that they've only begun to realize they have. Next to your emotional sophistication, their attempts can look quite feeble. Don't let that make you unkind. If a man tries to expose his inner self and is met with ridicule, condescension, or punishment, he's unlikely ever to try again.

Most women say they want men to be more sensitive. I suspect that what many of them really want is for men to be more tuned in to them and their feelings. Period. But sensitivity doesn't work that way. In order to be more caring with you, a man must explore emotions in all areas of his life. He'll need to talk about people and situations outside your relationship. Most specifically, he'll need to confide in you the desires, feelings, and fears he has surrounding his job. Men try to resolve problems at work by talking about them outside of work, often in boring and seemingly endless detail.

This is probably not the romantic exchange that you had hoped for. Nevertheless, men really do need to discuss their work. So as he begins the next conversation about his boss, his most current assignment, the coworker who's making his workday miserable, or the promotion he didn't get—take a deep breath and listen. Remember: this is the world in which his highest-pitched emotions develop and operate. If you want him to love and need you, then you should talk about that world with him. Learn to accentuate the positive about him. Don't dwell on his defects. Accept his negatives and play up his positives. Everyone likes to believe that they're unique and important, and your man will appreciate you more when you recognize these qualities within him.

Rule Number Four: Women Hear Love When You Say Romance; Men Hear Sex When You Say Romance.

Sex experts tell us that the key to a fulfilling, long-lasting relationship is communication. Yet men and women differ. There is a sexual double standard. Traditional views on sex include "Nice girls don't!" and if they do, they absolutely shouldn't be expected to enjoy it. Yet women are called "frigid" if they don't respond enthusiastically to a man's sexual style. In the nineties, women know they are sexually entitled to everything a man receives. At the same time, women are cognizant of the real need to protect their image. Some men feel threatened when some women express their sexual needs. These men tend to internalize a female's request to do something different as suggesting that they are lousy lovers and not manly. Remember, men are dealing with their own set of insecurities and need to be perfectly capable. (The good news is that men really do want to please women.) Both sexes must learn to recognize that sex, like most aspects of a relationship, involves negotiation and open communication toward a mutually fulfilling outcome. Leave your egos out of the bedroom.

FIVE THINGS THAT TURN MEN OFF

Have you ever known an attractive, bright, and charming woman who never seems to maintain a relationship for longer than a few months? There are millions of single women like that: apparently too perfect to be alone. In fact, their sheer number has given rise to paperback guides, weekend workshops, and private-practice therapy groups—all intended to explain the reasons why such a thing should happen. They "love too much," some say. Others tell us they're the victims of narcissism. Or feminism. Or sexism. Or professionalism.

Ultimately, though, all those explanations are just complicated descriptions of the five personalities that turn men off. Review them, and if you see yourself between the lines, you may want to make some changes.

Turnoff Number One: The "Whatever-You-Want-Honey" Woman

When you say what you want, you take responsibility for what happens as a result. Many otherwise appealing women are so intimidated by that kind of responsibility that they prefer to let men do all the deciding. In simple things (like saying they prefer to see one movie rather than another) and in the expression of major needs (like refusing to move to a new city just because their lover gets a better job offer there), they fear accountability. They don't want to make a wrong choice. They don't want their desires to cause a fight. Most of all, they don't want a bad outcome to reflect on them.

Of course, women who play this game pay a high price. They're never right about anything! Still, they're never wrong, and there's a security in that.

Sometimes women like this will try to justify their unwillingness to make choices. They'll say that men like to make the decisions, or that it's feminine to let a man take control. Well, they don't, and it isn't. Within courtship, men are looking initially for a date and later a mate. Both these roles are best filled by an adult, and adults assume responsibility.

Turnoff Number Two: The Wet Blanket

Another way that women sometimes avoid a direct approach with men is to rain on their parade (even while they offer no alternative to what's being suggested or done). These women will never come right out and disagree. Instead, they point out all the flaws with the man's position, and do so publicly. Men hate to be wrong, especially in public. If you absolutely feel some issue is vitally important, my advice is to wait and save it for airing when the two of you are alone. Insults are another no-no! They are rude remarks and can only damage your lover's self-esteem. This type of woman needs to balance her criticism with praise. Studies show that for every negative comment we should also voice four positives as a balance.

Here's an example of the wet blanket: A man phones his girl-friend and invites her over for dinner. "I've already done the shopping for a great Italian meal. I thought I could try out the pasta machine I got from my sister for my birthday." The woman's response might go something like this: "Well, okay. But you've never used it before. It's probably going to take too long and I'm really hungry. Are you sure you want to try it out on me? You know how sensitive I am when it comes to food. And I was really in the mood for something else! You always do this to me." Of course, as she talks, her voice becomes increasingly shrill and caustic. Up against such obvious hostility, the guy's probably going to offer another option. Yet, true to form, the wet blanket won't allow for that. "No, that's okay. Let's just stick with your plan."

It's a turnoff! And there's nowhere for the poor guy to go with it because she won't even let him change plans. He has only two options. He can confront her directly—which rarely works because she'll hide behind her willingness to go ahead with the plan anyway and still hold a grudge against him. Or he can ignore her complaints and swallow the resentment he feels over

For Women Only

her lack of enthusiasm. Either way, the relationship is on a slippery slope sliding downhill fast.

Turnoff Number Three: The Saboteur

She's the passive-aggressive type, the woman who undermines her partner at every opportunity. She's a little like the "wet blanket" because she manages to destroy even the best thought-through plan. But she's more vicious about it. She keeps a guy moving along on one set of assumptions only to zing him good at the last minute. For example, she accepts an invitation to the opera, although she'd rather go to the drive-in movie. But when her date shows up, she's dressed in (expensive) jeans and a casual cotton blouse. Or despite the fact that she likes her home to be an exercise in "creative clutter," she promises to straighten up her apartment before hosting his out-of-town relatives for dinner. But at 5:30 that evening, when guests are due to arrive at 6:00, she's just heading home from work to start the cleanup.

These are women who, in the final analysis, do exactly what they want, when they want to do it, in precisely the way they want it done. They make it seem as though they're giving up their own desires in favor of a man's. But they aren't. In the worst possible way, they're having their cake and eating it, too. They get to ruin his plans without taking the blame for their mean-hearted actions.

Turnoff Number Four: The Seductress

The femme fatale of modern mating is another turnoff. She's the woman who stares unblinkingly into the eyes of every man she meets, who asks endless questions about the most ridiculous facets of his life, who essentially congratulates him every time he can tell her what time it is. She manipulates men for her own advantage. She capitalizes on their vanities and vulnerabilities. She becomes his indispensable mate through manipulative techniques. She's not really interested in men; she's interested in what they can offer her. She could also be a gold digger.

One of the biggest lies going (and it's frequently perpetuated

225

by women) is that men are too stupid to know when they're being abused in this way. Actually, they do realize what's happening, at least most of the time. It's just that they don't care. The caricatured seductress is after what she can get from us. So men go for what they can get from her. (And you can bet it's not emotional commitment.)

Turnoff Number Five: The Nag

There is a fine line between being assertive and being a nag. Men hate to be reminded; to them it's nagging. They hated it when Mom did it to them, and they'll hate it when their significant other "mothers" them in this manner. Any kind of reminding, whether it's commitments, obligations, or household responsibilities, can all too readily signify nagging. And they view this as criticism.

Nagging chips away at men's sense of self-esteem, competence, and sense of comfort.

DON'T WAIT TO FEEL IT

In matters of the heart, we all want our feelings to guide us. Women in particular don't like to act out of calculated theory. They don't want to feel that they're manipulating a romantic relationship. They prefer to respond more honestly to what's going on inside through open communication. Women do what they feel. That's one of the things about them that men like best.

But there are a lot of women out there in today's singles scene who fake it. Just as men have learned a basic strategy for getting what they want from women, some women use their emotional know-how to get what they want from men. They play with a man's head and his heart. They pretend to find him bright, amusing, unique, and desirable. All the while, they actually think he's a silly fool who can't tell the difference between true respect and insincere flattery.

From the moment they're born, little girls learn to be emotionally superior to boys. Still, a sense of superiority won't keep you warm at night. So if you want to try to change your luck with men, you've got to find a way to understand and accept men for who they are. After all, how long can this charade continue? If you wait for that understanding and acceptance to come from within, you may have to wait a very long time at great sacrifice to your true needs—not just superficial, materialistic comforts. Instead, change your behavior. Begin to think and act in new and more constructive ways toward men. They want to please you as much as you want to please them. Treat them like insensitive idiots, and they're sure to fulfill your worst expectations. Have positive expectations. Treat them like your emotional equals, and there really is a very good possibility that they will rise to the occasion. Men tend to be a bit unsteady on their feet initially, but a lot of them want to please you—for all the right reasons!

PUT IT INTO PRACTICE

If your luck with men has been less than impressive, you need to think about whether some of the "blame" lies with you. It's true: men can be incredibly nearsighted when it comes to love. But other women manage to get the best out of them. So this exercise asks you not to think about your ideal man. Instead, it asks you to imagine the ideal woman. What do you think a man's Dream Lover would be like?

Again, use your notebook, and divide a page into three sections. The first should be entitled "Personality." It's your space to describe the ultimate fun woman to have as a mate. Don't focus on deep-down qualities. Concentrate on outward temperament. How would this fantastic woman act? Is she quiet? Or gregarious? Serious or a little batty? Be as specific as you can, and explore the traits that you think a man would find really wonderful in a woman.

Now make a section for "Emotions." Here's the space to write down what the perfect 10 would be like on the inside. What's in her heart? How does she express her love? And what about her anger? When is she most open? What makes her back off and give a man some emotional room to move? Does she want a serious commitment? Or just a loose but loving affair?

The last section should be "Your Assessment" of how you compare to this great lady. In the last chapter's "Put It into Practice," I asked men to be both fair and realistic. I would ask the same of you. The point is not to give yourself a final grade, or to rank yourself on some arbitrary scale of good and bad. All I want is for you to imagine what you think a man would want, and see the ways in which you do (and do not) match that image. Lastly, write what you actually can fulfill comfortably. The point is to remain the basic you, but accentuate your positive qualities, and play down or eliminate those negative qualities that bring excess baggage into the relationship. Present yourself honestly; just emphasize the positive. Remember, a man looks for a relationship with a woman where he can forget his own mental conflicts and feel better about himself. He wants a friend, companion, and sex partner who, because she feels good about herself, can help make him feel good about himself.

Should you change? Should you deliberately set out to make yourself over and into the image you've described? No. I don't believe in makeovers. I believe in people knowing and accepting themselves. I believe in your looking for someone who can accept you as you are. So I'm not asking you to change. I'm asking you to see yourself and, just maybe, gain a new insight into what's not working for you with the men you meet.

ANSWERS TO THE QUIZ

1. c
2. b
3. d
4. d
5. c
6. c
7. a
8. c
9. b
10. a

12 Twelve Secrets About Finding Love and Commitment

"If we do not change our direction, we are likely to end up where we are headed."
—ANCIENT CHINESE PROVERB

*T*he purpose of this entire book has been to convince you that romance and love can come into your life . . . *if* you get real, *if* you take control, and *if* you make the right moves.

Today, like never before, you have to seek people out and take the risk that comes with letting them know you might be interested. The greatest hoax ever played on humankind is the myth of how romantic attachment will fall into our laps. Religion and politics may separate us, but believe me, we're all raised to believe that love will triumph. From earliest childhood, we're told that in the end, good people of honest intent will somehow chance upon each other and live happily ever after.

Well, guess what: it's never been true. It's just that today more of the world is within reach. So it's easier to see the enormous lie within the myth. Think about it: the one "old maid" or "confirmed bachelor" that every family knew a generation ago has miraculously multiplied.

In such a high-pressure mating market, it's essential to have a strategy. Don't bother to check your astrological forecast. Don't consult with a therapist or bartender, either. I can tell you for free what they would charge you to say, "Yes, today might be your lucky day." But only if you put one foot in front of the other and move deliberately toward the goal you have in mind. You need a plan that outlines the basic rules of the game. You also need to follow the plan step-by-step. This book has tried to lay out that plan. I've passed along the bottom-line message from various statistical research reports and surveys, from scholarly studies and from real-life singles just like you. Every story and every quote comes from real life. Each has been presented in a sincere effort to convince you of the one fact you most need to accept: that long-lasting love is not likely to fall into your lap. No matter how wonderful and deserving you are, it's not going to happen without your actively going for it.

I know that's discouraging. It's infuriatingly unfair. It has probably made more than a few readers angrily accuse me of insensitively interpreting the facts, or of not being a romantic. I accept that. In fact, it doesn't even bother me. My purpose is not how much you like hearing what I have to tell you. My concern is that you believe it *and* act upon it. If you continue to put your trust in out-dated assumptions about love, you'll almost certainly wind up frustrated and alone.

Before concluding, I would like to review the most concrete and vital points of the book:

SECRET NUMBER ONE: DON'T ASSUME NUMBERS WILL WORK IN YOUR FAVOR.

Numbers can be deceiving. That's certainly true about the statistics on American singles. At first glance, they suggest that there has never been a better time to be unattached. In fact, there has never been a *harder* time.

It's true that there are more available men and women than ever before. It's also true that the vast majority of them want to be half of a couple. Nevertheless, more and more eligible men and women are finding themselves alone every Saturday night. Why? Because they're waiting for fate to do what they must do for themselves: make love happen.

Today, a majority of singles are mature, independent, self-aware, and selective about just what they need in a partner. They deliberately delay a serious romantic involvement so that they can spend more time clarifying their personal values and emotional concerns. That's all well and good, but there is one problem with the plan. By the time a lot of us figure out what we want and when we're finally ready to look for Mr. or Ms. Right, the parade of prospects has passed us by. We're deep into our adulthood, with all its time-consuming responsibilities, and we simply don't make enough time for meeting and dating people.

Even those of us who are willing to deliberately take the time often discover that the methods of introduction that worked a decade (or two) ago are now obsolete and ineffective. College classmates are a part of our past. Synagogue and church are introduction services only for the religious. Friends and relatives are either paired off (and out of touch with other eligible singles) or still in the market (and saving the best prospects for themselves).

This all boils down to one disheartening conclusion: despite the increased number of available men and women, your access to desirable candidates is actually shrinking.

SECRET NUMBER TWO: DON'T "REMAKE" YOURSELF—EVEN IF YOU'RE NOT MEETING THE RIGHT PEOPLE.

When you're lonely, and you've been that way for a while, there's a natural tendency to figure that it must be your fault. We beat ourselves up. We figure that we must be doing something wrong. We feel we're not lovable, and not worthy of love. If you venture into the self-improvement section of your neighborhood bookstore, you will find a lot of support for that assumption. Lose weight, gain weight, change your hair, buy new clothes, muscle up, drive a different car, move to a better area of town—these are just a few of the suggestions you may come across in your effort to transform yourself into a more "desirable" man or woman.

Sometimes, of course, authors focus on the need for a personality change. One psychologist will tell you to be more assertive. The next will encourage you to be less pushy. It seems there's a book for everyone: women who love too much, men who can't commit, Peter Pans, Cinderellas, Casanovas, narcissists, and sexists.

Don't fall for contrived explanations or complex makeover plans. The time and effort you spend recasting yourself only sets you up for an endless cycle of transformation and disappointment. Why? Because when the "new" you fails to find happiness and romantic excitement, you'll be forced back to the drawing board to try re-creating yourself again. You're fine the way you are; perhaps you're just going about looking for love in all the wrong places!

The truth is, you don't need to change the way you look, where you live, what you drive, or the way you behave. You don't have to be smooth, sexy, or especially charming. You just need to get out there, exactly as you are, and go about it more intelligently.

SECRET NUMBER THREE: MEET AS MANY PEOPLE AS YOU CAN, IN ANY WAY YOU CAN.

The biggest obstacle to your romantic happiness stems from an inability to meet enough available people. Studies show that most of us are emotionally compatible with only one out of every twenty-five people. And when you figure in physical chemistry, lifestyle interests, and basic values, the odds of your just stumbling across your soulmate are virtually zilch. That means you need to get to know a lot of singles before you can reasonably hope to find someone you really like.

Again, there's a popular answer to this roadblock: lower your
standards of acceptability. Settle for less than you want, and then
you won't be so disappointed. Not a smart strategy! You deserve
to be with someone wonderful who will give you what you need
and who will be able to fulfill your greatest expectations.

The more intelligent solution to your problem is obvious:
you've got to meet more people. Give yourself "decent exposure," in any and every way possible. Let people know you're
available and looking. Think of your single status as something
positive, rather than something that embarrasses you and makes
you hide from others. Get out there! You have so much to offer
someone, but no one will know it unless you expose yourself.
Join a health club. Look for any charitable organization that has
a high number of singles who participate in doing charity work.
Take a continuing education class at your local high school or
college. Join a reputable dating service. Start a silly conversation
with somebody at the grocery checkout, a bookstore, or the
mall. Anywhere. Anytime. Consciously maintain a positive attitude with great eye contact and a ready smile. Say something to
someone who seems interesting. Anything. Remind yourself
over and over again that when you appear interested you are not
admitting desperation. You're just intelligently eliminating the
twenty-four noncompatible people and, just maybe, finding the
one with whom you click.

But our ancestors didn't have to stoop to such drastic meas-
ures, you might be saying. They just lived their lives until good
fortune stepped in. This is what I call the "destiny" approach,
and it's still the most popular myth about meeting people. My
advice is to forget it altogether. Depending upon your perspective, it was either the luxury of past generations to wait for fate to
put people together (who were not necessarily "made for each
other"), or the accepted mind-set to let destiny control their love
lives. For men and women of the nineties, courtship begins only
when singles actively and purposefully initiate it.

• • •

Secret Number Four: Take Risks. The Bigger a Risk You Take, the Better Your Chances for Finding Romance.

I understand why so many people still want to believe in the old approach. They're afraid of the rejection that might follow an open declaration of availability. Forty years ago, when men and women met in high school and at local community events, they could talk and pursue each other without clearly admitting that they were "interested." They could fall back on the structure of classes, choir practice, or a neighborhood get-together to justify their presence and, to some extent, even their friendliness.

Today, those façades are hard to come by. Modern singles must go for it aggressively! They need to come out from wherever they've been keeping themselves to meet in places and in ways that reveal their interest in connecting with someone. Singles' bars, personal ads, singles' activities clubs, and dating services exist *solely* to bring men and women together. When you decide to introduce yourself in one of these ways, you can't hide your motives for being there, so make the very most out of these. Why else would you join? Don't do an incomplete job; put all of yourself into the experience.

If it's any comfort, remember that the bigger a risk you take, the better your chances of meeting somebody who's really right for you. Romance and risk are closely linked. You almost never get one without the other. After all, it's hard to pursue people. Period. It's even harder to go after them romantically. You might be turned down and then have to deal with red-faced embarrassment or blue-hearted pain. Who needs it?

By the same token, if you want a fulfilling relationship, it's foolish to surround yourself with people who are looking for just one night's passion. It's more frightening, but much smarter, to find ways of meeting other available singles who are as willing as you to show their interest in a serious romantic partnership. So personal ads are generally a better bet than office parties. And a reliable dating service is likely to work best of all because of its members' expectations for commitment and your access to information.

SECRET NUMBER FIVE: TRUST SEXUAL CHEMISTRY AND LEARN TO READ THE SIGNALS YOU SEND AND RECEIVE.

In recent years, scientists have proved beyond all doubt that sexual attraction is very real. It makes your heart race, your pulse pick up speed, your muscles gently quiver, and your brain produce hormones to signal a bizarre combination of terror and bliss.

Research has also shown us that romantic chemistry is totally irrational. You can't make it happen just because everything else about her is perfect. You can't stop it from happening even if he's all wrong for you. That's because the indescribable rush you get when you're around someone special isn't about ideas or reason. It's about your intangible and indescribable basic human drives and instincts.

Does that make it too unpredictable to count on? Absolutely not. In fact, mutual attraction really is the best predictor of long-term romantic compatibility.

Unfortunately, it's not always mutual. You can be uncontrollably drawn to somebody who barely knows that you're alive. So you've got to learn to interpret consciously the sexual signals that men and women have been sending, receiving, and unconsciously responding to since the dawn of time.

The most dependable of those signals is a series of five behaviors that always take place when shared sparks are flying in the air:

1. *Initial approach.* Someone comes close, usually about three feet away.
2. *Subtle turn.* The other person silently turns toward the pursuer with sustained eye contact.
3. *Talk.* Either of the two people initiates it.
4. *Touch.* This is the most crucial of the five steps (and the one that most often breaks the ritual because neither person is willing to take the risk). Finally, when two people are mutually attracted, they begin to:
5. *Mimic.* Without realizing it, they begin to mirror each other;

e.g., they may cross their legs together, recline in their chair in the same manner, and eventually their speech patterns and breathing become in synch.

Don't rush heart first into a steady relationship simply because you're swayed by the power of sexual attraction. Nevertheless, realize that without its force working in your favor, the most "appropriate" love affair is doomed to fizzle before it ever really gets started.

SECRET NUMBER SIX: EXPECT THAT EVERY FIRST DATE WILL BE A BIT AWKWARD.

When you finally land a date with somebody you genuinely want to spend time with, there's a tendency to place a lot of expectations on that first encounter. It's your big chance to impress and be impressed, right?

Wrong! Even when everything is as perfect as it can be, a first date is going to be a bit stilted, awkward or uncomfortable. In fact, the more attracted you are to somebody, the more stressful the experience will most likely be. You've got some very strong impulses pushing you in one direction, while your own internal indecisiveness and a fairly strict set of acceptable social behaviors limit your actions every step of the way. If your date is equally drawn to you, the initial hours you spend together can be like wrestling with a tiger. You'll doubt that you have the strength to hold on, but you sure won't want to let go.

Remember, a first date is simply an opportunity to check chemistry and whether there's a potential for a relationship. It's the chance for you both to confirm or reject your original suspicion—that this could be the start of something really special. In that sense, it is a test. The best preparation is a positive outlook. Look over what you wrote in "Notes for Myself" in Chapter 2 to affirm what wonderful qualities you bring to any date. Anticipate something good. After all, every new person we meet really does have something we can learn from. So relax and treat a date as a chance to have a good time and expand your horizons.

Don't worry about trying to show off your fabulous sense of humor or sharp intelligence. When you get back home and review the date, don't lose sleep over the funny joke you didn't tell during dinner, or the brilliant point you failed to make after the play or movie. Don't even worry about the many awkward moments of silence in your conversation. A first date leads to a second when two people find that their original attraction is reinforced by even a brief and clumsy get-together. If the buttons are still being pushed, you'll get together again. If they aren't, you won't, no matter what you said or did. You'll probably be no worse off for the experience.

Still, you can cut down the tension by planning a first date that distracts you both from the "interview" process that's going on. Too often, people imagine that an intimate dinner or midnight sailboat ride are the romantic ways to initiate courtship. These make terrific subsequent dates. Sometimes it's better to plan on a three-ring circus, sporting event, botanical garden, or chaotic street fair. Do anything that offers lots of sights and sounds to fill in when conversation takes an unavoidable turn toward the ridiculous. You may even want to schedule a daytime date. There's less pressure and sexual tension when you meet in the light of day. And, if everything goes that well, you'll figure out a way to extend the date into the evening.

SECRET NUMBER SEVEN: DON'T EXPECT AN EASY CONNECTION AND TACKLE THE ART OF CONVERSATION ONE STEP AT A TIME.

There's a common myth that tells us that people in love can talk for hours about almost anything at all. There's another that encourages us to believe that lovers owe it to each other to be up front about their thoughts and feelings. "Tell it like it is!" Put it out there. Be honest; anything less is dishonest . . . or so we're told.

I agree, but only to a degree. Honesty is a wonderful element in a love affair. But it doesn't have to come rushing from your mouth like lava from an erupting volcano, especially on a first date. You don't have to turn yourself inside out examining deep life issues with a stranger you've just met. I call these heartfelt discussions "date-killers." My point is for you to be 100 percent honest, but keep some mystery about you. *Take your time.* By tackling conversation in small and progressively more serious steps, you give yourself and your partner some time for intimacy to grow and to decide whether or not it's worth the effort to respect differing opinions.

Under the best of circumstances, two people find themselves simply falling into conversation with comfortable ease. If that happens to you, count your blessings. It's a wonderful experience to feel that kind of connection right off the bat. By the same token, you shouldn't write off a new relationship just because you're finding it somewhat difficult to carry on a free-flowing conversation. Some budding love affairs take a little more time and a bit more conscious effort in this department.

The next step is getting acquainted on a deeper level. When should you move from idle chatter to more revealing conversation? When you both feel at ease with the idea. If that sounds too vague, make a rule out of it. Aim to keep verbal exchanges fairly light on the first two dates. Ask personal questions and be prepared to reciprocate and answer some when they are directed your way. If your partner moves into areas that you find uncomfortable, be casually direct and say something like, "Oh, let's not bog down a good time with such serious stuff—at least not yet." The content of conversations tends to become more substantial as both parties begin to form a closer connection. It flows naturally when they feel this closeness.

Depending on the conversational and behavioral styles of both of you (introverted and extroverted) after the third date or so, you should feel the desire to shift gears. Ask about career goals, long-term life ambitions, and even basic personal values. It's probably still too early to ask about fundamental personal questions of religion, politics, and the desire to have children. Resist the temptation, as there will be plenty of time to discuss these issues if you feel the relationship has real potential. These, after all, are very intimate topics. Eventually, of course, it will be

important to cover them for the relationship to become a significant and serious one. Still, you've got all the time in the world.
So don't rush.

SECRET NUMBER EIGHT: DON'T EXPECT SEX TO COMPENSATE FOR GAPS IN A RELATIONSHIP.

Sexual attraction is the fuel that ignites and moves a romance. It
helps you distinguish between a good friendship and a romantic
relationship. Remember that acting on sexual attraction changes
the relationship forever. Until you are sexually intimate with
someone, the nature of your relationship is basically undefined
(except, of course, to those who clearly and absolutely believe
that sex before marriage is immoral). Are you casual dating partners? Buddies? Significant others? It's a matter of opinion, and
there's a certain freedom that comes with leaving the parameters
open-ended. Once you have sex, you've crossed the line of just
being buddies. The emotional content inherent in sexual intimacy tends to set up expectations whether conscious or not.

When both people seem to be in agreement that the chemistry feels right, that doesn't mean that either is immune from
the peril of premature sex. Instant sexual intimacy does not necessarily mean that the two people share a connection of their
hearts. If both don't already have a strong foundation for satisfying communication, as well as similar expectations for where the
relationship is headed, then they are likely to find their road to
romance chock-full of emotional obstacles and disappointments.

In many new courtships there's someone who pursues and
someone else who gets chased. In general, the person being pursued is the one left most vulnerable after the relationship becomes sexually intimate. That's because in theory the courtship
has peaked. After sexual intimacy has occurred, the balance of
power tends to shift because the pursuer has been satisfied. The
prize has been won. Next the pursuer usually takes a giant step
back and away from the relationship. That leaves the person who
finally surrendered a bit confused and tending to question what

he or she did wrong. Actually it was probably nothing.

It's important to remember that courtship is not a smooth ride. The dynamics are ever changing and you must be willing to go with the flow of the ride. Sometimes you are the pursuer, and other times you'll be pursued.

In fact, every solid relationship has to go through this rite of passage. There will come a certain point when a new romance needs to be put to "The Test" of whether sexual intimacy will make, break, or change your relationship.

Most recent surveys indicate that a growing number of men and women want to wait longer before they add sex to the romantic picture. People want more foreplay, in every sense of the word. They want to discover each other intellectually, socially, and even emotionally before committing to a sexual relationship. That's a big adjustment for some of us who came of age during the sexual revolution, when people had sex first and then got to know each other. But it's now the order of the day. It's part of safe and healthy courtship rules in the nineties.

SECRET NUMBER NINE: DON'T WORK AS MUCH. PLAY MORE.

A recent national survey on singles found that the foremost concern among men and women is career advancement. Hardly a shocking piece of news, especially when you stop to consider that in today's world, we all need to put a major push on professional achievement just to keep our workplace and financial heads above water.

As a result of today's reality of career frenzy, a lot of us are virtually addicted to job responsibilities and the added stress that goes along with them. In fact, workaholism is the most prevalent addiction among single Americans. It's also a major stumbling block to a fulfilling romantic relationship. Typically, when you work a minimum of ten hours a day, and then squeeze in an early morning workout (to lower your risk of heart disease or improve your appearance) and an evening extension class (to increase your chances for a good promotion), you won't have the time or energy left to meet many people, much less fall in love with someone . . . unless, of course, your activities are filled with single people of the type that you'd like to meet and who are in the same rut as you.

If you recognize that you're an overachiever, believe me when I tell you one of your innermost secrets: you do tend to have difficulty with personal relationships. Your commitment to perfection—which serves you well in the work world—will chip away at and ruin one romance after another for you. Maybe you focus on the imperfections of your new partner and decide you really deserve better. Maybe you obsess on the deficiencies in your own feelings and call things off simply because you don't feel as committed as lovers "should." Either way, your promising career is always right there, eager to take advantage of the extra time you suddenly have on your hands.

The best offensive strategy in this arena is a good defense. Don't allow yourself to work so much. Instead, work smarter. No seven-day work weeks. Reject the dictum "If you can't show up on time for the 7:00 A.M. Saturday meeting, don't bother showing up for Sundays!" No business calls after 7:00 each night. And if you're prone to bring your work home with you nightly, limit yourself. You need to set aside a small amount of quiet, nongoal-oriented time each and every day, making this a time to relax and sort through the things in life that matter most to you. You need to expand your social circle. Depending on your job, to make that possible is almost like waiting for your fairy godmother. So try to resist an office romance temptation. Dating someone you meet through work will make your life more insulated, complicated, and potentially explosive.

SECRET NUMBER TEN: KNOW THAT THE THREE THINGS WOMEN WANT MOST FROM A MAN ARE STRENGTH, COMMUNICATION, AND HONESTY.

According to one recent survey, four out of every five married women in America would refuse to form a relationship with their partner if they had the chance to do it all over again. Their reason? Because, they say, the men in their lives can't open up and share their feelings.

Women of the nineties don't want Rambo, James Bond, or the Marlboro Man. They want 100 percent of their man, imperfections and all. When they say they're fed up with wimps and looking for that rare creature—a truly strong man—they're not referring to biceps or pectoral muscle size. They're talking about masculine self-assurance, the ability to build intimacy, and the strength to open up emotionally.

When they tell us they want honesty, they're not asking us to constantly reveal our every thought and feeling. They are, however, demanding that we overcome our ingrained fear of emotions. They want us to talk less about events or facts and more about points of view and personal outlook. They're less interested in the mechanics of our job than in the human behavior dynamics that occur at work each and every day.

All this demands that men develop a new kind of dating sophistication. Most of us grew up thinking it was manly to be strong and silent. (It worked for Clint Eastwood, didn't it?) Now, available single men are required to express what's going on inside. If we don't know how we feel this can be particularly difficult. It calls for a lot of self-analysis and, eventually, requires that we begin communicating our deepest thoughts and feelings to a woman. If we do an inadequate job at it, we stand to lose the interest, respect, and admiration of the person with whom we most want to become close.

Increasing communication may sound like a prescription for a major romantic risk. It is. But it's the only way to get what you're after: love and bonding with a special woman.

Secret Number Eleven: Know That the Two Things Men Want Most from Women After Physical Attractiveness Are Spontaneity and Enthusiasm.

Let a woman's romance fall into trouble, and her best friend is likely to tell her to make a delicious dinner, pick up a new-release video, and have him over for a quiet evening. Comfort, don't confront him. Flatter him. Make him feel that he's the most important thing in your life.

Well, I hate to argue with female wisdom, but it's the wrong course of action. These men really don't want a partner to offer them a safe sanctuary. They want a woman to offer them an exciting diversion. They don't want relaxation more than anything else. They do want escape and fun. They want a gregarious and enthusiastic playmate, as well as a sweet companion to enjoy life with. And, of course, along with this they enjoy the flattery!

Oddly enough, a man usually has to fight the urge to squelch the very qualities in a woman that draws him to her. He'll unintentionally find himself making fun of her exuberance and putting down her free spirit—especially if she shows too much independence. Yet, even as he does that, he's attracted by these traits because they signal liveliness in her. Typically men aren't comfortable with constant emotional intimacy. They move back and forth between the desire for attachment and the need for independence and freedom. If a woman clings too much, they tend to feel suffocated. If she lets go and concentrates a lot on the outside world, they feel less trapped and more inclined to seek her affection. Remember, men are goal-oriented and enjoy the chase.

So the smart woman of the nineties gives only a tiny bit more than she receives. It's a no-win situation to demand a strict fifty-fifty split on who gives how much to a romance. Each should be given a full 100 percent. However, women who are willing to go way beyond their fair share often wind up compromising their own needs. They become involved in go-nowhere love affairs with men who pay more attention to the weekend ballgame than to their partner's emotional fulfillment.

SECRET NUMBER TWELVE: CHANGE YOUR BEHAVIOR AND YOUR HEART WILL FOLLOW.

What should come first: feelings or behavior? Should we act the way we feel, or behave the way we *wish* we felt? In matters of modern romance, it's best to change your modus operandi and wait for your emotions to follow suit.

If you know you act in ways that trip you up with prospective partners, then make up your mind to take a different tack. Even when your heart tells you to stay home and lick wounds you suffered in your last painful affair; even when some inner voice tells you to try too hard, demand too much, or accept too little; even when every cell in your body demands that you laugh at his silly attempt to express himself or demean her vitality—fight back! Put your brain in control, and make your actions follow its orders. If you can alter your behavior and get yourself to act the way you wish you really were inside, you will find yourself mysteriously becoming the person you would like to be. The behavioral experts claim that the first step is to wear a smile even if you're not happy. By having a smile on your face you'll face others more positively. Your smile is contagious and likely to get positive reactions. Like all creatures of habit, we can be trained to respond according to the wishes of our master, and we are our own masters. So we must consciously decide to adjust our behavior. You'll feel yourself increasingly comfortable with the new set of actions because they'll bring you positive reactions.

Put It into Practice

That's it. That's my system for dating success. It's my best advice to date. Of course, I'm always learning, and as I get more or better information, I look for ways of getting it to you. So keep your eyes and ears open. I'm sure you'll be hearing from me in the near future.

In the meantime, there is a single message I'd like to reiterate one last time. The easiest temptation in the world is to do nothing. Politicians almost always take this path of least resistance, and the world remains plagued by injustice. Sometimes parents do it, and they watch their kids fall into ever more dangerous habits. Some married people do it, and they keep themselves locked in miserable, unfulfilling relationships. A whole lot of single people do it, and they remain alone.

Your last assignment is probably your most important. Write down at least five new approaches that you're going to take to increase your exposure to the opposite sex. Besides all the information that I've given you throughout the book (especially in Chapter 5), there are some helpful tips in the first appendix ("Ninety Ways to Find Love in the Nineties"). I suggest that before putting this book away you consider the following: What are you going to do to find the love of your life who *is* out there waiting for you to find him or her?

Change is hard. It's filled with clearly visible danger and, perhaps worse, with the terror of the unknown. So do whatever it takes—do everything it takes—to make it happen. You'll make mistakes. You'll embarrass yourself. Worst of all, you'll probably get hurt a time or two. But remember: being hurt is the sign of a heart still open to love. There's nothing admirable about emotional armor so thick that nothing penetrates. When heartbreak is no longer possible, neither is ecstasy.

A *Ninety Ways to Find Love in the Nineties*

1. Get an attitude adjustment. Want love? *Get real!*
2. Become more assertive in everything you do.
3. Do your grocery shopping from 5:00 to 7:00 P.M., when singles do their shopping and families are home having dinner.
4. Look for *every* opportunity to meet the opposite sex.
5. Find a local gourmet coffee shop and become a regular; the conversation is a lot more stimulating than the depressing alcoholic banter and environs of a bar.
6. Try to become a more positive thinker in all that you do.
7. If a parent, join the PTA or local kids' parents' groups (it's a good place for nonparents, too!).
8. Hit the health club during prime-time hours; people are everywhere, and even when you wait in a line to use a machine or for your class to start, it's a natural for you to strike up a conversation.
9. Always carry business cards, or make cards with only your name and phone number on them.
10. Find out what local events happen in your area and offer your time as a volunteer.

11. Host a potluck dinner party with friends, where everyone must bring both someone new and something to eat.
12. Volunteer some time to a nonprofit organization.
13. Make an extra effort to meet new people each week. Sure, it might feel contrived, but no less than if you were planning a new business venture.
14. Buy a new car or major toy; it could contribute to renewed confidence.
15. If you own a business, join the Chamber of Commerce; they can have great mixers.
16. If you're a mom or dad, become an assistant coach of your child's Little League, soccer, or basketball team (full-time coaching might take up too much of your time).
17. Stop spending your weekends with your relatives, unless they're out and about doing fun things and don't nag you about your singleness.
18. Update your wardrobe, even if it's just a few pieces; new clothes can help give you a fresher and more energetic attitude.
19. Join a bowling league; it's a great way for meeting other singles.
20. For men, consider taking cooking classes, which are typically filled with women, and also give you more confidence about what to do when you start a relationship with someone wonderful.
21. If you're a woman, how about taking an automotive class? (It's typically filled with men.)
22. Do something out of character, like hang gliding, rock climbing, or river rafting.
23. Consider taking occasional night classes; they'll widen your education, and could expand your social horizons.
24. If you like to sing, join a temple or church choir.
25. Join a professional organization in your field because they often give you exposure to new people who could help you in both your business and social life.
26. Go out even when nobody wants to go along. Part of being single and wanting a significant other in your life means you've got to strengthen your inner resolve and reduce your sense of isolation and anxiety.

27. Try to think younger and more progressive. Younger isn't always better, but it can easily open you up to new ideas that older people might summarily dismiss as risky or immature.

28. Create a dining club and try your city's fine restaurants.

29. Learn to play cards and get a group together. Make sure to invite some new people each week even if it means adding another card table.

30. Take minivacations to locales in your area; it's amazing how many wonderful things exist in your own backyard that only the tourists seem to appreciate.

31. Pamper yourself at a spa for a weekend; you'll end up with an invigorating new spirit.

32. Take a vacation to a fun place for singles.

33. Start doing your laundry at the Laundromat—many younger singles don't have a washer or dryer.

34. Call some of your old friends from high school or college.

35. Take western dance lessons; they're packed with people who might ordinarily feel out of place at a rock 'n' roll nightclub. And they usually attract a more fun-loving crowd.

36. Get a dog and take it for walks through the park or on the beach.

37. Visit happy hours at a karaoke bar. Singing has a tendency to break the ice very quickly with strangers.

38. Push yourself to go out even when you are tired.

39. Take a singles cruise, but make certain that your age group is well represented.

40. Get a group of people together to go river rafting or to do some other very challenging activity.

41. Take a self-improvement class.

42. Add some culture to your life by visiting a museum, a gallery, or the theater.

43. Take up tennis and get on a tennis ladder.

44. Plan more walks on the beach or parks, which are great for meeting people.

45. Join a hikers' group for weekend hikes.

46. Host a "bring-a-new-friend-to-dinner" party.

47. Become more active in your temple or church.

48. Rent a sports car for the day and visit a nearby resort.

49. Get a group together for a sporting event and plan a tailgate party.
50. Try to eat more healthfully.
51. Find a cultural center that offers poetry reading.
52. Take a bag lunch and eat it in the park.
53. If you wear glasses, try contact lenses; it might give you a whole new outlook on the world.
54. If you are a man, consider taking aerobics classes.
55. Give yourself a total makeover, from head to toe; a new look could inspire you to make even more changes in your life.
56. Take a nutritional food preparation class, which is typically filled with singles.
57. Learn to play beach volleyball.
58. Go kite flying in the park.
59. Take sailing lessons.
60. Try going on a trail ride at a local stable.
61. Attend charity benefit dinners, especially bachelor auctions.
62. Visit Las Vegas; it's a great spot to meet singles.
63. Decide what you want in a mate.
64. Participate in a weekend bike ride.
65. Create "The Dutch Club," where everyone pays individually to go to movies, dinner, or a sporting event.
66. Join an active political organization.
67. Donate time at a local hospital.
68. Create an alumni association in your town for alumni from your college.
69. Take acting lessons.
70. Create a social group with friends from work, even if it's just an after-work opportunity to share a drink.
71. Ask friends to introduce you to their friends.
72. Create a single-friend pyramid in which each person attending a planned event must bring a single friend.
73. Get informed by reading anything you can get your hands on which makes for stimulating conversations.
74. If you are a woman, learn to understand sports, which will help you enjoy them more.
75. Men should be less consumed with sports on the weekends.
76. Try wearing your hair a different way.

77. Get creative with opening lines, especially ones that won't elicit a simple "yes/no" response.
78. Get up early on the weekends and compete in a ten-kilometer race or walk.
79. Initiate a conversation with people whom you wouldn't ordinarily talk with.
80. Try to become more approachable and you will be approached more often.
81. Try to become an expert at a variety of things, such as wines, cultures, or languages.
82. Start going to swap meets, which are great places to meet singles.
83. Consider going to comedy clubs; they're generally filled with groups of friends of the same sex, and you're typically seated with people you don't know.
84. If you admire someone, let that person know how you feel.
85. Next time you need to buy something, go to the mall; there are plenty of people everywhere.
86. Do a little research; find out what men or women like to hear.
87. Go to a rock concert from your music era.
88. Take classes to become a massage therapist.
89. Do anything to keep from sitting at home watching television.
90. Take up a new hobby, such as biking, rollerblading, golf, or tennis.

APPENDIX

B *Singles in America: What's Changed Since 1900?*

THE FACTS

	No. of singles 18+ years old	% of singles in population	Median age at first marriage	Marriage rate per 1,000 population	Divorce rate per 1,000 population
1900–1959	1900 M: 12,329,000 1900 W: 10,764,000 Total: 23,093,000		1900/Men: 26.1 Women: 22	1910: 10.3 1930: 9.2 1950: 11.1 (Highest point: 11.1–1950)	1900: .8 1930: 1.6 1950: 2.6
1960	M: 18,630,000 W: 21,765,000 Total: 40,395,000		Men: 22.8 Women: 20.3	8.5 (Lowest point: 1959–62)	2.2
1970	M: 24,390,000 W: 29,972,000 Total: 54,362,000		Men: 23.2 Women: 20.8	10.6	3.5
1980		36%	Men: 24.7 Women: 22	10.6	5.2 (Highest point 5.3–1981)
1990	Total:	42%	Men: 26.3	9.8	4.7

	Best places to meet singles	Economics of dating	Single-parenting issues	Worst sexually transmitted disease	Attitude toward sex outside of marriage
	75,618,000	Women: 24.1			
2000	85,000,000±	50±%	???	???	???

SINGLES LIFESTYLE ISSUES

	Best places to meet singles	Economics of dating	Single-parenting issues	Worst sexually transmitted disease	Attitude toward sex outside of marriage
1900 –1959	Dances, Neighborhood, Church socials, High school, Arranged marriages	Man always pays.	The mother always gets custody.	Syphilis, Gonorrhea	"No!"
1960s	Singles bars, Organizations, Political rallies	"Men pay; shouldn't they always?"	The mother always gets custody.	Syphilis, Gonorrhea	"Shhh!"
1970s	Discos and bars	"Let's try Dutch treat."	Importance of father's role is taken into consideration.	Herpes	"If it feels good, do it!"

1980s	Health clubs, Singles network mixers, Personal matchmakers, Classified ads, Video dating	"Who should pay for dates? If it's us men, then we kind of expect something in return."	How to handle shared custody? How to handle dating as a single parent?	Herpes, AIDS	"It's part of my personal growth. Besides, everyone else is doing it?"
1990s	Video dating, 900 phone nos., Religious organization socials	Continued confusion about who should pay, but men still pay on first dates	How to handle blended families?	AIDS	"Is it worth dying for?"

HOW SINGLES ARE PERCEIVED—PART 1

	Gender roles	Popular singles on TV	Popular films about singles	Popular books about singles	Motto of the decade's singles
1900 –1959	The man is the provider and courts the "little lady."	There were none.	*And God Created Woman; An Affair to Remember*	Kinsey's *Sexual Behavior in the Human Male*	"Marry and live happily ever after"
1960s	Things begin to change; women start asking questions about equality and their power	John Forsythe in "Bachelor Father" and Fred MacMurray in "My Three Sons"	*A Man and a Woman; Sex and the Single Girl; Love with the Proper Stranger*	Helen Gurley Brown's *Sex and the Single Girl*	"Is the grass greener on the singles side?"
1970s	Women start asserting their rights in both business and personal areas	Bill Bixby in "Courtship of Eddie's Father," Marlo Thomas in "That Girl," Mary Tyler Moore	*Love Story; Kramer vs. Kramer; An Unmarried Woman*		"I've got to be me!"
1980s	Men uncertain about what is expected of them;	Ted Danson in "Cheers," "Oprah," "Designing	*Annie Hall; Starting Over*	Warren Farrell's *The Liberated Man*	"Can we get together?"

	Women start to enjoy and suffer from their new rights	Women"			
1990s	Uncertainty about who is supposed to be "strong and aggressive"	Candace Bergen in "Murphy Brown"	*When Harry Met Sally; Sleepless in Seattle*	They are still being written.	"We've got to be you and me."

HOW SINGLES ARE PERCEIVED—PART 2

	Singles' perception about their single life	Public perception about single life	Business & consumer marketing perception	Fiscal industry perception
1900–1959	"No problem; I'm going to be married soon."	"The nuclear family is everything."	If you're single and over 25, what's wrong with you?	Very difficult to obtain credit or loans
1960s	"What other relationships might work better than marriage?"	"The family is the most important element in American culture."	College kids and old ladies	Singles don't care much about money; they want peace, love, and sex.
1970s	"It's my choice and I don't want to get married!"	"Is it normal to be single?" "Is s/he gay?"	Swinging singles are not a viable market for mainstream business targeting.	Do "these people" really have any money to spend?
1980s	"I don't fit in . . ."	"What's wrong with that person?"	Relationship books and issues sell.	Yuppies with high disposable incomes
1990s	"I feel okay being single . . . but I sure wouldn't"	"You are what you are."	What's wrong with being single? Don't we target	No question that singles have high buying power

mind finding
someone to love."   this group?

PARENTING ISSUES

	% children under 18 living with two parents	% children under 18 living with one parent	No. of children under 18 living with one parent	% households headed by single parent	% of single parents over 30
1970	85.2	11.9	8,199,000	5	7.8
1980	76.7	19.7	12,466,000	7	17
1990	71.7	25.5	16,624,000	9	34.2
2000	Smaller no. than before	Bigger no. than before	Bigger no. than before	12+	More than 34.2

C Recommended Reading

Adler, Robert
Sharing the Children: How to Resolve Custody Problems and Get on with Your Life, Adler & Adler, 1988.

Cabot, Tracy
How to Make a Man Fall in Love with You, Dell, 1984.
How to Keep a Man in Love with You, McGraw-Hill, 1986.
Marrying Later, Marrying Smarter, Dell, 1990.

De Angelis, Barbara
Make Love All the Time, Dell, 1987.
Secrets About Men Every Woman Should Know, Dell, 1990.
Are You the One for Me?, Dell, 1993.

Faludi, Susan
Backlash, Anchor Books, 1991.

Farrell, Warren
Why Men Are the Way They Are, McGraw-Hill, 1986.
The Myth of Male Power, McGraw-Hill, 1993.

Fisher, Helen
Anatomy of Love: The Natural History of Monogamy, Adultery and Divorce, W. W. Norton, 1992.

Garreau, Joel
Edge City, Doubleday, 1991.

Godek, Gregory J. P.
1001 Ways to Be Romantic, Casablanca Press, 1991.
1001 More Ways to Be Romantic, Casablanca Press, 1992.

Gosse, Richard
Singles Guide to America, Marin Publications, 1989.

Reingold, Carmel Berman
Re-Marriage, Harper & Row, 1976.

Reinisch, June M.
The Kinsey Institute New Report on Sex, St. Martin's, 1990.

Sills, Judith
Excess Baggage: Getting Out of Your Own Way, Penguin Books, 1993.

Tannen, Deborah
You Just Don't Understand, Morrow, 1990.

Ullman, Dana
The One Minute (or so) Healer, Jeremy P. Tarcher, Inc., 1991.

Viscott, David
Emotionally Free, Contemporary Books, 1992.

Warren, Neil Clark
Finding the Love of Your Life, Focus on the Family Publishing, 1992.

Whipple, Beverly
Safe Encounters: How Women Can Say Yes to Pleasure and No to Unsafe Sex, McGraw-Hill, 1989.

Great Expectations
D *Centre Locations*

Atlanta
320 Interstate North,
Suite 110
Atlanta, GA 30339
404/956-9223

Austin
9037 Research Blvd.,
Suite 100
Austin, TX 78758
512/837-3000

Aventura
20803 Biscayne Blvd.,
Suite 102
Aventura, FL 33180
305/936-1910

Baltimore
40 York Rd., Suite 500
Towson, MD 21204
410/938-8989

Birmingham
(call 411 for address and
phone number)

Boca Raton
4800 North Federal Highway,
Suite B 103
Boca Raton, FL 33431
407/393-6666

Boston
210 South St.
Boston, MA 02111
617/338-6500

Bucks County
2607 Interplex Dr.
Trevose, PA 19503
215/244-9800

Central New Jersey
(Call 411 for address and
phone number)

Cherry Hill
One Cherry Hill, Suite 600
Cherry Hill, NJ 08002
609/667-6673

Chicago
350 West Ontario St.,
Suite 500
Chicago, IL 60610
312/943-1760

Cincinnati
8044 Montgomery Rd.,
Suite 151
Cincinnati, OH 45236
513/793-7733

Clearwater
15950 Bay Vista Dr., Suite 150
Clearwater, FL 34620
813/538-9331

Cleveland
6300 Rockside Rd., Suite 200
Independence, OH 44131
216/642-8855

Columbus
1103 Schrock Rd., Suite 101
Columbus, OH 43229
614/431-8500

Dallas
14180 Dallas Parkway,
Suite 100
Dallas, TX 75240
214/448-7900

Denver
400 South Colorado Blvd.,
Suite 200
Denver, CO 80222
303/321-1516

Detroit
25925 Telegraph Road,
Suite 145
Southfield, MI 48034
313/354-3210

Encino
17207 Ventura Blvd.
Encino, CA 91316
818/788-7878

Hartford
2189 Silas Deane Hwy.
Rocky Hill, CT 06067
203/257-3336

Houston
50 Briar Hollow Dr.,
Suite 100
Houston, TX 77027
713/623-6495

Huntsville
7529 South Memorial
Parkway, Suite C & D
Huntsville, AL 35802
205/882-3045

Indianapolis
3500 West Depauw Blvd.,
Suite 2070
Pyramid II, 7th Floor
Indianapolis, IN 46268
317/471-0580

Jacksonville
4348 Southpoint Blvd.,
Suite 210
Jacksonville, FL 32216
904/281-0999

Kansas City
7501 College Blvd., Suite 110
Overland Park, KS 66210
913/451-3711

King of Prussia
150 Allendale Road, Bldg. #3
King of Prussia, PA 19406
610/768-7000

Las Vegas
4045 South Spencer St.,
Suite 105
Las Vegas, NV 89119
702/734-6000

Los Angeles
1640 S. Sepulveda Blvd.,
Suite 100
Los Angeles, CA 90025
310/477-5566

Mexico City
Andres Bello No. 10, Piso 7
Col. Chapultepec Polanco
Mexico, D.F. C.P. 11560
011-52-5-282-9070

Milwaukee
16650 West Blue Mound Rd.,
Suite 100
Brookfield, WI 53005
414/796-5100

Minneapolis
3300 Edinborough, Suite 300
Edina, MN 55435
612/835-9590

Mountain View
2085 Landings Dr.
Mountain View, CA 94043
415/964-2985

Nashville
312 Blue Bird Dr.
Goodsville, TN 37072
615/370-0222

New Orleans
(call 411 for address and
phone number)

Newton
29 Crafts St., Suite 550
Newton, MA 02158
617/332-7755

Northern New Jersey
(Call 411 for address and
phone number)

Orange County
18818 Teller Ave., Suite 110
Irvine, CA 92715
714/476-1986

Orlando
2101 West State Road #434,
Suite 201
Longwood, FL 32779
407/788-0009

Philadelphia
1341 N. Columbus Blvd.,
Suite 402
Philadelphia, PA 19125
215/634-3339

Phoenix
5635 North Scottsdale Rd.,
Suite 190
Scottsdale, AZ 85253
602/941-0500

Pittsburgh
Seven Parkway Center,
Suite 678
Pittsburgh, PA 15220
412/928-5575

Portland
5331 SW Macadam Ave.,
Suite 225
Portland, OR 97201
503/226-3283

Raleigh/Durham
3714 Benson Dr., Suite 200
Raleigh, NC 27609
919/872-4888

Sacramento
2277 Fair Oaks Blvd.,
Suite 195
Sacramento, CA 95825
916/927-2700

St. Louis
2458 Old Dorsett Rd.,
Suite 200
Maryland Heights, MO
63043
314/291-6789

Salt Lake City
(call 411 for address and
phone number)

San Antonio
8131 IH 10 West, Suite 225
San Antonio, TX 78230
210/979-7500

San Diego
3465 Camino del Rio South,
Suite 300
San Diego, CA 92108
619/283-6400

San Francisco
330 Pine St.
San Francisco, CA 94104
415/982-4500

Schaumburg
1701 E. Woodfield Dr.,
Suite 400
Schaumburg, IL 60173
708/706-9889

Seattle
10900 N.E. 8th St., Suite 230
Bellevue, WA 98004
206/454-1974

Stamford
(call 411 for address and
phone number)

Upland
450 North Mountain, Suite B
Upland, CA 91786
909/985-2733

Walnut Creek
1280 Civic Dr., Suite 300
Walnut Creek, CA 94596
510/944-4900

Washington, D.C.
8601 Westwood Center Dr.,
2nd Floor
Vienna, VA 22182
703/847-0808

Each Great Expectations Centre is independently owned and operated.

Jeffrey Ullman is available to speak to groups on a variety of subjects dealing with how romance is changing in the 1990s. If interested, please contact:

Michael Olguin
Olguin & Associates
619/234-0345

or

Assistant to the President, Great Expectations
818/788-5200

Index

Love and Romance Are Just a Phone Call Away!

Wouldn't it be great if you could make one phone call and immediately change your life? You've already made that possible by reading this book. The key question you're facing is: **Should I make this call now?**

Since you've already made the choice to find romantic commitment, I'd like to help you reach your love goal as soon as possible . . . and I truly mean **as soon as possible!**

There are no guarantees in life, especially in dating. But there is one indisputable certainty: Unless you get active in your quest to find a suitable mate, you are destined to be alone.

If you want someone meaningful in your life, **you** can determine your destiny! Right now you don't have to be a creature of circumstance—you can choose to be the **creator** of your circumstance!

Believe me, you aren't alone. I have helped many people find love by providing a relationship service, Great Expectations, where thousands of marriages and millions of dates have started.

Just pick up the phone and call any one of our Membership Centres located throughout North America (see list on pages 260–63) to see how you can make your greatest expectations come true.

And to show my further commitment to you, just bring in your copy of this book when you visit a Great Expectations Centre and you can receive a 25 percent Author's Special Discount on the Membership of your choice.

Love and romance are just a phone call away.

Jeffrey Ullman
Founder, Great Expectations

This offer expires December 31, 1996